ELIZABETH BISHOP

Edgar Allan Poe & The Juke-Box

ELIZABETH BISHOP (1911–1979) is one of the great, most beloved poets of the twentieth century. Her work has been awarded the Pulitzer Prize, the National Book Award, and the National Book Critics Circle Award. *The Complete Poems, The Collected Prose,* and *One Art: Letters,* among others, are published by FSG.

ALICE QUINN is the poetry editor of *The New Yorker* and executive director of the Poetry Society of America. She also teaches at Columbia University's School of the Arts.

ALSO BY ELIZABETH BISHOP

POEMS

North & South

A Cold Spring

Questions of Travel

The Ballad of the Burglar of Babylon
with woodcuts by Ann Grifalconi

The Complete Poems (1969)

Geography III

The Complete Poems: 1927–1979

PROSE

The Diary of "Helena Morley"
translated from the Portuguese

Brazil
with the editors of *Life*

The Collected Prose
edited by Robert Giroux

One Art: Letters
edited by Robert Giroux

ANTHOLOGY

An Anthology of Twentieth-Century Brazilian Poetry
edited with Emanuel Brasil

PAINTINGS

Exchanging Hats: Paintings
edited by William Benton

Edgar Allan Poe & The Juke-Box

Laddy & Love - key

~~[illegible]~~

239

EDGAR ALLAN POE & THE JUKE-BOX

The juke-box fumes; the music falls
heavily through the darkened room.
Starlight, La Conga, all the dance-halls
in the block of honkey-tonks,
cavities in our wavering moon,
strung with bottles and blue lights
and silvered coconuts and conchs.

As easily as the music falls,
the nickels fall into the slots,
the drinks like lonely water-falls
in night descend the separate throats,
and the hands fall on one another
~~down~~ darker darkness, under
~~the~~ tables. Everything descends,
descends, falls, – much as we envision
the helpless earthward fall of love
descending from the head and eye
down to the hands, and heart, and down.
The music pretends to laugh and weep
while it descends to drink and mind.
The burning box can keep the measure
strict, always, and the ~~[illegible]~~ down-beat.

Poe said that poetry was exact.
But pleasures are mechanical
and know beforehand what they want
and know exactly what they want.
Do they obtain ~~that~~ single effect
Can be calculated like alcohol
or like the response to the nickels.
~~Just~~ how long does the music burn?
like poetry, or all your horrors
half as exact as horrors here?

Blue as gas,
blue as the pupil
of a blind man's eye

Edgar Allan Poe & The Juke-Box

Uncollected Poems, Drafts, and Fragments

ELIZABETH BISHOP

EDITED AND ANNOTATED BY ALICE QUINN

Farrar, Straus and Giroux / New York

Farrar, Straus and Giroux
19 Union Square West, New York 10003

Distributed in Canada by Douglas & McIntyre Ltd.
Printed in the United States of America
Published in 2006 by Farrar, Straus and Giroux
First paperback edition, 2007

" 'A lovely finish I have seen . . . ,' " "After the Rain," "Breakfast Song," " 'Close close all night . . . ,' " " 'Dear, my compass . . . ,' " "Florida Deserta," "Foreign-Domestic," " 'In a cheap hotel . . . ,' " "Keaton," " 'One afternoon my aunt and I . . . ,' " "Something I've Meant to Write About for 30 Years," "The moon burgled the house—," "The Street by the Cemetery," "Vague Poem," and "Washington as a Surveyor" were originally published in *The New Yorker.* "Apartment in Leme" was originally published in the *London Review of Books.* "Current Dreams," "Dear Dr.—," " 'Don't you call me that word, honey . . . ,' " "Dream—," "(Florida Revisited)," "Edgar Allan Poe & The Juke-Box," " 'From the shallow night-long graves . . . ,' " " 'I had a bad dream . . . ,' " " 'In the golden early morning . . . ,' " " 'It is marvellous to wake up together . . . ,' " "Letter to Two Friends," "On the *Prince of Fundy,*" and " 'We hadn't meant to spend so much time . . .' " were originally published in *American Poetry Review.* "In a Room" was originally published in *Conjunctions.* "For M.B.S., buried in Nova Scotia," "Florida," "Just North of Boston," and "Key West" were originally published in *The Atlantic Monthly.* "A Drunkard," "Salem Willows," and "Suicide of a Moderate Dictator" were originally published in *The Georgia Review.* "Syllables" and " 'We went to the dark cave of the streetcorner' " were originally published in *The New York Review of Books.* "A Short, Slow Life," "Good-Bye—," "Hannah A." (in a slightly different form), "Homesickness," " 'I introduce Penelope Gwin . . . ,' " and "Villanelle" originally appeared in *The Paris Review.*

All facsimiles from Elizabeth Bishop's papers appear by permission of Special Collections, Vassar College Libraries, and Alice Methfessel, executor of the literary estate of Elizabeth Bishop.

The Library of Congress has cataloged the hardcover edition as follows:
Bishop, Elizabeth, 1911–1979.
Edgar Allan Poe & the juke-box : uncollected poems, drafts, and fragments / Elizabeth Bishop ; edited by Alice Quinn.— 1st ed.
p. cm.
Includes bibliographical references.
ISBN-13: 978-0-374-14645-0 (alk. paper)
ISBN-10: 0-374-14645-4 (alk. paper)
I. Title: Edgar Allan Poe and the juke-box. II. Quinn, Alice. III. Title.

PS3503.I785E34 2006
811'.54—dc22

2005011511

Paperback ISBN-13: 978-0-374-53076-1
Paperback ISBN-10: 0-374-53076-9

Designed by Jonathan D. Lippincott

www.fsgbooks.com

10 9 8 7 6 5 4 3 2 1

Contents

Introduction

To visit the Department of Special Collections, Vassar College Libraries, and explore the abundance of Elizabeth Bishop material is to enter a universe of fascinating proportions. In the boxes that preserve more than thirty-five hundred pages of Bishop's writing are brief, indelible character sketches. ("Loved the wrong person all his life / lived in the wrong place / maybe even read the wrong books—"), bits of overheard dialogue she found irresistible, notes for stories, commentary on poetry she revered (by Herbert, Hopkins, Stevens, and Moore, particularly), wholly arresting, distinctly characteristic bits of description ("the bureau trapped in the moonlight, like a creature saying 'oh' "; "Begonias ghostly in a galvanized bucket"), accounts of dreams, drawings, menus, shopping lists, and hosts of fascinating remarks on the art of poetry, as well as the occasional withering comment on a poem, an essay, or a literary attitude or viewpoint she deplored. Of Robert Bridges, Poet Laureate of England and friend to Hopkins, for instance, she writes, "The reasonableness of all his ideas is too much—not a touch of the fanatical. He seems to have made himself into a poet out of wisdom—after deciding, sensibly, it was the best profession life had to offer him." There are also—especially in her notebooks from the 1930s and '40s, when she was often desperately uncertain about the direction of her work and her life—anguished *cris de coeur,* indicating how much courage and bedrock stamina her survival entailed.

Many of the titles set down in the notebooks are referred to just once, including early groups with marvelous descriptive tags indicating Bishop's ideas for them. Her post-college journal, which she began on the island of Cuttyhunk off the coast of New Bedford, Massachusetts, in July 1934, lists the following on one page: " 'The

Citrus Fruit'—love & friendship, 'The Emblem in the Eye'—6 sonnets, 'Flags and Banners'—motion in dreams, and 'An Individual Island for Everyone' (breakfast foods, etc.—satire)."

And there are innumerable fragments and drafts of poems, work that she did not complete to her satisfaction or considered trifling; drafts with phrases that haunted her, showing up again and again in her notebooks over the course of years; drafts with lines written out in a rush but accompanied by a chosen rhyme scheme; fragments that showcase verbal gestures familiar to Bishop readers from the more successful resolution of those gestures in the poems we know—all of it work that for one reason or another she chose not to publish but did not destroy.

Thinking about poetry in the highest terms was instinctive for Bishop and meeting her own standards was almost impossible, and this may account for the extraordinary quality of her unpublished work. In a letter to Marianne Moore dated December 5, 1936, the twenty-five-year-old Bishop discusses her reaction to a new sequence by Wallace Stevens, "Owl's Clover," making clear how deeply she is pondering what poetry can and ought to do: "What strikes me as so wonderful about the whole book—because I dislike the way he occasionally seems to make blank verse *moo*—is that it is such a display of ideas at work—making poetry, the poetry making them, etc. That, it seems to me, is the way a poet should think." In another early letter to Moore, she asks, "Can you please forgive me and believe that it is really because I want to do something well that I don't do it at all?"

Early on, editors understood her perfectionism and regularly tried to goad her to let go and send them her poems. She began publishing in *The New Yorker* in 1940 at the age of twenty-nine, and on March 9, 1955, Katharine White wrote to her, "As usual, this letter is a plea to let us see some of the Elizabeth Bishop manuscripts that I feel certain are on your desk, all finished if only you could bring yourself to part with them." Many years later, on May 26, 1972, Howard Moss, who had succeeded White as Bishop's editor and who became her friend, wrote exuberantly to her about a poem he had seen in draft years before: " '12 O'Clock News' is marvelous and we're delighted to have it . . . I was particularly happy to see that 'unicyclist' back. I've been waiting for him for years . . . Like Beethoven's father, I'd simply put you in a room and make you work all the time if I could. Of course, I wouldn't be that strict. A little gin, a few sandwiches . . ."

In a talk about poetry prepared but not presented in Rio in the 1960s (and included in full in the appendix), Bishop writes of the challenges as she conceived of them: "Off and on I have written out a poem called 'Grandmother's Glass Eye' which should be about the problem of writing poetry. The situation of my grandmother strikes me as rather like the situation of the poet: the difficulty of combining the real with the decidedly un-real; the natural with the unnatural; the curious effect a poem produces of being as normal as *sight* and yet as synthetic, as artificial, as a *glass eye*."

None of the material here was stamped by Elizabeth Bishop for publication with the notable exception of her villanelle "One Art," which is included here in the appendix along with the sixteen available drafts of the poem as numbered by the Vassar archive. There is disagreement among scholars about the sequence of the drafts—see *Elizabeth Bishop: Life and the Memory of It* by Brett C. Millier and *Elizabeth Bishop's Poetics of Intimacy* by Victoria Harrison (both noted in the bibliography)—but the set as it is offers a unique opportunity to study a Bishop poem from inception to fulfillment. The poem was written within months as distinct from the sometimes decades-long separation between a poem's beginning and Bishop's satisfaction with it. Bishop kept the drafts together. And it seems the appropriate candidate for inclusion—for the sake of contrast and study—in this book of unfinished work.

The illustrated poem that opens the book, " 'I introduce Penelope Gwin . . . ,' " a portrait of the artist as a young girl, must have pleased Bishop when she wrote it, but where could it have found a home in her oeuvre while she was alive except in an essay on her juvenilia?

In a letter dated January 20, 1938, when she was about to turn twenty-seven, Bishop sent "Money," one of the slighter poems collected here, to Marianne Moore. She referred to the poem as "a sort of joke (made out of a sentence in Dostoevsky's *House of the Dead*: 'Money comes and goes like a bird.')" Graduating from college during the Depression, though, Bishop had cause to ponder the subject seriously, and her conclusion—that money's "migratory habits" are "stern, both ignorant and wise"—is captivating even if the poem is too tidy and circumscribed to have passed muster with her. The little poem also shows the kind of phrase that could hook Bishop and motivate her to begin a poem.

Bishop's notebooks from the 1940s are full of touching evocation of Mrs. Hannah Almyda, her housekeeper in Key West, whom she described lovingly in letters to friends. But it's at the moment when Bishop seizes upon a powerful metaphor—"the Pelican, self-sacrificing, tearing feathers from its breast to line its nest"—and writes "for a poem?" in the margin that the depth of her regard for her friend and the scale of her own dependence become manifest.

On a draft of "Hannah A." Bishop writes "stiff," and yet what she sets down allows us to experience how rhyme—which she describes in an early notebook entry as "mystical"—helped her marshal and explore her thinking, and how poetry, as she remarks in a letter to May Swenson, is "a way of thinking with one's feelings."

This book opens with two poems from girlhood followed by a number of poems written just after college, in the mid-1930s when Bishop settled in New York and set about methodically reading English poetry on her own, working on her knowledge of French at Columbia, and studying the clavichord with Ralph Kirkpatrick. These early poems reflect her interest in allegory and her pressing need to explore the subject of love. These are followed by poems drafted on her travels to Ireland, France, and Spain, and a fragment jotted down on her first trip to Florida in December 1936.

The kernel of the book derives from two notebooks dating, roughly, from 1937 to 1947, which Bishop entrusted to a close friend, Linda Nemer, as she left Brazil in 1970–71 after what she later described as "the fifteen happiest years of my life." Nemer showed the notebooks to the poet and scholar Lorrie Goldensohn on a visit Goldensohn made to Ouro Prêto in the spring of 1986. As Goldensohn recounts the episode in her book *Elizabeth Bishop: The Biography of a Poetry*, "Bishop emptied the contents of her desk in Rio, and told Linda that she was likely to outlive her: she must keep these papers. Sell them if she liked, but if so, get a good price for them." Goldensohn initiated arrangements for the purchase of these materials by Lisa Browar, who was then curator of the Department of Special Collections, Vassar College Libraries. Most of the poems in the third section of this book come from these two notebooks, referred to in the notes section as the Key West notebooks and identified by their folder numbers, 75.3a and b and 75.4a and b, in the Vassar archive. The title poem, "Edgar Allan Poe & The Juke-Box," is the last developed draft in the first of the notebooks. Many years after she left Key West, Bishop showed the poem to Robert Giroux, her editor from 1956 until her death, saying that she had envisioned it as the concluding one in her second collection. Her letters and journals of the period (abundantly quoted in the notes) testify to the role Poe had in her thinking in the late 1930s, and the poem is also biographically significant, pointing up the considerable anguish she was experiencing before her move to Brazil in 1951.

Dating drafts is challenging and sometimes impossible. Bishop famously began poems and set them aside for years. "The Moose," we know, had its origins in a bus trip the poet took in 1946, and she continued to work on the poem after reading it in June 1972 at the Phi Beta Kappa ceremony at Harvard. Every trip to Vassar yields new insights about the material presented here. Bishop's prose account of a newsreel she watched in September 1954—see "Suicide of a (Moderate) Dictator," in the appendix—also contains reference to a poem, "Dicky and Sister," which she continued to work on in a notebook from the 1970s, the draft of which appears here on page 168.

The two Key West notebooks of the thirties and forties are numbered. It's clear that Bishop did not fill one notebook before beginning the other—both have entries from the late forties—and yet because of references to historical events, to a change of residence, or to travels that have been documented elsewhere, in letters or other writing, it appears that she used the one identified as 75.4a and b mostly in the earlier period, from the mid-thirties through the early forties, and the second, identified as 75.3a and b, from the mid-forties up through 1947. The notebook page numbers provide a rare if far from foolproof framework, and the drafts in Section III are sequenced accordingly, with a clutch of poems written around 1942 placed between the drafts in the first and second notebooks. In the notes section, I quote the source material that dates these poems positioned between the first and second notebooks to 1942 or thereabouts, but there was considerable guesswork involved.

A number of drafts from the Key West notebooks are accompanied by the notation "Bone Key" or "Key of Bone," which Bishop evidently contemplated as a title for either a sequence or a collection of poems about Key West. A notebook page with lines from the draft "After the Rain" indicates some of her thinking:

"one of the children thinks—

Bone Key

Key West, Largo Hueso, *Key of Bone.*
& sees a key like one to the front door
made of white bone. The island is
the white coral bone key to
                    the sea,
the depths of the gulf—

More evocative description of Key West follows, some of it again from "After the Rain":

(The kites are flown;
the puddles are gone.)

The palm trees will make their entrance
into the evening sky. The water-tower
is silvered with metallic paint,
moon on stilts.
The moon-flower wilts.

The drafts earmarked for "Bone Key" include " 'From the shallow night-long graves . . . ,' " "The Street by the Cemetery," "Florida Deserta," "Edgar Allan Poe & The Juke-Box," and "After the Rain," which she continued working on after she moved to Brazil, writing to her editor at Houghton Mifflin in September 1953 that she intended to include it in her second collection.

To order drafts in subsequent sections, I've depended on the dates Bishop gave them or that Vassar affixed to them, on the testimony of Bishop's friends, on references provided in her letters and journals, on the conjectures of established scholars to whom I'm greatly indebted, and on my own sense of chronology derived from an immersion in Bishop's papers for many years. But it must be explicitly stated that the ordering of this material is in no manner definitive.

I wanted to share my experience in the archive at Vassar. Therefore, the selection is inclusive and thoroughly representative, ranging from extensive drafts to fragments I found compelling. In transcribing the work, I sought to present the most coherent, intact drafts, and I've indicated in the notes whether a draft is singular or one of several extant. Facsimile representation seemed the best way to reflect the state of some of the drafts (and the challenge of transcription) as well as the most exciting way to present them. (The note on the text which follows provides a more detailed description of sequencing, transcription, and other editorial decisions.)

Much, if not all, of the material assembled here has been quoted in the many excellent books on Bishop's poetry published in the years since her papers were graciously made available for study by her literary executor, Alice Methfessel. It's my hope that this book will provide an adventure for readers who love the established canon, enabling them to hear echoes and make connections based on their own intuitions and close reading of both the finished and the unfinished poems.

A Note on the Text

Contents

Everything in this book is located at the Vassar College Libraries in the Department of Special Collections, where Elizabeth Bishop's papers are housed. Sixty-five of the drafts are grouped in the boxes listed by the archive as "Unpublished Poetry." Two of the poems, "Dear, my compass . . ." and "Close close all night . . ."—first published by Lloyd Schwartz in his article "Annals of Poetry: Elizabeth Bishop and Brazil" in the September 30, 1991, issue of *The New Yorker*—are in the folders dedicated to articles about Bishop. The remainder can be found in the boxes and folders listed as "Fragments" and in the boxes that contain Bishop's many notebooks and journals from 1934 to 1978. The vast majority of the legible, developed drafts in the archive are gathered here, but the selection is not exhaustive. I have not reproduced all of Bishop's uncollected juvenilia or work that is restrictively fragmentary, that does not indicate to a certain degree something of her artistic ambition for it or otherwise command interest because of its biographical significance.

The State of the Manuscripts

This is not a facsimile edition, although some facsimiles are included to illustrate the range of manuscript material. Most of the drafts represented are legible in manuscript. Even if Bishop drew an X across a handwritten draft, it's most often possible to see every word very clearly underneath it and even easier to do so if the draft was typed, and quite a number of the drafts are fair copies to begin with. But in all cases, I present the most coherent, intact draft—the fullest and/or most legible available—rather than opt for a less decipherable or less complete version of a more advanced draft. In the notes to the individual poems, I have reproduced many of the revisions and variants I found.

There are a few extreme cases. The extensive revisions visible in the facsimile for "Florida Revisited" show just how difficult it is to reliably set forth any single version of this poem—the stanza at the top of the facsimile is accompanied by the notation "2nd or 3rd"—but the draft as printed does give us a sense of the arc of the poem as Bishop envisioned it, and I've followed her instructions on the page in ordering the legible parts. In the case of "Dicky and Sister," nearly every page of drafted material in her notebook is represented because there is no one copy indicating her design for the poem. Instead, we have a portrait of evolving lines and scenes, and the result is so beautiful that had she finished the poem it would have been as central to her oeuvre as "Sestina."

Chronology

Dating drafts can be difficult and is sometimes impossible. Where Bishop noted a date on a manuscript or notebook page, I've registered that either on the page with the draft or in the note to the draft. Otherwise, I've done my best to determine when Bishop most likely wrote the drafts reproduced here by studying her notebooks, her letters, the many excellent books about her work, and the two principal biographies, *Elizabeth Bishop: Life and the Memory of It,* by Brett C. Millier, and *Remembering Elizabeth Bishop, An Oral Biography,* by Gary Fountain and Peter Brazeau. I have assumed for the sake of guidance (sometimes wrongly, I'm sure) that drafts are roughly contemporaneous with letters to friends or notebook entries with similar phrasing. In the notes, I cite the material that provided me with the evidence, or guesswork, that helped me to order the drafts.

Brackets and Other Symbols

Slashes. Bishop's handwriting is challenging. It's possible to mistake "love" for "lose," in which case context is the only guide. Where indicated, I've registered my uncertainty by enclosing guesses within slash marks. Slash marks enclosing empty space indicate illegible words or phrases.

Square brackets. As Bishop revised a poem, she often crossed out words without replacing them. I have restored the crossed-out words within square brackets where it is helpful to see them in order to make sense of the lines.

A short horizontal line. This indicates lines or phrases omitted as too partial to suggest her intentions. (See "Hannah A." as an example.) The wider horizontal lines replicate hers on the manuscript or journal pages.

Parentheses

The revisions Bishop wrote in parenthesis are reproduced that way. I have not attempted to represent all the variants on pages where they are extensive, as doing so might have overwhelmed the intact drafts embedded in these pages, but I have included select revisions where manageable and have registered others in the notes.

Emendations

I have corrected Bishop's spelling in cases in which it is obvious she would have made the corrections herself—"loathe" instead of "loath," "lavender" instead of "lavendar." But I have retained her spelling preferences in certain cases—the British versions of "marvellous" and "travelling," for example. I occasionally did not feel the need to dehyphenate a word ("wheel-chair," for instance) or to hyphenate a word she didn't hyphenate. (In "I introduce Penelope Gwin . . . ," the young Bishop did not hyphenate "self-expression.") In all cases, I placed the apostrophe where it should be, as clearly indicated by the text. I added periods at the end of sentences, capitalized the first words of new sentences, and closed parentheses. In general, with respect to regularly punctuated drafts, I feel there is nothing to be learned from omitting punctuation where it is clear she would have employed it. Where very rough drafts are concerned, I proceeded cautiously, representing her creative punctuation so as to preserve the feeling of the draft.

Italics

Bishop wrote the following in her Key West notebook from the 1930s: "(effect produced on me as a child by the italicized words in the Bible—not knowing what they signified. *Italics* have a natural effect—requires no explanation.)" Everything Bishop underlined in her notebooks is italicized with the exception of the titles she affixed to poems and drafts. Her titles are regularly indicated by single, double, and occasionally triple underscores.

The Appendix

Everything located in the Appendix is related to a draft or fragment, as noted on the initial page of each item.

Drafts Included That Were Entirely Crossed Out by Bishop in Her Notebooks and Papers

A Warning to Salesmen
Washington as a Surveyor
In the Tower
Valentine V
"What would be worst of all . . ."
"Under such heavy clouds of love . . ."
Money
"We hadn't meant to spend so much time . . ."
The Street by the Cemetery
For A.B.
The Salesman's Evening
Edgar Allan Poe & The Juke-Box

I

Poems from Youth

Don't go so fast, dear little bee
Said Mary with a laugh & a chuckle
                                        of glee.
I know you're making honey
                    to carry to your hive
To let them know you are still
                                                  alive.

I introduce Penelope Gwin,
A friend of mine through thick and thin,
Who's travelled much in foreign parts
Pursuing culture and the arts.
"And also," says Penelope
"This family life is not for me.
I find it leads to deep depression
And I was born for self expression."
And so you see, it must be owned
Miss Gwin belongs to le beau monde.
She always travels very light
And keeps her jewels out of sight.
"I will not let myself be pampered
And this free soul must not be hampered
And so besides my diamond rings
I carry with me but two things:
A blue balloon to lift my eyes
Above all pettiness and lies,
A small and compact potted plant
To hide from a pursuing Aunt.
(Just as they took my photograph
I saw one coming up the path.
That's why my eyes are turned away,
I mostly look the other way.)
My aunts I loath with all my heart
Especially when they take up Art.
And anything in the shape of one
Can make me tremble, turn, and run."

Our Heroine

An Aunt

Madame D.–

Miss Gwin will give a little talk
And tell of her amusing walk
Through country lanes and sixty states
Of really quite astounding gates–
With running water, nice hot tea,
And chats with Europe's royalty..
"Once in the gardens of Tuileries
I met this dear friend in the trees.
With flowers and little birds galore
She quenched her thirst for nature lore.

She fed grilled almonds to the birds
And spoke to them with honeyed words."
Notice her frank and honest eyes.
(It is Miss E. in disguise)
"Upon the Tiber catching fish
I chanced on Madame D'ienis.

Miss E. in disguise

Russian Aunt-Eater

You recognize her, I suppose?
(Notice the parasol of rose
To keep the sunlight from her nose)
But Russia was, I bring to mind,
The place I made the biggest find.
A Russian Aunt-Eater it was–
Large appetite–and lovely jaws.
An Aunt will look at him and faint,
Even the kinds that sketch or paint.
Of course, while in Romantic France
I met with Cupid and Romance.
One glimpse at my rejected suitor–
He was a vagabond German tutor.
But no! I would be no man's wife.
The stark reality of life
For me, and he was past his prime.
His mouth hung open half the time.
It gave my whole life quite a jolt
To find he had begun to molt....
I leave you with this little thought:
"What is not is and what is not"
(Spoken by Cardinal Richelieu
As I am sure you didn't know) Adieu."
I'm sure we all admire Miss Gwin.
How very sweet and kind she's been....

German Tutor

"I introduce Penelope Gwin . . ."

I introduce Penelope Gwin,
A friend of mine through thick and thin,
Who's travelled much in foreign parts
Pursuing culture and the arts.
"And also," says Penelope
"This family life is not for me.
I find it leads to deep depression
And *I* was born for self expression."
And so you see, it must be owned
Miss Gwin belongs to *le beau monde.*
She always travels very light
And keeps her jewelry out of sight.
"I will not let myself be pampered
And *this* free soul must not be hampered
And so besides my diamond rings
I carry with me but two things:
A blue balloon to lift my eyes
Above all pettiness and lies,
A neat and compact potted plant
To hide from a pursuing Aunt.
(Just as they took my photograph
I saw one coming up the path.
That's why my eyes are turned away,
I mostly look the other way.)
My aunts I loathe with all my heart
Especially when they take up Art.
And anything in the shape of one
Can make me tremble, turn, and run."

Miss Gwin will give a little talk
And tell of her amusing walk
Through country lanes and sixty states

At really quite astounding rates—
With running water, nice hot tea,
And chats with Europe's royalty.
"Once in the gardens of Tuileries
I met this dear friend in the trees.
With flowers and little birds galore
She quenched her thirst for nature lore.
She fed grilled almonds to the birds
And spoke to them with honeyed words.
Notice her frank and honest eyes."
(It is Miss Ellis in disguise)
"Once on the Tiber catching fish
I chanced on Madame Dienis.
You recollect her, I suppose?
(Notice the parasol of rose
To keep the sunlight from her nose)
But Russia was, I bring to mind,
The place I made the biggest find.
A Russian Aunt-Eater it was—
Large appetite—and lovely jaws.
An Aunt will look at him and faint,
Even the kinds that sketch or paint.
Of course, while in Romantic France
I met with Cupid and Romance.
One glimpse at my rejected suitor—
He was a handsome German tutor.
But no! I would be no man's wife,
The stark reality of life
For me, and he was past his prime.
His mouth hung open half the time.
It gave my senses quite a jolt
To find he had begun to molt. . . .
I leave you with this little thought:
'What is not is and what is not'
(Spoken by General Richelieu
In case you didn't know) Adieu."

I'm sure we all admire Miss Gwin.
How very sweet and kind she's been. . . .

"Once on a hill I met a man . . ."

Once on a hill I met a man
    With silver beard and starry cloak
And pointed shoes—and all his words
    Hung round me like a magic smoke.

He said he'd take me far away
    To Babylon or Shadow-land.
He sang a little tuneless song
    And led me upwards by the hand.

And as we went the birds flew round
    His head and whistled quick and gay,
And all the trees laughed at some joke
    And rabbits hopped along the way.

It wasn't night, it wasn't noon,
    Just grey and nothing and aloof.
We came upon a tiny house—
    Four walls, a little door, a roof.

He led me in and left me there
    And shut the door without a sound.
Then stood outside and said—I think
    It was the Lord's Prayer wrong way round!

Then through the keyhole, very slow,
    "What foreign land is this?" he hissed.
The lock clicked twice; a little wind
    Sobbed once, and he was gone like mist.

I cut my knuckles on the walls,
    I bruised my shins upon the door,
I said each witch-word that I knew,
    And then I cried upon the floor.

And morning never comes, nor night;
    The shadows never slide away.
Always the four walls are alike—
    Indefinite and gleaming grey.

There are three windows in the walls,
    But when I want to look outside
The world slips off some other way,
    As if it had been told to hide.

I never get a look at it;
    Its face is never turned to me,
Although I sometimes catch a glimpse
    Of snowy hill or lonely sea.

If I extend I do not see,
    Along the walls there moves a frieze
Of shadow people, shadow beasts
    And curious and shady trees.

Pale faces hang there, as a dream,
    If I but turn my head too soon,
And knights and princesses and bats,
    And people from the fabled moon.

It is a wondrous way to live.
    I know that it will never end.
The strange man left me here for good
    And that small, sobbing wind for friend.

I am afraid to touch the walls
    Or push against the window, for
Above the wind I heard a sound.
    I heard you sing outside my door.

Who are you out there with the wind?
    Is yours a face that palely gleams
Among the throngs upon my walls,
    Among my quaintly trooping dreams?

I guess you better go away.
    I might break down the door for you.
And if he came and found me gone
    And his house spoilt, what would he do?

II

1929–1936

College, New York, Europe, Florida

Perishable, adorable friends
each sometime ends

“A lovely finish I have seen . . .”

A lovely finish I have seen
upon a sand-flat glassed with sky—
or with a gold-leaf film of sea
re-brushed, re-grained by random cloud.
Can one accuse of artifice
such finishes and surfaces?

When in the dawn you turned to speak
& waited for my teeth to touch
the sugared coolness on that cheek,
—the other cheek—I found in such
deliberation of caress
the utmost of your worldliness.

1929

Good-Bye –

You are leaving the earth
Already a little distance
a [illegible], your flight –
or a slow [illegible] bow of your head
Look on the earth, and describe it –
But just that much is an [illegible] to do,
it has cost centuries of effort
and is costing us centuries of grief
In the late, crowded, terminal
we both look smaller, older.
Your gardenia smells like [illegible].
Have a martini. The great effort is yet to begin.
Our eyes blur the way
slightly tearful
we made lists on a half-wet paper napkin –
But here we, in this world,
in this noisy restaurant –
just by the misty window
a dirty heavy wrapper slow
it wants to regret
it will deposit you like a seed –
Hold on
Hold on, as I love you –

[1931–34]

Good-Bye—

You are leaving the earth
but only a little distance
a hairsbreadth, your flight—
or a short /curly/ hair of your head
laid on the earth, would describe it—
but just that much is so hard to do,
it has cost other people centuries of effort
and is costing us centuries of grief.
In the hot, crowded terminal
we both look smaller, older,
your gabardine suit looks shabbier.
Have a martini. The great effort is yet to begin.
Our eyes bleary & /   /
slightly tearful
we made lists on a half-wet paper napkin—
What are we, in this mob,
in this noisy restaurant—
just at the misty window
the /slick/ heavy wings slow
it waits to /negotiate/
it will deposit you like a seed—
hold on
hold on, as I lose you.

For a Pair of Eyebrows—

Once Justice was enthroned by Love
    Upon a certain Lady's brows,
To read his sentence and to prove
    Some reason in her whys and hows;
In Justice's hands he bravely laid
The scales, the emblems of her trade.

And thus Love weighed his lightest wit,
    The Lady's pity estimated,
And if the balance tipped a bit
    He cursed himself and hesitated,
And if perchance the scales went down
Love wept the weight of that sweet frown.

Apologia

Thou asks'f me, Margaret, why I have forgot,
      If e're I value thee, thy natal date?
I answer, unembarrassed by the thought,
      That now more justly can I celebrate,
            Though rather late.

Time cannot add the past month to thy age,
      Count on his fingers as he will, because
Thus I've subtracted it, and though he rage
      The sum is changed; my Mathematick laws
            Will give him pause.

I tell thee, Margaret, I have warded off
      Thy doom some thirty days or so, and when
Creeps on the cautious wheel-chair and the cough,
      Watch them advance—but to retreat again,
            And thank me then.

A Warning to Salesmen

Perishable adorable friend,
I saw the fields outside the city,
The colorless hills with spare margins of trees.
I watched a few crows bend
Over the bare fields, closely examining the stubble,
And a few more walking among the stubble with unbent knees.
The farmer was home, putting away vegetables in sand
In his cellar, or talking to the back
Of his wife as she leaned over the stove. The farmer's land
Lay like a ship that has rounded the world
And rests in a sluggish river, the cables slack.

See the fragment entitled "City Stars," the epigraph of this section, in the note on this poem.

Washington as a Surveyor

Lord, I discovered when I discovered love
That day a continent within the mind,
Unstable on the sea, boundaries unlined
Which now I slowly take the measure of.
The coast's determined; the mountains do not move;
Natural harbours and clear springs I find,
Shade trees and fruit trees, everything of its kind—
Even for an empire more resources than enough.
My favorite flowers, besides, some of each,
Yes, and wild animals who stand and stare;
Rivers that run beyond my present reach
The other way, and clouds that glitter in the air.
Love's flag quickly I planted on the beach
While I explored, but the one I love is not there.

Three Poems

I

From the eighth floor, from the twenty-eighth floor;
Face to on the sidewalk or in front of a store;
Off and below, through wires, /somewhere/ on a road;
At the end of the sky; at the edge of the wood;
Under a bird's eye, close to the parted hair,
Discovered by headlamps of a speeding car;
Sighted, a speck, from ship; sighted, a speck, from shore;
Small, as the numbers on watches; huge /   / and /   /
/   /; or making on the mountain
Something as slender as a scratch with a diamond;

—Infinite angles of shooting. We do not move,

In this agile camera, the wide eye of love
Fresh from the cinema, our posture is this
Always: always the clasp, the kiss.

II

Love's eye alone is stereoscopic,
Seeing in vistas many more dimensions,
And where he dotes, leans on abysses
In a flat town. He scorns machines
To take him places, but he could make
Enamelled wheels from alarm clock faces
If he cared to. In cheapest music
His ear discovers interesting dissonance.

He only speeds through sleeping cities,
Finding highways to the beaches,

Finding fun in dead amusement parks.
Sees nothing sad about neglected breakers
That keep on falling in the dark all night.
Flames through the Steeplechase, the Lido;
With happy mouth wide open and shut eyes
Rides the bleak roller-coaster.

III

All passionate words that meet the mind's approval
The heart rejects and will not listen to,
Even those chosen not from love, but art or science.
The heart sits in his echoing house
And would not speak at all.

The mind goes on to say: "Fortunate affection
Still young enough to raise a monument
To the first look lost beyond the eyelashes."
But the heart sees fields cluttered with statues
And does not want to look.

Younger than the mind and less intelligent,
He refuses all food, all communications;
Only at night, in dreams seeking his fortune,
Sees travel, and turns up strange face-cards.

Song—for the Clavichord

Love is not here;
He has not gone away;
He has not found
A better place to stay.
He is not places anyway.

He is not old;
He is not new,
He is not what you think;
He is not you,
Nor you, nor you. He's you.

In the Tower

The snow lies on the sky light,
Angels' faces looking down
Featureless; impersonal, thoughtless,
Undistinguishable, spotless,
Knowing neither smile or frown,
Pressed there between glass and twilight.

Valentine V

When Love goes hunting, who is he
That so can terrify his game
Winded and stumbling, still they flee?
Has a report
Of Love's fantastic sport
Been spread before him, and they see
Between the trees not death approach but shame?

Not from his arrows do they fly,
For those they might meet with their hearts
If only he would let them die.
They know that Love
Their curled horns will break off.
Pluck as a prize the living eye
And toss among the leaves the private parts.

"The past . . ."

The past
at least
is polite:
it keeps out of sight.

The present
is more recent.
It makes a fuss
but is unselfconscious.

The future
sinks through water
fast as a stone,
alone alone.

1935–36?

"We went to the dark cave of the street-corner . . ."

We went to the dark cave of the street-corner
And the kiosk was bare.
A cold wind drove the people off the streets
Then blew their doors ajar.
But two white-faced angel-newsboys
With black mouths were there,
With their speckled wing-sheaves of newspapers,
And they prophesied "War! War!"

Then we noticed a bright light
At the end of the street where we stood,
And we saw that the street stretched to Africa
Where a round African sun burned red.
There in the hot sands of the Circus
Sad, sand-colored lions stood,
And in the middle of the Circus was
An ancient Roman fountain, filled with blood.

LUXEMBOURG GARDENS

Doves on architecture, architecture
Color of doves, and doves in air –
The towers are so much the color of air,
They could be anywhere.
Here histories, cities, politics, and people
Are ~~all~~ made presentable
For the children playing below the Pantheon.
The Queens of France,
Female diplomats and flirts,
~~With~~ ^together their long legs ~~hid~~ quiet in ~~stony~~ marble skirts,
Smile, and pounce on the carousel dance. burnt wood
Stock-still, the fountain, a half-gone candle,
With wax-white drops fallen to one side.
Then; ~~by~~ with ~~the~~ a capricious puff of wind,
The wick begins to bend;
It gasps, and scatters itself
~~Like~~ a broken string of glass beads.
The puff came from Guignol,
Or then among the trees,
~~But~~ and Which he meant to mock was not the fountain
But the Pantheon.
He proposes to set it free; he puffs again
Now the big, half-filled balloon
Slowly rises and floats away;
And the children, not surprised, point and say
"It will get to the moon."

Luxembourg Gardens

Doves on architecture, architecture
Color of doves, and doves in air—
The towers are so much the color of air,
They could be anywhere.
Here histories, cities, politics, and people
Are made presentable
For the children playing below the Pantheon.
The Queens of France,
Female-diplomats and flirts,
Their long legs quiet in marble skirts,
Smile, and ponies on the carousel dance.
Stock-still, the fountain, a half-gone candle,
With wax-white drops fallen to one side.
Then: with an ingenious puff of wind,
The wick begins to bend;
It snaps, and scatters itself
In a broken string of glass beads.
The puff came from Guignol
Over there among the trees,
And what he meant to mock was not the fountain
But the Pantheon.
He proposes to set it free; he puffs again.
Now the big, half-filled balloon
Slowly rises and floats away,
And the children, not surprised, point and say
"It will get to the moon."

IN A ROOM AND MY CAT THE PARADES

Sept. 1936

IN A ROOM

There was a stain on the ceiling
Over the bed,
Shaped like a rhinoceros head
With a jagged horn and a trumpet in his mouth.
The trumpet had blown, without "feeling,"

all the gilt plaster-work, hoarsely,
from his jaw.
In the morning I saw
Over my head the brilliant results of his music:
A molding, constructed as coarsely

As an opera-house balustrade.
Off-center because
one room now was
three or four rooms of unequal size,
the chandelier displayed

Its large, branched star, snow-flake plan,
brassy-gold,
but with no lamp to hold.
Under the molding the two rusted pipes
the plumbing arrangements ran

to the closet in the corner and bored
within it.
Several times every minute
the toilet trickled and splashed, flushed
of its own accord.

The floor was dark red stone, damp and uneven.
Near one wall
a heavy iron chain hung half-way down from the ceiling,
giving a medieval sensation of heaven.

One electric light bulb alone was provided.
Under the light
Perpetually, day and night,
All the time I there, five flies held a dance.
In unhurried orbits they glided

Like five planets, only they both back and forwards:
On their track
They let themselves drift ~~buzzing~~ back,
Then began again. Their sound was a boring sentence
Emphasized over and over on the wrong words.

I dried my stockings on the balcony and kept
Untidy piles
Of newspapers on the red tiles
In the beautiful white marble fire-place, with its ~~mantle~~ shelf ?
Upheld on scallop shells. At night I slept

On the great lumpy bed, in a range of mountains,
and had
— the ~~[illegible]~~ bad ?
Dreams of my ~~whole~~ life, while from the water-closet
Came ~~the~~ sounds of far-off squalls and fountains.

When not sleeping, I observed that
All night
Fine gold whiskers of light
Spread over the ceiling from the next room, pricking out
That molding, like a curious cat.

A man and his wife sat up late in there; I could hear
Them fighting
In low voices, and a continuous writing,
"Scratch - scratch - scratch," going on, while they drank
Bottle after bottle of beer.

In the darkness ~~the~~ the five flies spoke
Of Revelations
In their hopeless conversations,
Of the gilded beauties of heaven, and the blackness of hell, too,
till thinking
"But here I am in my room," I awoke.

AND MY CAT

lived in the room with me — [illegible]

E. Bishop

[illegible]

Naples, Fla—'36

Today the birds all carry rings in their beaks that they have stolen from the ring-machine on the merry-go-round. The children go away without any, sobbing hard. They try to console themselves with the sweet, ruby-stoned peaches, set thick in the round peach-trees, but the leaves curl over them like little scimitars and the poor children cut their fingers and cry harder than ever. Who will comfort the children, who can possibly comfort them now for their ringless and bloody fingers? The merry-go-round's horses' nostrils grow redder, their eyes fill with tears. They would like to run away, they are so angry. They wrench at the nails fastening their hooves to the circular floor, but the calliope plays louder and louder, and round and round they go, until they are too dizzy to be indignant any longer.

III

1937–1950

Key West, Washington, D.C., Yaddo, Nova Scotia

Prose = land transportation
Music = sea transportation
Poetry = air transportation (in its present state)

It is hard to get heavy objects up into the air; a strong desire to do so is necessary, and a strong driving force to keep them aloft.

Some poets sit in airplanes on the ground, raising their arms, sure that they're flying.

Some poems ascend for a period of time, then come down again; we have a great many stranded planes.

—c. 1937

"What would be worst of all . . ."

What would be worst of all
Would be to be lost from you
As in a dream it often is—
—In a crowd, or a forest, or [some] national disaster—

The laws of chance to
Horrible, horrible
Knowing that you were looking for me
Not able to stand still & wait—
And you, kindness itself, helping the refugee,
Taking the other /lost/ to the people
                    they loved
Amusing them

And you and I missing each other

I have no home   neither have you

I feel we best prepare some scene like
                    this

Villanelle

After receiving the message from the police department as to the date of the trial, Louise had a bad dream. (Aug. 18) She dreamed she was a prisoner & condemned to death, but on the fatal day they let her go. She was dressed in bright red — trousers & shirt — and she was going somewhere on a train. She was to be executed at a certain hour — but not formally — anyone could do it when the right minute came — on the train, in the station, etc., etc.

(a)
b
a²

a
b
a¹

a
b
a²

a
b
a¹

a
b
a²

a
b
a¹
a²

when the opponents fell together.

2 "Aunt" poems

Villanelle

After receiving the message from the
police department as to the date of the
trial, Louise had a bad dream.
(Aug. 18) She dreamed she was a
prisoner & condemned to death, but
on the fatal day they let her go. She
was dressed in bright red—trousers
& shirt—and she was going some-
where on a train. She was to be
executed at a certain hour—but
not formally=anyone could do it
when the right minute came—
on the train, in the station, etc., etc.

"Under such heavy clouds of love . . ."

Under such heavy clouds of love,
    O be ashamed.
You supervise but really yield,
While all around the villages,
The little cottages, the fields,
    Are ransacked and deformed.

Give up, give up that uniform,
    O shameless lover,
And choose again without remorse
Your Dictator. For while in love
There is so much to lose, of course,
    But more, still, to discover.

Dream—

I see a postman everywhere
Vanishing in thin blue air,
A mammoth letter in his hand,
Postmarked from a foreign land.

The postman's uniform is blue.
The letter is of course from you
And I'd be able to read, I hope,
My own name on the envelope

But he has trouble with this letter
Which constantly grows bigger & bigger
And over and over with a stare,
He vanishes in blue, blue air.

Florida

Look at the Lears upon the beach!
No beards, but gray hairs on their chests
    Like city-snow,
    All gently blow.
Each upon his elbow rests,
With a young lady stretched by each,

In pale blue tights her lovely form;
Ophelia prostrate by the sea
    Casts large, sad eyes on
    The bright horizon.
The sun /invades/ all those who flee
Far from the love-affair, far from the storm.

Money

Money comes and money goes,
    Like a bird it flies,
Its migratory habits stern
    Both ignorant and wise.

In the season, I have watched
    Its wonderful gyrations,
Swift and fierce, and boldly close
    To human habitations.

Under the arches of the vaults
    Are built the hidden nests.
What instinctive fears and faults
    Govern those silver breasts?

Valentine

See, here, my distant dear, I lie
Upon my hard, hard bed and sigh
    For someone far away,
Who never thinks of me at all
Or thinking, does not care.
Banging the doors into the hall,
The roomers go to take the air
    —It is a lovely day.

The Negroes play harmonicas
But I am desolate; because
    Of what, I cannot tell.
The palm trees rattle happily,
Pink bloomers hang upon the line;
The roomers whistle cheerfully . . .
Oh please accept a valentine
    From one who loves you well!

"We hadn't meant to spend so much time . . ."

We hadn't meant to spend so much time
    In the cool shadow of the lime.
You played with three green leaves all afternoon,
    —Three green leaves and a red heart.
    Now it is growing dark.
I can't stand your arrangements anymore.

They are that shadow; real dark is the truth:
    The lime tree is a little booth
Outlined with leaves, one clotted heart displayed,
    On the outskirts of a sad suburban fair.
    Now look behind the dirty curtain where
Harlequin lies drunk in his checquered clothes . . .

"From the shallow night-long graves . . ."

Bone Key

From the shallow night-long graves
of the sleeping town,
from a graveyard's thin gray soil
springs the stubble of sound:

  A voice calls out,
  "Where is he at?"

Someone at the corner whistles.
Nothing is expected
of us yet, but what was that
the mirror just reflected?

  Hush, shut up,
  the sun's not up.

Pale small face without make-up,
small /arms/ along the sheets;
but there,—the lying eyes and there
the sun's peremptory reach,

  imposing his
  responsibilities

The Street by the Cemetery

Bone Key

The people on little verandahs in the moonlight
    are looking at the graveyard
    like passengers on ship-board.
How did it happen on this warm & brilliant night
    that steerage passengers
    were given deck-chairs?

They are admiring the long row of white oleanders
    inside the graveyard paling.
    The moon goes sailing,
and hypnotized they sit on the verandahs
    with nothing much to say
    to the neighbors three feet away.

The gravestones do not move; but in the blended motions
    of the oleander
    its white blossoms stir
like pieces of paper in those dark accumulations
    floating in a cluster
    in the dirty harbor.

It is marvellous to wake up together
At the same minute; marvellous to hear
The rain begin suddenly all over the roof,
To feel the air suddenly clear
As if electricity had passed through it
From a black mesh of wires in the sky.
All over the roof the rain hisses,
And below, the light falling of kisses.

An electrical storm is coming or moving away;
It is the prickling air that wakes us up.
If lightening struck the house now, it would run
From the four blue china balls on top
Down the roof and down the rods all around us,
And we imagine dreamily
How the whole house caught in a bird-cage of lightning
Would be quite delightful rather than frightening;

And from the same simplified point of view
Of night and lying flat on one's back
All things might change equally easily,
Since always to warn us there must be these black
Electrical wires dangling. Without surprise
The world might change to something quite different,
As the air changes or the lightning comes without our blinking,
Change as our kisses are changing without our thinking.

Florida Deserta

Bone Key

Oh summer clouds that come so low, come down,
come down the streets of the tourist-deserted town,
    shade the houses,
    soothe the eyes,
come down so every head can wear
    a cold compress,
descend, surround, and dissipate the glare,
banish the break-bone fever.

& Summer stars, refrangible though aloof,
converge invisibly on each tin roof:
    each shiny scale
    of that whole shoal
of sleeping tarpon; meet within,
    be colorful,
restore to every sun-bleached, spectral brain
its coldest blue and green.

For A.B.

The pale child with silver hair
Sat on the sofa all afternoon
And in the softest Southern accent
Read Hans Christian Andersen,

And laughed half-scared and too high-pitched
Showing pallid little gums;
Cried because the Snow-Queen came,
Her temples hollowed with bad dreams,

Wept for the interrupted story:
The woodsman's child who grew so weary,
The Princess dressed in white, the orphan,
The child who died and lay in the white coffin.

The Salesman's Evening

Seen by twilight, it is a beautiful town,
  (We cannot give the name)
And, as far as beauty goes, it is proud to own,
  It is exactly the same
As it was /two/ hundred years ago. But then
There were no ugly shops, there were no travelling salesmen.

On the buildings the classical ornaments
  Show in the gray air
Bleached like driftwood, and a whitened monument
  In the central square
/Rears/ contemptuously against its background of general neglect.
The salesman thinks sand-blasting has produced that antique-effect.

Under the gas-lamps and the /oil-/lamps he searches
  For a souvenir
To take home to his wife, [but] everything he tries to purchase
  Proves to be too dear,
And there is nothing really pretty, anyway, it is all imitation,
Imitation-leather bags, papier mâché ash trays, or a rayon combination.

Although he makes fun of the objects he has already sold them,
  They could not be such junk
As what they already have, and he believes what he told them.
  He is so lonely he decides to get drunk.
He orders something at his hotel, but it costs too much there
So he goes to a little place still open across the square.

Naturally the drinks are smaller
  At such a down-at-the-heel café
But really his glass there looks like a little crystal pillar

Slightly worn away
In the center of the capitol by the action
Of rain storms, or sand and winds' friction.

Or a bar-keeper sharpening his /   / there. In this small depression
Lie his tiny drinks
A brightly colored, adulterated procession.
The salesman thinks,
"Yellow, then red, and now I'll have a yellow."
People at the next table are pitying the poor fellow

Who then plays right into the hands of his assailants.
But now he can pity
The buying betrayed inhabitants
Of the beautiful, beautiful city,
"This is a dead town. Why that horse out there
Is more alive than they are—and those white curlicues on the buildings
around the square."

Edgar Allan Poe & The Juke-Box

Neddy & bone-key

blue as gas,
blue as the pupil
of a blind man's eye

Easily through the darkened room
the juke-box burns; the music falls.
Starlight, La Conga, all the dance-halls
in the block of honkey-tonks,
cavities in our waning moon,
strung with bottles and blue lights
and silvered coconuts and conches.

As easily as the music falls,
the nickels fall into the slots,
the drinks like lonely water-falls
in night descend the separate throats,
and the hands fall on one another
[down] darker darkness under
tablecloths and all descends,
descends, falls,—much as we envision
the helpless earthward fall of love
descending from the head and eye
down to the hands, and heart, and down.
The music pretends to laugh and weep
while it descends to drink and murder.
The burning box can keep the measure
strict, always, and the down-beat.

Poe said that poetry was *exact.*
But pleasures are mechanical
and know beforehand what they want
and know exactly what they want.
Do they obtain that single effect
that can be calculated like alcohol
or like the response to the nickel?

—how long does the music burn?
like poetry, or all your horror
half as exact as horror here?

Key West

I

They have set up the carnival, the carnival,
In the back-lot of the burnt-out cigar factory,
And the high-diver, before he leaps to his canvas pool
From the ladder festooned with colored lights, can see
Down into the ruins, and then all over the town,
Over the tin roofs to the blacked-out ocean,
The surrounding water, like sheets of carbon paper,
Used and re-used. With display of mock emotion
He sets a match to himself: flaming, he falls
Like a wagon of war past the gutted stucco walls.

II

Where six hundred men used to work at rolling cigars
To fill the boxes with the ornate lids
That showed a woman with roses in her hair
And tulle-draped bust—a woman like her bids
The citizens to come and see her dancers,
Guaranteed to wear nothing but feather fans and jewels,
And a man with the face of an educated ape
Lures them to see the educated mules.
While Negro children, who are not allowed,
Look on solemnly from among the crowd.

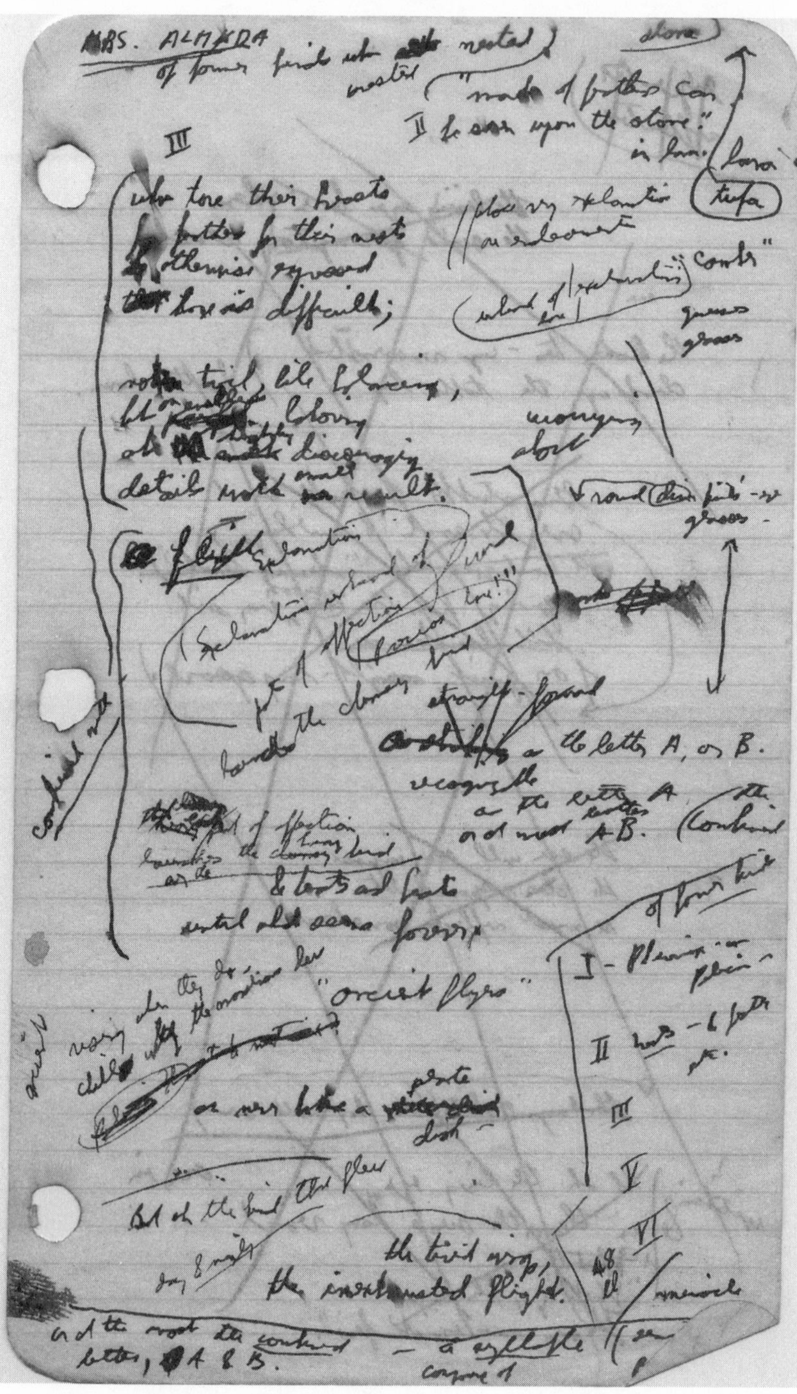

Notes and an outline for the poem entitled "Hannah A." in the legible draft transcribed on the following page.

Hannah A.

Of former birds who rested
on ice-floes, who resisted
dragons, who nested
by the streams of lava
where they lived alone,
where marks of feathers can
be seen upon the stone
or in the crumbling tufa,

———

who tore their breasts
for lining for their nests
or otherwise expressed
that love was difficult;
no trick, like balancing,
but endless worrying
at such discouraging
details with small result,

who cared for, much too long,
the one ungainly young
who couldn't learn his song,
or a stupid mate
whose only active thought,
—to flap his wings, & fight—
kept quarreling half the night
for rotting meat;

[Love, heavy flight & heavier
the body to manoeuver
as necessary over
the foil-tipped leaden waves
& frost-tipped feather
through the frost-clouded air
to the great rock where
the loved one really lives.]

After the Rain

Key West

After the rain the puddles are blue.
As St. Theresa said of Grace:
"There are little pools for children,
there are pools for all,
some large, some small."

The school-house in its gritty playground,
built of cement-blocks, stained with rain,
is turreted, and crenellated,
a two-dimensional
cardboard castle

where little captives, like fair ladies
mirror-charmed, gaze into blackboards.

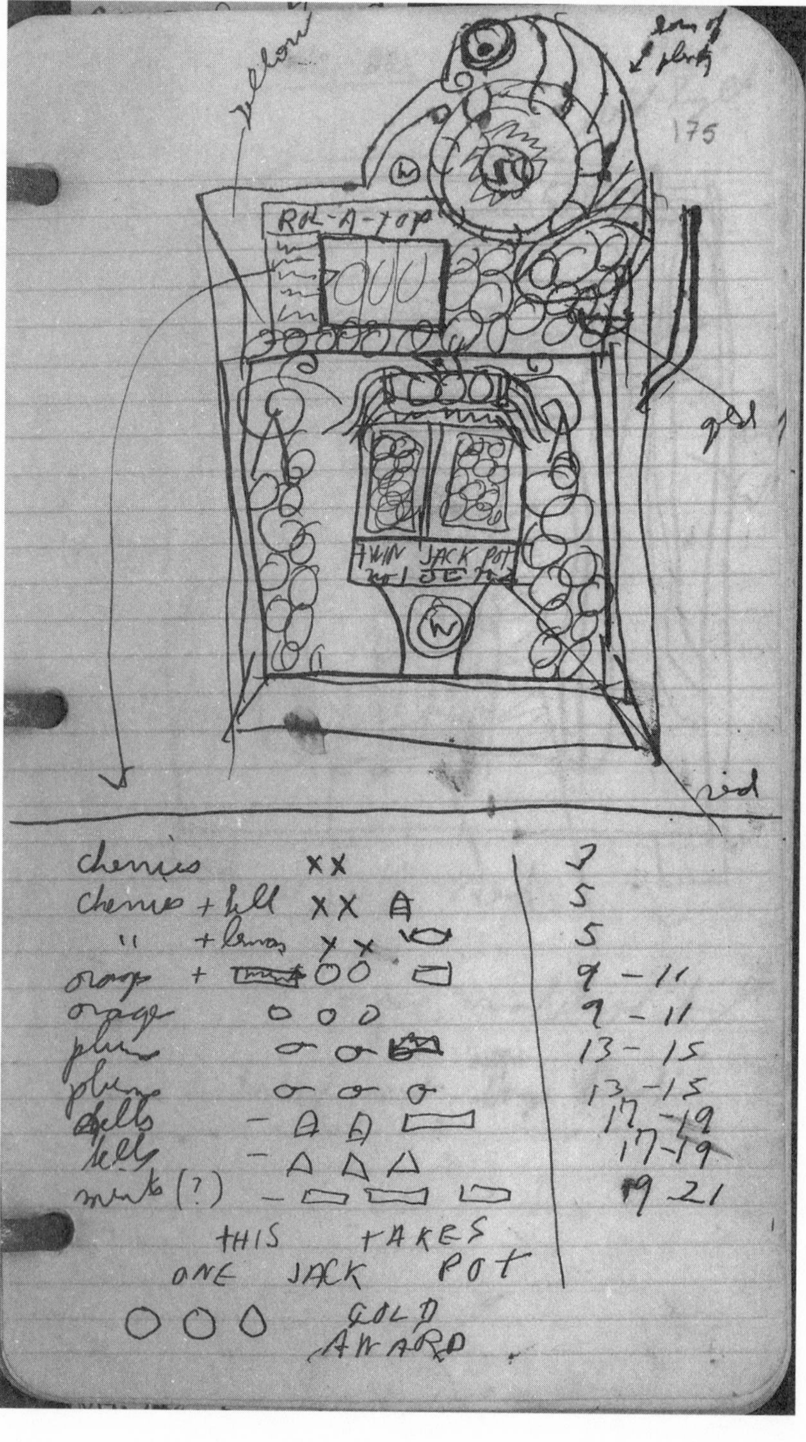

yellow
175
ROL-A-TOP
TWIN JACK POT
gold
red
cherries XX 3
cherries + bell XX 5
" + lemons XX 5
orange 9 - 11
orange 9 - 11
plums 13 - 15
plums 13 - 15
bells 17 - 19
bells 17 - 19
mints (?) 19 - 21
THIS TAKES ONE JACK POT
GOLD AWARD

The Soldier and the Slot-Machine

I will not play the slot-machine.
  Don't force the nickel in my hand.
I will not play the slot-machine.
  For all the nickels in the land.

I will not ask for change again.
  The barkeeper can see me dead
Before I'll try to meet those eyes
  That move like money in his head.

The slot-machine is all embossed
  With horns of plenty done in gilt;
And out of them all down its front
  Stream dummy coins supposedly spilt,

Like medals for its cleverness,
  As if the slot-machine could cough
In nickels down its tunic, but
  One cannot pick the dummies off.

They are symbolic of the whole
  It seems to me, and I should know
Since hundreds of times, thousands of times,
  I've added mine onto that row

Moving along here in this groove
  Towards that hole they all fall through.
The slot-machine is who is drunk
  And you're a dirty nickel, too . . .

Its notions all are preconceived.
　It tempts one much to tear apart
The metal frame, to investigate
　The workings of its metal heart,

The grindings of its metal brain,
　The bite of its decisive teeth.
Oh yes, they decorate the top
　But not the awful underneath.

The slot-machine is full of —.
　The slot-machine's materiel
And if you squint your eyes it looks
　A little like a general.

And even if generously inclined
　Its money all will melt, I'm sure,
And flow like mercury through the cracks
　And make a pool beneath the floor . . .

It should be flung into the sea.
　It should be broken up for junk
And all its nickels taken away.
　The slot-machine is who is drunk.

I will not play the slot-machine.
　Its pleasures I cannot afford.
Whoever got the Twin Jack-Pot?
　Whoever won the Gold Award?

Full Moon, Key West

The town is paper-white:
the moonlight is so bright.
Flake on flake
of wood and paint
the buildings faint.
The tin roofs break
into a sweat
of heavy dew
dripping steadily
down the gutters
click click.
Listen!
All over town
from black gaps
in bedroom gables
from little tables
behind the shutters
big alarm clocks
tick tick.
A spider's web
glints blue, glints red,
the mirrors glisten
and the knobs on the bed.

The island starts to hum
like music in a dream.
Paper-white, drunk,
the sailors come
stumbling, fighting,
mumbling threats
in children's voices,

stopping, lighting
cigarettes
with pink dull fires,
in groups like hands
and fingers on
the narrow sidewalks
of cement
that carry sounds
like tampered wires,
—the long strings of
an instrument
laid on the stream,
a zither laid
upon the flood
of the glittering Gulf.

"The walls went on for years & years . . ."

The walls went on for years & years.
The walls went on to meet more walls
& travelled together night & day.
Sometimes they went fast, sometimes slow;
sometimes the progress was oblique,
always they slid away.
In passing
one could write down a word or two
a whole page or a joke
gone the next morning.
Think of them sliding edgewise through
the future holding up those words
as something actually important
for everyone to see, like billboards.
The ceiling was tiresome to watch
overburdened with fixtures & burning lights
but the floorboards had a nice perspective.
They rose a little here, sagged there
but went off alas under the wall.
Did they flow smoothly on or meet
in the next room in a crash of splinters?
The morning light on the patches of raw plaster
          was beautiful.
It was crumbled & fine like insects' eggs
or walls of coral, something *natural.*
Up the bricks outside
climbed little grill-work balconies
all green, the wires were like vines.
And the beds, too, one could study them,
white, but with crudely copied
plant formations, with pleasure.

The clothes we wore like angels' clothes,
angels are no more bothered with buttons.

One day a sad view came to the window
                                        to look in,
little fields & fences & trees, tilted, tan & gray.
Then it went away.
Bigger than anything else the large bright clouds
moved by rapidly every evening,
rapt, on their way to some festivity.
How dark it grew, no,
but life was not deprived of all that sense
of motion in which so much of it consists.

REGULATOR
IDEAL
FANC

Stoves & Clocks

The stoves stand all along the walls, the clocks
   are fixed on high,
   the constellations in the sky.
The dirty, sagging floor
supports the stoves that might be rocks
or crocodiles or islands or
some other fixtures of a world.
   The clocks are still, the stoves are cold.
   Both clocks and stoves are old.
   Silent the shop,
   silent the clocks,
   cold the stoves,
   extinct and terrible the world.

Where the blue gas made [flourets]
   it sank back,
   sucked back down the /   / black
pipes, like blue eyes with cataracts
   for one moment, and gone.
Where the stove-lids glowed red-hot
   the fires left

                                        an ancient pot

a few stains of paint or henna—

mysterious

Little Thaw in January

The snow is thinning & melting
& the bright icicles are thinning
            & falling.

Over every brick chimney a
   wavering column in the air
   (column of wavering)
where the aerials and branches
   look as if
seen through faulty
   window-panes.

The housewives come out to
sweep their porches in their
   cotton house-dresses.

All colors are prized equally,
   employed sparingly

& the new pale blue object all tangled up
   in the old elm trees—

the young auburn dog trotting down
the bluish, now bare, wet
   sidewalk,

& the blue shadows, too much like a
   poor water-color, perhaps,
   but beautiful nevertheless—

Heart please give up, let it go!
Relax, as they say. Let it go like
                    the snow
that vanishes under one's eyes simply be-
   cause there is no possibility
   of its staying.

2.

   [It was an] impossibility,
Impermanence, from the very start,—
Go, & with the sun delicately shining—

   Now the grass starts showing
through the snow—like stubble
getting longer on a man's chin—

"Onliest" as they say in K.W.—
—a nice endearment

& you, dear Mistake,—

" " " " , mistaken
            one—

"Don't you call me that word, honey . . ."

Don't you call me that word, honey,
Don't you call me that word.
You know it ain't very kind & it's also
                    undeserved.

I could take that to court, honey,
I could certainly take that to court,
But maybe I misunderstood you, and besides life is much too short.

Current Dreams

I

From all confusions come
different dreams for each:
on a long wild beach
with breakers rolling in
on a sullen ledge of rock
as dull & smooth as flint,
there has been a bombardment
and where the shells have fallen
the flint has turned red-hot
in irregular patches under
an inch of clear black water,
beautiful stains, like Chartres;
and at the edge of the waves
where the stains burn ragged red
and the water hisses, a crowd
of hesitant little children
pick their way along
in fastidious concern
in order not to burn
cold, wet, white feet.

II

Will it go off or will it forget?
We labor at the indicators.
They burnt the fingers. We examine
the cluttered back.
Somebody says in a scolding voice
"Don't be so stupid about an old alarm clock!
Don't you know that everything is an alarm clock?

Children, houses, churches, books and pictures?
Yes, everything in the world is set,
Set, and will go off, *brrrrr,*
[Right to the second!"]

III

The sea [is a deceptive footing]
& we search its drunken, shifting sidewalks.
The air turning to salt-water on the way,
we descend some creaking stairs
drawn by music of marimbas
to a cellar-cabaret.

But when we get there it is silent.
Around us impetalled fish swim seriously;
it is not a cabaret at all.
It is an endless wax-works, dimly lit,
where rows of lonesome figures sit
whose fresher tears, naturally, cannot fall.

IV

He is reading the funny-papers
in a long ante-room
and continues reading them
right in an auditorium
where they are making speeches
and hammering mahogany hammers.
Seated in the large audience
he reads the Katzenjammers.
What goes on up on the platform
seems to concern economics.
It is all very embarrassing.
He keeps reading the comics,
crying, & holding them close
so the little dots of red
that make up the small pink faces
really look like blood.

He holds them close to his face.
What a wretched situation
—the paper gets all wet
with his tears of mortification.

The Museum

Dear—please let's go back
to that little provincial museum,
& through its little rooms again,

gray-green beads & various valises
other objects worthless value
or unauthenticated

Please let's go back

No I can't imagine what
those stone things were ever used for.
& This time let us translate
the labels more carefully

on brownish paper, as if scorched
printed in a quaint /black/ type. 19th cent.

Some of them had slipped
to the bottom of the cases & lay
face down, or stood on one corner.

Some of the rooms were dim
dry smell or a damp smell

A column of sunlight fell
clear & thin & alive
almost like a stream of water—
alive as a stream of water
as if it lived there
commenting fastidiously on lighting—

THE TRAVELLER TO ROME

If he saw it again,
the sagging historical dome
staring down at the traveller
to Rome
in [illegible] wrinkled clothes
now that he knows
as much and his mind is richer
would he notice more detail,
would it be more beautiful
than it was then?

And if he saw again
the cold courtyard
cobbled as if by the weight
of centuries of cobwebs,
would he see below a crowd
cross like the shade of a cloud,
a crowd [illegible] of famous and great,
now that he thinks he knows
whose the authentic shoes,
[illegible] who wore them when?

The Traveller to Rome

If he should see it again,
the sagging historical dome
staring down at the traveller
to Rome
in rumpled clothes
now that he knows
so much and his mind is so much richer
would he notice more detail,
would it be more beautiful
than it was then?

And if he should see again
the grave courtyards
cobbled as if by [the] weight
of centuries of cobwebs
would he also see a crowd
[cross like the shade of a cloud,
a crowd of famous and great,
now that he thinks he knows
whose the authentic shoes,
who wore them when?]

If the first time were the last
would he not have recognized
first the first fact is the fact
galvanized
of being there,
of the mortal stare,
of presence and the import
[of] eyes neither dying nor dead,
full-face in a profile head
[that] solemnly bulge from their past?

The traveller to Rome
[—one need have no regrets—
could note in his second experience,
one suspects],
or succeeding visits
to similar sites,
scarcely as much difference
as lies in the fractional depth
of the layers and layers of gold-leaf
(over) the dome.

Dear Dr. —

Yes, dreams come in colors
and memories come in colors
but those in dreams are more remarkable.
Particular & bright   (at night)
like that intelligent green light in the harbor
which must belong to some society of its own,
& watches this one now unenviously.

Slant rhyme 167

I had a bad dream
toward morning, about you.
You lay unconscious
It was to be
for "24 hrs."
Wrapped in a long blanket
I felt I must hold you
even though a "lord of guests"
might come in from the garden
at a minute
I see us lying
with my arms around you
& my cheek on yours.
It was warm – but I had to
prevent you
from slipping away
from your body, your cheek
from the wound-round blanket. –
gross dark morning

Thinking of you
a thousand miles away,
how I tried to hold you
with the mere arms of a dream

in the deep of the morning
the day coming

that loneliness like falling on
the sidewalk in a crowd
that falls [illegible] with stones. sore
slow, elaborate shame.
the sidewalk rises, roars
like absolute despair

"I had a bad dream . . ."

I had a bad dream,
toward morning, about you.
You lay unconscious.
It was to be
for "24 hrs."
Wrapped in a long blanket
I felt I must hold you
even though a "load of guests"
might come in from the garden
[at] a minute
& see us lying
with my arms around you
& my cheek on yours.
It was /warm/—but I had to
prevent you
from slipping away
from your body your cheek
from the wound-round blanket—
                    grave dark morning.
Thinking of you,
a thousand miles away,
how I tried to hold you
with the numb arms of a dreamer

in the deep of the morning
                              the day coming
that loneliness like falling on
  the sidewalk in a crowd
that fills [one with shame], some
                              slow, elaborate shame.
The sidewalk rises rises
like absolute despair.

"In the golden early morning . . ."

In the golden early morning
you came to take me to the airport.
There was an unusually heavy dew
even for there; the brick walk looked like plums
& the newspaper was wet outside.
M— & I stood & waited
& made some kind of conversation.
Then I looked at the paper & learned of the crash
the day before; some women & babies were killed.
After that I couldn't seem to think of anything to say
& she couldn't either. I kept wondering
why we expose ourselves to these farewells & dangers—
Finally you got there & we started.
It was very cold & so much dew!
Every leaf was wet & glistened.
The Navy buildings & wires & towers, etc.
looked almost like glass & so frail & harmless.
The water on either side was perfectly flat
like mirrors—or rather breathed-on mirrors.
I said oh look at the blue heron.
Several stood about in the shallow water & one white.
The road is very bumpy, & you drove fast
but for some reason I'm not afraid of your driving.
The little airport looked half-asleep.
Our voices sounded loud & clear & so like themselves
—if anyone knows what that means—
We had to wait & wait. There were 3 or 4 other people
A salesman and a very fat young Cuban girl—
Then we *heard* the plane or felt it
& it seemed to appear as if it were made out of
the dew coming together, very shiny.

When it landed the 2 pilots & the stewardess
walked in a sort of formation toward us
over the yellow sand.
I said to you that it was like the procession
at the beginning of a bullfight—it was exactly,
& you said "yes exactly only not so colorful."
M gave me a few last minute instructions & said
"Call me from Miami." You to my surprise
gave me a violent hug & a kiss on the cheek.
M kissed me on both cheeks & I knew she was about to cry.
So off I went & why do we undertake
these terrifying & cruel trips & why did I come here

In a cheap hotel
in a cheap city
Love held his prisoners — or my love
Love ~~[illegible]~~ the Night Clerk, the Negro bell-boy
~~[illegible] the [illegible] in the slot fan,~~
brought the pitcher of ice —
dropped the quarters in the greedy electric fan —
I remember the terrible carpet
& its smell, & the ~~[illegible]~~ bakelite telephone (pony)
with its ominous look, — look
(close to my head,) full full of the voices
of strangers
my head with one voice in it.
The bed, the motor — count below us — a ~~[illegible]~~ [illegible]

Six
It is you. my — stair.
almost [illegible] — fragments — Think (love)
~~[illegible]~~ & drops me
back ~~to [illegible]~~ bed
~~the fan [illegible]~~ (the ice clinks.)
~~The~~ chains me & berates me —

He chains us to this bed & he berates me.

"In a cheap hotel . . ."

In a cheap hotel
in a cheap city
Love held his prisoners   or my love
brought the pitcher of ice—
dropped the quarter in the spidery old electric-fan—
Love the Night Clerk, the Negro bell-boy
I remember the horrible carpet
& its smell, & the dog-eared telephone book

with its ominous look,
full full of the names
          of strangers close to my head,
my head with our name in it
                              or nameless embarrassment—
the bed, the motor-court below us

Six
Five yrs. ago   still
Almost every night   —frequently
[every night] he drags me
back to that   bed
the ice clinks, the fan whirs.
He chains me & berates me—
He chains me to that bed & he berates me.

To the Admirable Miss Moore

To the Admirable Miss Moore,
of whom we're absolutely sure,

knowing that through the longest night
her syllables will come out right,
her similes will all flash bright,

what can we give, yet not be rude,
to show the proper gratitude?

~~[illegible]~~

remote already, to impossible
Beneath the bed the big dog ~~thumped~~
his tail

HOMESICKNESS

c. 1900

~~So~~ She put up her hair & went to teach
~~a little~~
from home —
at Rose Phillips, thirty miles away

The pupils were —

Cousin Sofie —

Ugg
[illegible] !!

pan-
The salt pork & the buckwheat cakes
smelling like babyish —

headaches
the oil lamp — the sloping ~~bedroom~~
ceiling — in a loud print of wrongly
matched wall-paper

~~Finally~~
She missed
her father, her fateful mother & the
the [illegible] —

* ~~The~~ family dog to keep her company.

=

clenched
sleeping

not even realizing she was weeping
her face ~~[illegible]~~ nightgown drenched —

It was too late — for she, she did not know: —
already —, remote,
impossible (rhyme) impossible.

thumped
Beneath the bed the big dog ~~thwacked~~ his tail.

remote already & irreparable
Beneath the bed the big dog thumped
her tail

Homesickness

c. 1900

So she put up her hair & went to teach
[a little]   from home—
at River Phillip, thirty miles away

The pupils were—

Cousin Sofie—

The salt pork & the   buckwheat pancakes
smelling like frying—

headaches
the oil lamp—   the sloping bedroom
ceiling—in a low tent of sadly
matched wall-paper
Finally
She missed
her father   her fretful mother &
the jealous sisters—

* The family dog to keep her company.
—   clenched
—   sleeping
—

not even realizing she was weeping
her face   [her] nightgown   drenched—

It was too late—for what, she did not know.—
already—, remote,
irrepair*able* (rhyme) irreparable.

Beneath the bed the big dog thumped her tail.

The Owl's Journey

Somewhere the owl rode on the rabbit's back
down a long slope, over the long, dried grasses,
through a half-moonlight igniting everything
with specks of faintest green & blue.
They made no sound, no shriek, no *Whoo!*
—off on a long-forgotten journey.
—The adventure's miniature and ancient:
collaboration thought up by a child.
But they obliged, and off they went together,
The owl's claws lock[ed] deep in the rabbit's fur,
[not hurting him,] and the owl seated
a little sideways, his mind on something else;
the rabbit's ears [laid] back, his eyes intent.
But the dream has never got any further.

On the Prince of Fundy

We must weigh tons and tons and tons
with all those cars & cars & trucks
stowed below.
The cabin is pitch-black.
We gently gently rock this way and that.
Someone has a heavy tread, above.
Someone else—a woman—is singing. Why?
And why does she sing so high?
Everything creaks. And someone taps the pipes.
We gently rock. We *think* we rock because
there's nothing real to judge by.
I love you more today than I did yesterday.   apologetically
Isn't that nice?
[I thought I loved you. Now I know I do.]
Why are they walking around like that
and singing, too, at all hours of the night?
While we sway gently gently in the dark
(up, down and sometimes sidewise, too)   put it into *4's*

(We shall be arriving at Yarmouth, Nova Scotia in
approximately two hours and twenty-five minutes.)

IV

1951–1967

Brazil, Seattle, New York

Crossing the Equator

We all need the horizon, so it hardens
in its definition: *the horizon,*
(If it hadn't, as they say, we would imagine it;
rather, my dear, *you,* being practical, would have.)

Other things that you & I imagined
were not often so obliging.
Still the horizon is unbroken.

We needed the horizon, so it hardened
to *horizon,* into faultless definition.
(If it hadn't

imagination.)

Other spoken
were not often so obliging.
Still, the horizon is unbroken.

all the passive passengers with all their eyes on
our horizon: like a mighty hair it hardens.

holds us like a magic hair dragging our constant /love/
at the stern
south

in heavenly, watery imagery
pursues our
through watery, heavenly imagery—
headaches and exquisite *ennui,*

Young *Man in the Park*

Back. He put his legs through the back
of the park-bench, turning his back
Back.
He put his legs through the back
of the park bench,
turning his back   and turned his back
on the ships and the harbor.
He dropped his head down
and dropping his head
on the back
of his hands
The sun beat down
The sub-tropic sun beat down
on his head and his back
and the yellowing almond leaves   leaves of the false almond
   fell around him.   fell all around him.
Oh homesick young man
that's not the way
to conquer [the] country
The voyage is behind you
and here is your labor
No, he is fixed in his posture
his legs the wrong way around
facing the right way
sitting the wrong way round
Oh homesick young man, the steamers are nudging you inland
you refuse to look into your future
you have put the back of a park bench like a fence a barred gate
between you and the interior

He wants to go back all his feeling
is in his [bent] the long sun heated muscles of that back—

IMMIGRANT

Oh land-sick continent-sick

For M.B.S., buried in Nova Scotia

Yes, you are dead now and live
only there, in a little, slightly tip-tilted graveyard
where all of your childhood's Christmas trees are forgathered
with the present they meant to give,
and your childhood's river quietly curls at your side
and breathes deep with each tide.

"One afternoon my aunt and I . . ."

One afternoon my aunt and I
went picking blueberries. The sky

the line of marsh
like scribblings with green chalk
the berries were chalk-like, too
someone, perhaps Pythagoras,
had idly dotted over the pasture
with thick blue chalk, billions of dots

The men's rough voices
refined by the clear distance
the horses' velvet wickering
came to us clearly

She was
"a dirty picker" but very fast
The lard pail filled with berries
but also their thin blood-red stems
and thick little leaves, green or red
I was "clean" but slow
From the tin-mug to the lard pail
and from the lard pail to a basket

She wore a pair of overalls
her husband's, and an old straw hat,
called a "Cow's Breakfast."
          Note
a wicked family anecdote

our afternoon's addition
                    summer's sum

Haycock on haycock in the wagon
berry on berry in the pail
Pythagoras
One more
berry, one more baby, no more fuss.

the glaucous berries blind and blue
plop plop almost inaudibly
softly
a cricket held a high hot note
all afternoon

Syllables

Whatever there was, or is, of love let it be obeyed:
—so that the grandfather mightn't have been blinded,
the river never dwindled to what it is now,
nor the leaning big willows above it been blighted,
nor its trout been fished out;
nor, by the naked boys, the swimming hole been abandoned,
dissolved, abandoned, its terra cottas and gilt.
(—the boys who dove for white china doorknobs
stolen from the hens' nests;)
Whatever there is, or was, of affection
may it be said.

The barn swallows belonged to
the barns, they went with the church's wooden steeple.
& they flew as fast as they did because the air was so still—

That steeple—I can't remember—wasn't it struck by lightning?

“Where are the dolls who loved me so . . .”

Where are the dolls who loved me so
when I was young?
Who cared for me with hands of bisque,
poked breadcrumbs in between my lips,

Where are the early nurses,
Gertrude, Zilpha, and Nokomis?

Through their real eyes

blank crotches,
and /play/ wrist-watches,
whose hands moved only when they wanted—

Their stoicism I never mastered
their smiling phrase for every occasion—
They went their rigid little ways

To meditate in trunks or closets
To let [life and] unforeseen emotions
glance off their glazed complexions

A Short, Slow Life

We lived in a pocket of Time.
It was close, it was warm.
Along the dark seam of the river
the houses, the barns, the two churches,
hid like white crumbs
in a fluff of gray willows and elms,
till Time made one of his gestures;
his nails scratched the shingled roof.
Roughly his hand reached in,
and tumbled us out.

Suicide of a Moderate Dictator

For Carlos Lacerda

This is a day when truths will out, perhaps;
leak from the dangling telephone ear-phones
sapping the festooned switchboards' strength;
fall from the windows, blow from off the sills,
—the vague, slight unremarkable contents
of emptying ash-trays; rub off on our fingers
like ink from the un-proof-read newspapers,
crocking the way the unfocused photographs
of crooked faces do that soil our coats,
our tropical-weight coats, like slapped-at moths.

Today's a day when those who work
are idling. Those who played must work
and hurry, too, to get it done,
with little dignity or none.
The newspapers are sold; the kiosk shutters
crash down. But anyway, in the night
the headlines wrote themselves, see, on the streets
and sidewalks everywhere; a sediment's splashed
even to the first floors of apartment houses.

This is a day that's beautiful as well,
and warm and clear. At seven o'clock I saw
the dogs being walked along the famous beach
as usual, in a shiny gray-green dawn,
leaving their paw prints draining in the wet.
The line of breakers was steady and the pinkish,
segmented rainbow steadily hung above it.
At eight two little boys were flying kites.

To Manuel Bandeira, With Jam and Jelly

Your books are here; the pages cut.
Of course I want to thank you, but
how can I possibly forget
that we have scarcely spoken yet?

Two mighty poets at a loss,
unable to exchange a word,
—to quote McCarthy, "It's the most
unheard-of thing I've ever heard!" (1)

Translators of each other's tongue!
(I think that I may make this claim?)
The greater, relatively young,
sculptured in Bronze (2) and known to Fame!

Smiled on by Fame and Miss Brazil! (3)
Is this the man to keep so still?
The gallant man who rendered in
more graceful language, Elinor Glyn? (4)

Gave lovely Latin things to utter
to Tarzan, (5) who could barely mutter,
and polished Edgar Burroughs' brute?
Should such a man as this be mute?

And I, I am no *raconteur*,
my *repartee* is often weak,
but English-speaking friends, I fear,
would tell you I can *speak*,

and speak and speak, sometimes for days,
not giving any indication
of stopping or of feeling the need
of substitutes for conversation.

O conversations gone to pot!
—But please believe I've never thought:
"Your book is fine; I like it lots"
is best-expressed by apricots;

"You put all rivals in the shade"
is well-implied in marmalade . . .
—Nevertheless, accept and spread
these compliments upon your bread,

and, Manuel, may this silent jelly
speak sweetly to your poet's belly, (6)
and once more let me say I am
devoted with a jar of jam.

1. Recent remark of Senator McCarthy to the press.

2. O GLOBO, January 5th, 1955.

3. MANCHETTE, July 6th, 1954.

4. ITINERARIO DE PASARGADA, p. 100, n.

5. Idem.

6. If I may be allowed the expression.

The Grandmothers

I had three grandmothers, (one "great" one, understood)
three average Christian ladies of their day,
predominantly good;
they had their faults, but nothing serious.
But each one had one phrase she used to say,
so awful, so mysterious,
[it haunts their grandchild to this very day.]

without my realizing
a phrase is crystallizing
I've
started to employ it—

———

interrupt their conversation
& strike them dumb
baleful eye & confident
My day will come. enunciation—

What day, we wondered? asked her
And did it finally arrive?
She is no longer alive a kind of boast
/We'll never learn—/ & yet she had suffered, I think
no more than most—

The second

Nobody knows— It was true.

Nobody knew
—& nobody knew

what it was they were meant to *know*—

and ten years after the first one she died, too.

But the dear old great I'm afraid is worst of all.

Ho-hum. Ho-hum, hum-a-day—

it dismissed us all & all the future questions
& life & eating & sleeping & drinking

Give me thirty years, give & take a year,
What [terrible] phrase
  fill in here?

will my old lips have kept repeating, repeating?

St. John's Day

> "If St. John only knew it was his day,
> He would descend from heaven & be gay."
> —Old Song

A great and early sunset,
a classic of its kind, went unobserved,
although today the sun himself swerved
as far out of his course as he could get,

taking the opportunity
to see things that he might not see again;
letting the shadows poke their fingers in
and satisfy their curiosity.

Now, down below,
the darkness-level rises in the valley.
In the small tip-tilted town already
those gold cats' whiskers show

where six streets lie.
They shake, almost, to prove
to that withdrawing, orange presence above
the power of their electricity.

The valley's ceiling buckles;
a golden Roman candle surges;
down in alleys little demiurges
crack puff-ball knuckles.

But no, no prayer
can wake him. Is it cowardice?
He sleeps, he always sleeps away the solstice.
If he didn't his party might be gayer.

The moon burgled the house—

The end of the world
proved to be nothing drastic

when everything was made of plastic

we slept more and more even after
the pills gave out

and vast drops of the rivers ran
into the drying canyons of the sea

the sun grew pale as the moon and then
  a bit paler
although we still could see—

It was pleasant; it was lovely and
   languid
no one felt the urge to do anything,
even the children
we dreamed and dreamed all the cars
  were parked, no one went anywhere
they just stayed home and held hands,
at first, then stopped holding hands—

peace peace just what we've wanted all
  along—

the whole world turned like a
fading violet, turned in its death
gently, curled up didn't stink at
all but gave off a long sigh—sweet
                    sigh—

A Baby Found in the Garbage

Wrapped in the very newspaper
whose [headlines] she would make that day,   front page
newborn, she lay,
quite quiet, and the white fumes curled around her.
[The driver was so frightened that he ran away.]   (found her)

There are eighty apartments
in that apartment house built for the rich,
no one knew from which
she was cast down, or placed, upon that [pile]   [slipped down the chute]
[They think] she must have been a servant's

cried out and the white fumes curled around her.

[dressed in a towel, now, and
held by five shocked and babbling men]
talking

So she was spared the longer ride
out to the city limits and the dump,
where the buzzards and the poor join forces
in straggling double lines, and wait
to rally to each new-arriving truck,
to scrutinize, evaluate
/   /   varicolored muck.
[and the birds flap up and settle back again
and the people flap their arms to drive them off]
the people [flap] their arms; the [big black] birds
with naked heads and necks,
flap up and settle back. [again]   attack—

"Yours is a classic death, my dear."

In spite of everything they tried
she died, and scarcely having cried;
next day, wearing a diaper, inhaling strictest oxygen,
[and so was driven off again.—]

Then she was driven off again
It was a death almost Athenian—

Letter to Two Friends

Heavens! It's raining again
and the "view"
is now two weeks overdue
and the road is impassable
and after shaking all four paws
the cat retires in disgust
to the highest closet shelf,
and the dogs smell awfully like dogs,
and I'm slightly sick of myself,
and sometime during the night
the poem I was trying to write
has turned into prepositions:
ins and aboves and upons
[overs and unders and ups]—

what am I trying to do?
Change places in a canoe?
   method of composition—

The toucan is very annoyed.
Uncle Sam! Sammy! Shut up!
He stands up straight in his cage
with his bright blue eyes aglare
and shrieks in a perfect rage
[and] braces his tough blue feet
Maria do Carmo, please,   throw him a
give him a piece of raw meat—   small piece of meat

Marianne, loan me a noun!   Candida—
Cal, please cable a verb!   Paul—
Or simply propulse through the ether
some more powerful meter

The radio battery is dead,
for all I know, so is Dulles

the toads as big as your hat
that want to come in the house
and mournfully sit at the door
spotted, round-shouldered, and wet,
with enormous masochist eyes.
—The biggest snail seen yet moving
mysteriously to his fate
like a melting, white, dinner-plate,

left over from a *séance*
                                        tiered like the tower of Babel
with his brown, glazed house on his back

with no gift for languages
and even less for gesture
                                            but my dollar goes higher & higher—
exchange   anxiety
with a visa about to expire,
with a car with one good tire—   Brazil, "where the nuts come from"

New Year's Letter as Auden Says—

where the shoes don't fit my feet

hat and gloves and all
your picture on the wall
as if you had just said something,
something good I just missed

Dearest—[Cal,] you look,
up from the back of your book

Oh when the sun comes out—
the toucan spreads his wing
and re-oils every feather
and polishes up his bill
& the parrot calls
"[Lota!] Get out of the sun!"
(And naturally wants "A Coffee!"
instead of what we consider appropriate)

The small black birds that dance
like spots before the eyes

Look, the valley below
is like a bowlful of milk

frayed green silk
the Lent trees' mournful beauty

drink
an intense black cup or two
          pleasant

state of caffeinization—
        civilization

and try out your famous names
in the rarest diminutives—

merrily, merrily

confusing ends and means
in the country of coffee beans

If I cannot speak Portuguese.
shall I ever say Shibboleth?
—But
        With love, Elizabeth

Foreign-Domestic

I listen to the sweet "eye-fee."
From where I'm sitting I can see
across the hallway in your room
just two bare feet upon the bed
arranged as if someone were dead,
—a non-crusader on a tomb.
I get up; take a further look.
You're reading a "detective book."

So that's all right. I settle back.
The needle to its destined track
stands true, and from the daedal plate
[an oboe starts to celebrate
escaping from the violin's traps,
—a bit too easily, perhaps,
for the twentieth-century taste,—but then
Vivaldi pulls him down again.]

(Said Blake, "And mutual fear brings peace,
Till the selfish loves increase . . .")

MIAMI

Those building s you could poke y our fingers through,
yellowish, off-white,

glare
the brilliant, shoddy, glittering out there sleazy
across the bay the tattered screens of lines
of scorched Australian pines

The smell of fried potatoes from below

The hot air pulses the quaint old fan fed
the long-bladed fan, black and quarter-fed

from the bed

and at your head shakes over flowered
a ten cent store reading lamp two soiled telephone books
filled with their thousands of names
and none of them are ours thank God
in the dark drawer undoubtedly a Gideon Bible.
(and a rusted Gillete blade?)
Endless crowds in cottons, toilet waters,
b shoes at Burdines, place their bets, drink coconut milk-
take busses in gh heat -

As if by freshest brooks, in coolest shade
where shepherds sing
came sleep

love was

absurd, adulterous, and deep

ridiculous, adulterous, and deep.
flowered
The ten cent stor reading lamp shook (past tense)
on our heads
pretends to shake its petals on the two huge telephome books

stuffed with their thousand names besides our heads
that each holss only one each holding only one
the blue and sleazy glitter on the bay

the stores closed

As if by freshest brooks, in shades
where shepherds sing, they fell asleep
at five o'clock, lovers love
absurd, adulterous, and deep.

they fell asleep, with love that was
at thee at five o clock, and their love was
absurd, adulterous and deep.

As if by freshest brooks, in shades
where shepherds sing, they fell asleep
five o clock from love that was
absurd, adulterous, and deep.

Keaton

I will be good; I will be good.
I have set my small jaw for the ages
and nothing can distract me from
solving the appointed emergencies
even with my small brain
—witness the diameter of my hat band
and the depth of the crown of my hat.

I will be correct; I know what it is to be a man.
I will be correct or bust.
I will love but not impose my feelings.
I will serve and serve
with lute or I will not say anything.

If the machinery goes, I will repair it.
If it goes again I will repair it again.
My backbone

through these endless etceteras painful.

No, it is not the way to be, they say.
Go with the skid, turn always to leeward,
and see what happens, I ask you, now.

I lost a lovely smile somewhere,
and many colors dropped out.
The rigid spine will break, they say—
Bend, bend.

I was made at right angles to the world
and I see it so. I can only see it so.

I do not find all this absurdity people talk about.
Perhaps a paradise, a serious paradise where lovers hold hands
and everything works.
    I am not sentimental.

Mimoso, Near Death

The donkey named "Dainty"
(he's as tough as a—donkey)
    stands in the old blue truck-body
that lies on the hillside as if he were
ascending in it like Elijah
wheel-less   the sun—still sticks to the tops of the weeds—
    The tall weeds have all turned red
    up to his middle, up to his nose
some grow right through the truck bed growing
In the sunset as if he were standing in fine quiet flame—
a [cool], strange martyrdom   remote odd martyrdom—
a quaint cool martyrdom—
    He looks at me over his shoulder wistfully
What did he do? What did he believe? Where does he think he's going?
    On the rear of the truck its old messages can still be read—

    that once it flung back along the highways—

    it still is faithful to its old messages—

One to the left it says "I drive but God guides"   steers
To the right "There's no money in it but it's amusing"

"Come on, Dainty!"—"Come Dainty!"

    He looks like a saint—he looks like a sinner—

        bed-time!—dinner!

The weeds have all turned red.

Brasil, 1959

The radio says black beans are up again.
That means five hundred percent
in the past year, but no one quite believes it.
They're lying there, wherever they are raised,
those that do get to Rio are full of worms.
Somehow most come to terms   somehow
                                        and get a bellyful once a day
endless lines
waiting and waiting for the busses   gutters and drains
with "wash me" written on their tails
and now the rains   a woman drowned right in the city's heart
are doing it for them   right in the city's clogged old heart.

Floods,
the stations milling with men
and frightened secretaries
Send trucks. Why doesn't the army send us trucks?
And meanwhile far inland   to get us home
a fairy palace rises
a fairy palace small, impractical.

rises upon a barren field of mud
a lovely bauble, expensive as a jewel

The fly-blown meats
the butcher shop of "The Little Flower"
The starving cows parched

I saw the families camped in the old band-stand
the factory big as nights and days—
near the church beyond the cotton mills

night after night
among their rags and with a tiny fire
and all the color of the dirt of the north
oh
crooks crooks, stupid stupid stupid crooks

I see the families who've come on foot
You say what are you doing? ["Passeando"] "travelling," [or taking a
    walk—]

Meanwhile, you've never seen
a country that's more beautiful.
—or this part of it, anyway—
The delicacy of the green hills
the new bamboos unfurl   the edges
are all so soft against the pink watery skies
below, the purple Lent trees

Shall we change politicians?
An honest madman for a   swap the playboy for the honest
    madman?
And is he really honest? It's a kind of joke—

On the Amazon

Down the wide river
comes the soft rain
dark, dark-silver
racing forward
on pink water—down the wide river, comes the soft rain
a heavy sigh—
Gone again. and sudden a great soft sigh—
everywhere smudges
of rainbow and shafts
of soft sun backwards
rain over there now
crossing over
the dark blue line—the opposite bank—
and the river
erases it all
the world, all pink,
has dissolved at last
and is going somewhere
under a rainbow, too—
the rainbow has taken shape, but the world, all pink, strange to say
has dissolved at last
and is going somewhere, at last—
so *that* is the color of the world all together—
Air was never necessary—just water
and a little sun,
and a gentle acquiescent world—

The river, we are told, goes faster than the ship
tilts into [the sea tilting us, spilling us out to sea—]
(—if we keep our shape that long—)

(oh gentle crocodile
"embalmed and stuffed with straw"
with your head cruelly bent down to your breast
to look like a dragon, I suppose
no wonder you cry
tears of yellow varnish, [all] down your belly—)

Now it is clear. The water moves faster
a thin [glaze] of blue skin blue skin   thin loose blue skin
reflects, reflects—nothing—
A [sudden] line of birds
[flung up] like beads—   flings out
[and then]

A bar on stilts,
a bird on stilts
a boy on stilts—
stem the river with straws or toothpicks
stick a straw in the water for security
the neat palm thatch
the sitting hen on her individual platform—
the delicate hammocks—

"Let Shakespeare & Milton . . ."

Let Shakespeare & Milton
Stay at a Hilton—
I shall stay
At Chico Rei—

May 30th, 1960

(For the window-pane)

Dear Lilli, I liked this view,
I also liked to visit you,
but scarcely could prolong my stay
so bought the house across the way:
number twenty-eight. Now you
must visit me and see *my* view.

THE BLUE CHAIRS (that dream)

?.5 An awful night! so much more has happened
than happens in the most eventful day.
But just what happened really? ?
There was a curtain; there were those blue chairs.

All those blue chairs!

I longed for day —
Darwin said — "agony"

That was the way I longed for day to come
and now it be come — (dream song)
The light coming down at a list
in it that flood —

Gypsophilia

I like the few sad noises
left over in this smokey sunset.
That idiot dog!—He barks in *oblique* barks,
chop-chopping at the mountains with a hatchet.
They're flaking off in yellow sparks.
Or, no,—that's houses.

At Altenberg's, the orchid nursery,
somebody beats the hanging iron bar
until it sounds like farriers
down there, instead of flowers.
But the last clangs are
the last words of a bell-buoy out at sea.

Up here the air is thinner;
it's daylight still. And then the blue
deteriorates all at once. We're in
some dark sub-stratum of dew.
Dinner.
A child's voice rises, harsh and thin.

Manuelzinho's family: Jovelina,
Nelson, Nina
Jovelina bears   bends
a load of dead branches
her hair hangs down under her husband's old felt hat
a figure like a young witch's—
at a half-trot

Each child with an enormous sheaf
Of "Gypsophilia," "baby's breath"

Tomorrow, Saturday,
is market day—

We live aslant
here on our iron mountain. Venus
already's set.
Something I'm never sure of, even yet—
do we shine, too? Is this world luminous?
I try to recollect but can't.

To the Brook

My Nearest neighbor,
    we stretch in our beds,
    your muscles are longer
    but infinitely weaker;
    & they can't contract
    so you never could warm
    your feet in your hands,
    your hands in your armpits,
    and you twist and turn
    and constantly cough
    and are never at ease
    & if you stretch further
    your feet could fall off.

    I can /claim/
    my own toes if I please!
    I feel something hard.
    Oh: There are those hooks.
    But you feel nothing
    but nameless rocks.

All afternoon the freighters—*Rio*

All afternoon the freighters
kept rising from [a] sea
transparent as a sky.
The high white bridges
caught the sun,
[like calcimined] façades
[of] old Brazilian churches:
a diocese astray
in frail blue pastures.

Then fifteen whalers,
and after them the smoking
factory-ship.
It left a smear of grease,
so it was working.
They kill the whales with cannon. Can't
they leave the blessed whale in peace?
(Behemoth, ruminant,
goodbye, my dear:) Oh mates, Sailors

for your delight,
the sea & sky turn red;
& the [high] white bridges blush.
The holds are full of dying animals.
Don't worry, we'll consume them all
sooner or later. But how you have
roiled up the water! *Splash* . . .
What was that sound? The trash.
They throw it overboard at night.

Mimosas in Bloom

Dust from the floors of Heaven
that makes one sneeze and then smell honey.
What angels threw it out down here,
the lovely, yellow, air-light litter?

The gray-green leaves fold neatly back
like kittens' ears. The hillside's gold.
No, better than gold
this fine, soft, unmixed pigment.

Rainy Day, Rio.

Mountains should really not protrude
In city streets and brandish trees
At skyscrapers, nor should the seas
Roar at the business-man. So rude
Of Nature not to go away
But hang around the wondrous bay.

It rains and rains.

The chic dog and the not as chic   leak/ peak/ street

Umbrellas blot the wet mosaics

Apartment in Leme

1.

Off to the left, those islands, named and renamed
so many times now everyone's forgotten
their names, are sleeping.

Pale rods of light, the morning's implements,
lie in among them tarnishing already,
just like our knives and forks.

Because we live at your open mouth, oh Sea,
with your cold breath blowing warm, your warm breath cold,
like in the fairy tale.

Not only do you tarnish our knives and forks
—regularly the silver coffee-pot goes into
dark, rainbow-edged eclipse;

the windows blur and mirrors are wet to touch.
Custodia complains, and then you frizz
her straightened, stiffened hair.

Sometimes you embolden, sometimes bore.
You smell of codfish and old rain. Homesick, the salt
weeps in the salt-cellars.

Breathe in. Breathe out. We're so accustomed to
those sounds we only hear them in the night.
Then they come closer

but you keep your distance.

2.
It's growing lighter. On the beach two men
get up from shallow, newspaper-lined graves.
A third sleeps on. His coverlet

is corrugated paper, a flattened box.
One running dog, two early bathers, stop
dead in their tracks; detour.

Wisps of fresh green stick to your foaming lips
like those on horses' lips. The sand's bestrewn:
white lilies, broken stalks,

white candles with wet, blackened wicks,
and green glass bottles for white alcohol
meant for the goddess meant to come last night.

(But you've emptied them all.)

3.
Perhaps she came, at that. It was so clear!
And you were keeping quiet: [Oh, slightly] roughened,
greeny-black, scaly

as one of those corroded old bronze mirrors
in all the world's museums (How did the ancients
ever see *anything* in them?),

incapable of reflecting even the biggest stars.
One cluster, bright, astringent as white currants,
hung from the Magellanic Clouds

above you and the beach and its assorted
lovers and worshippers, almost within their reach
if they had noticed.

The candles flickered. Worshippers, in white,
holding hands, singing, walked into you waist-deep.
The lovers lay in the sand, embraced.

Far out, saffron flares of five invisible
fishing boats wobbled and hitched along,
farther [out] than the stars,

weaker, and older.

4.
But for now the sun. Slowly, reluctantly,
you're letting go of it; it slowly rises;
metallic; two-dimensional.

You sigh, and sigh again. We live at your open mouth,
with your cold breath blowing warm, your warm breath cold
like in the fairy tale

no—the legend.

Something I've Meant to Write About for 30 Years

The Florida East Coast Railroad; dawn.

one felt dirty, dirty, with swollen feet
and twisted clothes twisted under one
the scratchy plush scratchy sooty plush
the reek of beer and rye; a sailor's hat
hung on a seat arm. All the sailors were
passed out or sleeping & the soldiers, too—
in a mad ugly mess open mouths
and baby-faces, flushed

We stopped for just a moment, a small town
in southern Georgia? probably—
we jerked, backward and forward there
and I woke up—
Looking right into nigger-town
then back, then the same place again,
as if to make sure I'd really seen it
I'd really see it, and I did—
The light was lavender. The unpainted houses
were almost the color of the air
unpainted houses, air-color, almost—   sodden (this *was* the South)
bare muddy yards, black trees   all its black people were in bed
one porch with a wistaria
as if the air had started to crystallize there   dripping, half-crystallized
and melted again, dripped down—
But then it was a fence the fence, a fence
that took my eye—I saw it slide back   silently
then forward like a slide several times
a picket fence
Where the wistaria was (the picket fence

once whitewashed)
someone had fixed
with nails, half hammered in, then bent,
a piece of broken mirror to each picket top
gothic shape—
these fragments
catching the light, reflecting, white
and bluish, sadly, over and over again
as we shunted
only the mirrors seeing the morning coming
20 or 30 of them—I lost count   20 or more
a crazy iconography decoration why not *decorate* morning?
Irregular jagged jagg'd disconnected mad

For T.C.B.

Father's in the studio
  Painting hill and dale,
Mother's in the sitting-room
  Typing up a tale,
Hepple's in the pasture
  Looking at the rabbits:
Fairies, keep them in good health
  And faithful in their habits!

Hepple says the pasture
  Is your property,
Mother says he's wrong, it lies
  "As far as you can see,"
And Father paints a mile 'round that—
  But, really, it extends
Across the oceans, Thomas,
  To your very farthest friends.

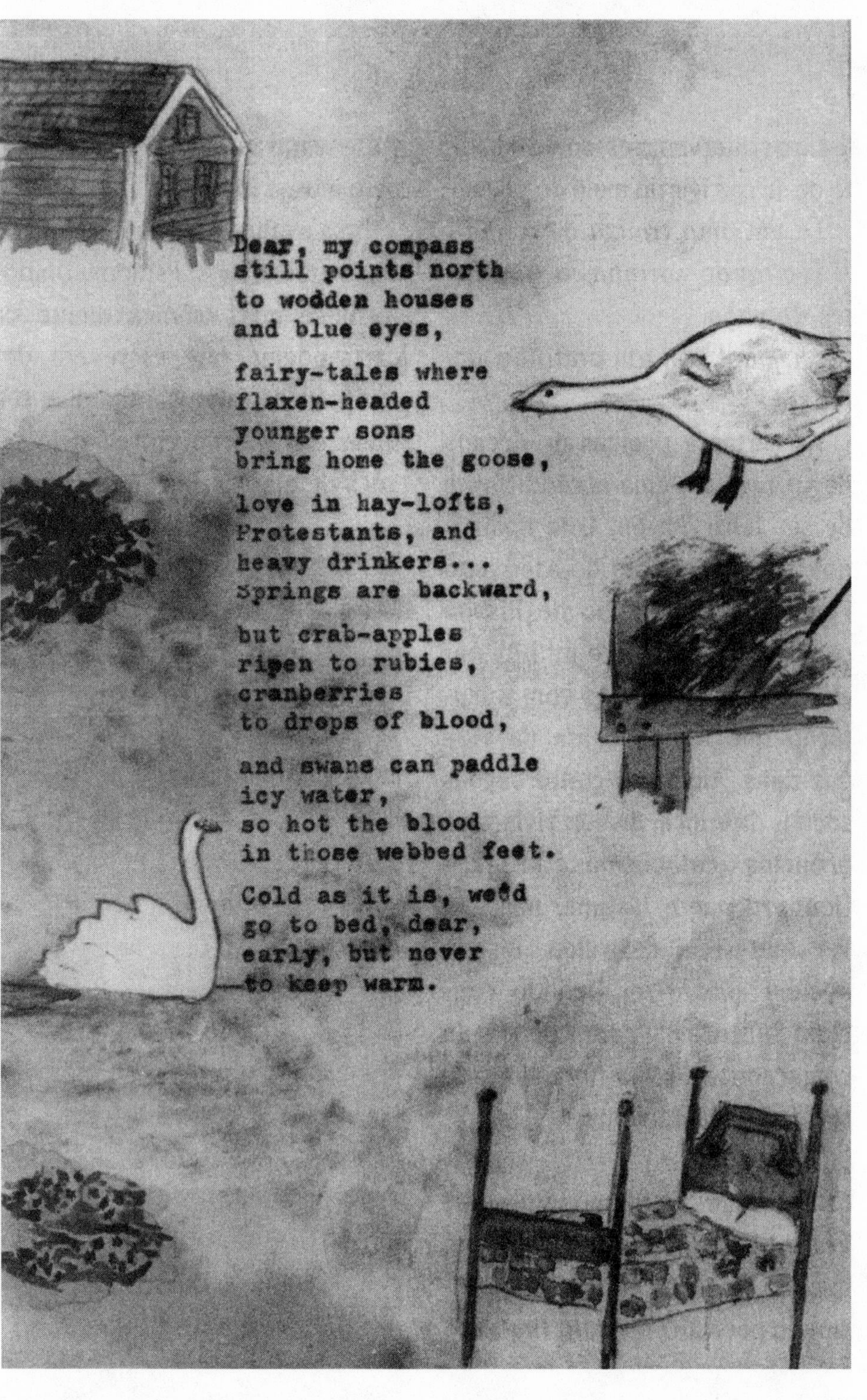

Dear, my compass
still points north
to wodden houses
and blue eyes,

fairy-tales where
flaxen-headed
younger sons
bring home the goose,

love in hay-lofts,
Protestants, and
heavy drinkers...
Springs are backward,

but crab-apples
ripen to rubies,
cranberries
to drops of blood,

and swans can paddle
icy water,
so hot the blood
in those webbed feet.

Cold as it is, we'd
go to bed, dear,
early, but never
to keep warm.

"Close close all night . . ."

Close close all night
the lovers keep.
They turn together
in their sleep,

close as two pages
in a book
that read each other
in the dark.

Each knows all
the other knows,
learned by heart
from head to toes.

The Pretender

The Pretender came to breakfast.
(We'd been notified two days earlier.)
He arrived at nine, on horseback,
—an eight-mile ride from the Palace.
(The second, "Summer" Palace, that is, very modest.)
The horse was sweating. *He* was like a daisy:
tall, big and blond, blue-eyed, guffawing . . .

His black-and-white checked breeches were rather loud,
a feather in his Alpine hat, a linen coat,
an ascot of white piqué;
his ascot pin, his cufflinks,
his shirt studs—all were *teeth.*
Hounds' teeth? Whose teeth?
Big and yellowed, set in gold.

He knew the name of each plant in the garden
and where they came from, [each tree on the hills.]
He knew the age and wood of each antique:
the jacaranda beds, chests of drawers, chairs—
he guessed who'd probably made the bed.
And if that isn't patriotism, what is?

[Something] left over from another age
—a Noble Savage armed with whip and boots.

He spoke about his children,
(five of them) and his wife,
whose name was "Esperanza." Unfortunately,
when they had married, the best cow of his herd
was also an "Esperanza." "So," he said,
"I had to change my cow's name, naturally."

INVENTORY

Bed, birdcage, and a chest of dr drawers,
the biggest shell, the flat and foot-shaped
piece of granite I found myself,
the paddle, and the portable ink-well;

the baby-book, the/coffe spoons the blue enamm the cloisonee
coffe spoons with blue enamel,

the living cat

where - where can I take them next? wand where
do we go next?

Oh let me not have looked
Let it somehow be that I never saw

& the cascade seems hurrying to some
climax, but really never cnages -

V

1968–1979

San Francisco, Ouro Prêto, Cambridge, Boston

"Far far away there, where I met . . ."

Far far away there, where I met
those strange affectionate animals
that seemed to like me too & ate the bread
but forgot me naturally the moment I left
oh that was a nice day, Rosinha, wasn't it . . .
one of the nicer ones. OH I hate memories
sometimes.
                    the bird that bowed to me

S F

light hexagons in tiers and tiers
honeycomb rifled by the bears
and left uneaten on the hills
all the bay windows unconnected
with the bay really, coincidence

the backyard = 2 TV antennaes still coming across it, my
two lovely big suspended dragonflies

and in the sudden rain 2 big roses on an unpruned tree
lash in the hissing rain but keep their petals on
alyssum ran wild there and geraniums
reach up the wooden turning fire escapes
such queer clapboarded faces, ladders, pipes,
and crooked porches
down there an unpruned avocado and a pine
and a rat runs beneath them in long grass

vanishes under the uncut grass

wooden fences, cramped houses with funny eyes
pipes, lines, grandma's big gray dress hung out to dry
and a long row of sheets (visitors there)

our cyclamen like a group
sisters of charity (OLD COSTUME)
the anemones turned shaggy now, about to fall

unhappy flower child

****

it was the moon & not the laundromat
that woke us love   whose   light   (woke me)

Aubade and Elegy

No coffee can wake you no coffee can wake you no coffee
No revolution can catch your attention
You are bored with us all. It is true we were boring.

1. For perhaps the tenth time the tenth time the tenth time today
and still early morning I go under the crashing wave
of your death
I go under the wave the black wave of your death

Your not there! not there! I see only small hands in the dirt
transplanting sweet williams, tamping them down
Dirt on your hands on your rings, nothing more than that
but no more than that-

the smell of the earth, the smell of the black roasted coffee
black as fine black as humus -
no coffee can wake you no coffee can wake you no coffee can wake you!

no coffee

No coffee can wwake you no coffee can wakeyou no coffee
can wake you

No coffee

A Drunkard

When I was three, I watched the Salem fire.
It burned all night (or then I thought it did)
and I stood in my crib & watched it burn.
The sky was bright red; everything was red:
out on the lawn, my mother's white dress looked
rose-red; my white enamelled crib was red
and my hands holding to its rods—
its brass knobs holding specks of fire—

I felt amazement not fear
but amazement may be
my infancy's chief emotion.
People were playing hoses on the roofs
of the summer cottages on Marblehead Neck;
the red sky was filled with flying motes,
cinders and coals, and bigger things, scorched black burnt.
The water glowed like fire, too, but flat.
I watched some boats arriving on our beach
full of escaping people (I didn't know that).
One dory, silhouetted black (and later I
thought of this as having looked like
Washington Crossing the Delaware, all black—
in silhouette—)
I was terribly thirsty but mama didn't hear
me calling her. Out on the lawn
she and some neighbors were giving coffee
or food or something to the people landing in the boats—
once in a while I caught a glimpse of her
and called and called—no one paid any attention—

In the brilliant morning across the bay
the fire still went on, but in the sunlight
we saw no more glare, just the clouds of smoke.
The beach was strewn with cinders, dark with ash—
strange objects seemed to have blown across the water
lifted by that terrible heat, through the red sky?
Blackened boards, shiny black like black feathers—
pieces of furniture, parts of boats, and clothes—

I picked up a woman's long black cotton
stocking. Curiosity. My mother said sharply
Put that down! I remember clearly, clearly—

But since that night, that day, that reprimand
I have suffered from abnormal thirst—
I swear it's true—and by the age
of twenty or twenty-one I had begun
to drink, & drink—I can't get enough
and, as you must have noticed,
I'm half-drunk now . . .

And all I'm telling you may be a lie . . .

Vague Poem (Vaguely love poem)

The trip west—
—I think I *dreamed* that trip.
They talked a lot of "rose rocks"
or maybe "rock roses"
—I'm not sure now, but someone tried to get me some.
(And two or three students had.)

She said she had some at her house.
They were by the back door, she said.
—A ramshackle house.
An Army house? No, "a *Navy* house." Yes,
                                    that far inland.
There was nothing by the back door but dirt
or that same dry, monochrome, sepia straw I'd seen everywhere.
Oh she said the dog has carried them off.
(A big black dog, female, was dancing around us.)

Later, as we drank tea from mugs, she found one,
"a sort of one." "This one is just beginning. See—
you can see here, it's beginning to look like a rose.
It's—well, a crystal, crystals form—
I don't know any geology myself . . ."
(Neither did I.)
Faintly, I could make out—perhaps—in the dull,
rose-red lump of, apparently, soil
a rose-like shape; faint glitters . . . Yes, perhaps
there was a secret, powerful crystal at work inside.

I *almost* saw it: turning into a rose
without any of the intervening
roots, stem, buds, and so on; just

earth to rose and back again.
Crystallography and its laws:
something I once wanted badly to study,
until I learned that it would involve a lot of arithmetic,
                    that is, mathematics.

Just now, when I saw you naked again,
I thought the same words: rose-rock, rock-rose . . .
Rose, trying, working, to show itself,
forming, folding over,
unimaginable connections, unseen, shining edges.
Rose-rock, unformed, flesh beginning, crystal by crystal,
clear pink breasts and darker, crystalline nipples,
rose-rock, rose-quartz, roses, roses, roses,
exacting roses from the body,
and the even darker, accurate, rose of sex—

For Grandfather

How far north are you by now?
—But I'm almost close enough to see you:
under the North Star,
stocky, broadbacked, & determined,
trudging on splaying snowshoes
over the snow's hard, brilliant, curdled crust . . .
Aurora Borealis burns in silence.
Streamers of red, of purple,
fleck with color your bald head.
Where is your sealskin cap with ear-lugs?
That old fur coat with the black frogs?
You'll catch your death again.

If I should overtake you, kiss your cheek,
its silver stubble would feel like hoar-frost
and your old-fashioned, walrus moustache
be hung with icicles.

Creak, creak . . . frozen thongs and creaking snow.
These drifts are endless, I think; as far as the Pole
they hold no shadows but their own, and ours.
Grandfather, please stop! I haven't been this cold in years.

meddle
model
paddle

Swan-Boat Ride

[Ballad of the Swan-Boats]

where the live swan paddles
dead water
*pontoons & pedals peanut—

my mother's hand
proffered a peanut from the bag (?)

Ungracious bird— Ungracious, terrifying bird!

Afloat, afloat suspended
the whole pond swayed
descended
madness & death

I saw the hole, I saw the blood.

set (designs)
The flower beds (in the same patterns)
—the State of Massachusetts seal

the State House Dome
its thinly crusted sun.

amniotic flood—

"A mother made of dress-goods . . ."

A mother made of dress-goods
white with black polk-dots,
black and white "Shepherd's Plaid."
A mother is a hat
black hat with a black gauze rose
falling half-open

A long black glove
the swan bit
in the Public Gardens

Hair being brushed at night
and brushed
"Did you see the spark?"
Yes, I saw the spark
and the shadow of the elm
outside the window
and

A naked figure standing
in a wash-basin shivering   half crouched
a little, black and white
in the sloping-ceilinged bedroom
with the striped wall paper

A voice heard still
echoing
far at the bottom somewhere
of my aunt's on the telephone—
coming out of blackness—the blackness all voices come from

The snow had a crust, they said, like bread—
only white—it held me up but it would not hold her
she fell through it
and said she'd go home again for the snow-shoes—
and I could slide in shine and glare while she
stepped wide
on the

Breakfast Song

My love, my saving grace,
your eyes are awfully blue.
I kiss your funny face,
your coffee-flavored mouth.
Last night I slept with you.
Today I love you so
how can I bear to go
(as soon I must, I know)
to bed with ugly death
in that cold, filthy place,
to sleep there without you,
without the easy breath
and nightlong, limblong warmth
I've grown accustomed to?
—Nobody wants to die;
tell me it is a lie!
But no, I know it's true.
It's just the common case;
there's nothing one can do.
My love, my saving grace,
your eyes are awfully blue
early and instant blue.

BELATED DEDICATION

I looked down
down through the two

Dwon through two open stove-lids
and saw the flames below
Then
I looked down through
two open stove-lids
and saw the flames below,

I looked down through
the graveyard's angels' eyes
blind circles without lids
as in the past I8d stared
in the past

down through the identical eyes
of the privy shameful muck
at the sad muck

shameless eyes
at that sad muck
littered papers

The blue tides had withdrawn
and left the red-veined mud carved into flames
The gusts of rain lifted only to show
Avernus
all apertures
lay below broken
in "classic fragment."

luminous
lumious
and any rainbow
and any rainbow, or a piece of it,
lay below, "a classic fragment," only -

sockets -

Under the rianbow's caress .
Its colored fingers are kind.
within it is the clean honest blue of your eyes
under it how noble, glowing
those brilliant crembs of houses,
those littered fields even, those suburbs and
level under the colored fingers
steady under the colored fingers,
under the promised hand.

steady below the visible fingers
the colored fingers of the hand
steady under visible colored f
fi ngers
forests -
land -

and the dead birds fell (and nobody saw them fall)
outwards, outwards and down,
in pairs like tears

likes tears, in pairs,

that you are there to thank,
and I thank you with all my heart.
Or the blue tides withdrew
swiftly -
and left their shallow sockets, filled with red mud carved into flames

Memory of Baltimore

We passed through about six o'clock
and avoided downtown Baltimore—
just before dark one spring evening—
[Some trick] of sunset where
   all the row houses [looked] lavender—

Do you know how, in the poorer sections of that town
they paint scenes on the window screens?
And as you drive by you catch the old-fashioned pictures
momentarily half-transparent, on the screens first from one side,
                          then the other, never straight on—
corny waterfalls and lakes
All of Baltimore I saw looked just like that—
   one could [almost] see through the bricks everything half-transparent

[Only] overhead
the lights came on—clear bulbs huge imitation diamonds
in white frills delicately bright in the long rose light—

light after diamond after diamond after diamond—

The macadam went up a slope and down
velvety pink gray pink
and all we saw of Baltimore
were the dissolving bricks

and the white stoops glowing row on row on row
like pearls—

   and Baltimore in tender veils   nacreous stoop!

the white stoops burning
with an inner light, yes really
angel-stoops, with no one on them   & no Jacob in the streets—
steps of pearl stepping stones of pearl, all up and down that
long long crepuscular street
[glowing to themselves]

and it was still daylight when we came out on the other side of
Baltimore—

those stoops of pearl

Travelling, A Love Poem (or just Love Poem?)

And here we must see:
"The Swaying Suspension Bridge,"
"The Exquisite Congregational Church"
(that's what it says),
And "The Octagonal House."
—None of these should tax the imagination!
Isn't it a beautiful day? It's a *beautiful* day. We almost always have good
weather, don't we?
Do you remember "October's bright blue weather?"
No. I can't remember who wrote it.
Want some more coffee? This toast is like Kleenex.
And then there's that fort
—you can see it out that window across the water.
They've left, across the hall. Let's get going.
Look, they've got the same pictures
but their carpet . . . that *aggressive* blue . . . Yucky.
Why do you suppose it was so *big*?
What war was it built for?
1812? Too late for the Revolution.
Perhaps that time we almost went to war
with Canada? Well, anyway—pre-Wright-brothers.
It says to "take flashlights" and "warm sweaters"
because most of it's underground.
Well, let's not. I can just smell the pee-pee.
Yes, *Mechanic* Street, I wonder why
—one sees lots of Mechanic Streets.
The sidewalk looks as if it had
melted, doesn't it, and hardened again.
My grandmother told me that kind is called "asphalt."
Yes, it looks as if it had melted and run
around those elm-trees.

How gold everything is—it's sort of nice.
All these towns have *some* nice old buildings.

Salem Willows

Oh, Salem Willows,
where I rode a golden lion
around and around and around,
king of the carrousel
and the other golden creatures,
around and around and around,
sumptuously, slowly,
to the coarse, mechanical music
of the gold calliope!

Round went the golden camel
and the high gold elephant
with his small red velvet rug,
around and around and around;
the staid, two-seated chariot,
gold horses and gold tigers,
but above all others
I preferred the lion,
and I mounted him astride.

His wooden mane was golden.
His mouth was open; his tongue
enameled red; his eyes
brown glass with golden sparkles.
His right forepaw was lifted
but the others wouldn't budge.
There were figures at the center—
front halves, plaster people.

From time to time, to the music,
they'd raise a flute, but never

quite to their lips; they'd almost
beat their drums; they'd not quite
pluck their upheld lyres.
It was as if that music,
coarse, mechanical, loud,
discouraged them from trying.

Around and around and around.
Were we all touched by Midas?
Were we a ring of Saturn,
a dizzy, [turning] nimbus?
Or were we one of the crowns
the saints "cast down" (but why?)
"upon the glassy sea"?
The carrousel slows down.
Really, beyond the willows,
glittered a glassy sea
and Aunt Maud sat and knitted
and knitted, waiting for me.

Back to Boston *Just North of Boston* [Draft 1]

Winter-

one doesn't know whether to laugh or cry

Back from the week=end - winter twilight
Now come the miles of ?????????
The miles of roadsigns-
one doesn't know whether to laugh or cry
onLights chasing each other round & round, lights
and screaming letters
An 18th century man-of-war, or half of one;
twelve plaster steerat slightly different angles,
wedding clothes for rent ;
a Chinese temple, maybe ?-
The lofty dou ghnut
The screen of a drive-in movie blank white
leaning over the slope - the letters all gibberish the steers
somewhere off there is the old Bay
at the intersection, just off -
a barn, a farmhouse - ten yards from the road
a big old farmhouse all the elms are gone
but one and it is dead
Let's hope the farhouse
is blind anddeaf - it looks it -

no one lives there -
someone sesll home made bread - what home/?
There;sa brown field, somrockes, a whole
brown hill
The jet-lines frazzle out so quick- there must be
a wind high up there -

a small brown hill - historic hill, no doubt -
the cops are parked there; the blue light revolves
and flashes an unnatural bright blue
even in the daytime
Far off, both sides, the willow trees
are puffs of yellow smoke
hopeless soft explosions- silent soft explosions
a blue-jay shrieks
the farmhouse, dumb numb and dumb, bright as a light, as those policar l
and let's hope, blind and deaf that policecar
The barn has just fallen down quite recently - light-

The original owners the real world the ??? unobtrusive
have given up not quite the ghost - the ghost is there -
~~(like Vuillard's sister in the wall-paper) NO~~ -
weak, stunned, dazed, pale, pining
"gone into a decline" "consumptive" consumed, all right -

* so that a Hereford's on th e top
temple roof
a headless bride is dangling inn the
doughbnut -
the howboy hat won't fit this
infant's head -

One can imagine a giant child
trudging along here, discovering
all these wonderful toys with whoops of
joy -
picking them up ~~and mxing~~ setting the
down, all mixed up

A Cowboy's hat, forty or ~~so~~ ft high
you can walk inside it

Draft one of two. The revised, more legible, but sadly abbreviated second draft follows.

Just North of Boston

Winter twilight: miles of advertising.
—One doesn't know whether to laugh or cry.
Lights chasing each other round and round;
lights running at us screaming letters.
If only we didn't know how to read,
or if they screamed Chinese or Arabic,
would we consider them more beautiful?
You say "It's possible."
But look—an 18th-century man-of-war
has run aground: She's struggling there
against the rocks, her lights still lit,

directing rescue operations. No—
it's worse: it's *half* a man-of-war.
Now come the wedding clothes for rent:
six brides are standing in a row,
dresses agleam like glare-ice; next, their grooms,
with ruffled shirt-fronts, pink or blue,
all on a brilliant stage, on stilts.
How can they meet? When will they marry?
Gold! *Gold.* A Burmese temple? Balinese?
An Oriental-something roof, with grinning
dragons. Just beyond,
an ice-cream cone *à gratte-ciel*
outlined in glowing yellow, glowing rose
on top—the ice-cream—strawberry.
Twelve Hereford steer, three Hereford calves
of sturdy plaster are deployed . . .

Dicky and Sister

"*Tweet.*" loud & coarse,
the equivalent of "Dry Up!"

Dicky & Sister sing & call,
argue & quarrel
He has the better disposition
Dicky & Sister quarrel & sing
The set tubs sit (or set),
Magee Ideal
sends out a chuff of coal gas
(the water tank is *full*)
the brass pipes shine,
the soup boils,
the Jello jells
& the alto voice
sings hymns & hymns
& "*Away down in a diving bell*
   At the bottom of the sea
   The nice little mermaids
   Pretty little mermaids
   All come a' courting me—

The fox got up in the summer night
& he looked at the moon both large & bright

my dear-oh—dear-oh—dear-oh"

(This is their dear-oh) all these things
live on together, day, night, day—

Still day

—the birds take baths
newspapers spread on the set-tub
They bill & coo a little
but Sister is not in the mood—

influencing each other—as much as they can

Sister makes for Dicky's cage
(She thinks it is better than hers—
if the silly bird can think)

She has to be ejected then
she shrieks, she shrieks,
& has to be removed entirely
from the kitchen for an hr—

the stove is *shaken down*
                              scraped out—
the 2nd scuttle

& the scuttles slightly scuttle

Sister's always had designs
on Dicky's cage. She finds it better (more
in some   than her own . . .
attractive,—

Dicky, a "roller", green,
sings his little head off:
Held high, it moves from side
to side. His throat-feathers
move separately, up & down;
& he shifts his hold on the perch
in his   efforts

At the other window
Sister flirts her tail
& turns her back. "*Tweet!*"
She throws her seeds about.

Once in a while the *tweet* goes wild,
—the equivalent of 'Dry up!'

Unsatisfactory wife!
Dicky sings on & on . . .

In the kitchen
of the old wooden
"double-decker", top floor—
Winter Sunlight coming in
[from the right,] from afar—
Two windows, two canaries
    Dicky and Sister.
A stove: *Magee Ideal*

The sink, the 'set-tub'—
The pairs of faucets, staggered.
The table, the sewing machine
covered with an old red tablecloth
the list of someone's peculiar (DIET) foods

brass—
& at right angles—
the paired brass water pipes
up to the ceiling—
the linoleum—&
a hooked rug—very worn—
& towels behind the stove—
over the table a calendar
—a picture of a baby
cut from "The Ladies Home Journal" cover
& a list—someone's *diet*

[the gentle mistress of this]

the owner of all these things—

proprietor of the pedal Singer
of the *Stove*—

At night who knows what happens?
The birds don't know—
Only perhaps the mice know
& the occasional [cock-] roach—?

Do the set tubs still set—
the brass pipes cling to the wall?
The faucets stay turned off?

At night what happens? Who knows?
Dicky & Sister have put their beaks
under their wings, they're covered up
at night, the Singer cover covers Dicky—
it also seems to cover the bread
whenever left to rise

Magee Ideal dances
jigs a [little] on her tiny black claw feet—

the Singer pedals furiously
furious, trapped, the Singer pedals—

(*the smell of yeast*)

The bread rises—
The brasses shine
The moon   that bosses
or *Magee Ideal*'s   oven door—
her broken thermometer   cyclop-eye
or the thermometer   one eye
that doesn't register right—
                    see straight—

the towels dry   at last
& the scuttles *scuttle*

Its coals gleam black, blue, gold—
Ashes & coals lie under the grate
Coals then gray ashes
lie beneath the grate—
The water tank—hisses with greenish tarnish

The Singer sings, everything sings
in its own way—
          silently—
hum themselves to sleep
sleep humming in the partial dark

Wait for the sun,
the tea-kettle   comfortably

                        All long ago,
                        All long ago.

~~the gentle [illegible] of the (restless)~~

the owner of all these things —

proprietor of the [illegible] signs
of the Store —

2. At night what happens? Who knows?

[illegible] [illegible] put their [illegible]
[illegible] [illegible] [illegible] [illegible]
(at night, the signs cover [illegible] [illegible] —
it does [illegible] to cover the [illegible] / [illegible]
left to [illegible]) [illegible] for ?

1. At night who knows what happens?
The birds don't know —
Only perhaps the mice know
& the occasional cock-roach — ?

Do the red tables still [illegible] —
the brass pipes cling to the wall?
The faucets stay turned off?

[illegible] [illegible] [illegible] [illegible] boxes
[illegible] a [illegible] [illegible] by [illegible]
they [illegible] clean [illegible] —

the signs [illegible] furiously —
furious, trapped, the signs [illegible] [illegible] →

[the smell of gas]

The bread rises —
The brasses shine
The moon   the basses ←

on baroque bedstead   our door —

the towels dry   and hot
& the scuttles scuttle —   ?
its the coals glow blood, & blue, gold —
Ashes & coals lie under the grate
use   Coals the ~~ashes~~ grey ashes
lie beneath the grate —
The water tank — hums with greenish
~~green~~
tarnish —

The dogs sleep; eighty dogs
in into our ways —
silently —
hum themselves to sleep,
~~sleep humming in the partial dark~~
Wait for the sun,
the tea-kettle   comfortably

has broken thermostats   cyclops-eye
on the thermostats   one eye
that doesn't register right —
see straight —

All long ago;
All long ago.

(FLORIDA REVISITED)?

The coconut palms still clatter;
and the pelicans still waddle, soar, and dive,
and the sickly-looking willets pick at their food.
The sunset doesn't color the sea; it stains
the water-glaze of the receding waves instead.
At night the "giant dew" drips on the roof
and the grass grows wet and the hibiscus drags
folded, sad and wet, in the morning
And it still goes on and on, more or less the same
as it has, apparently, for over half my life-time-;
Goes on after, or over, how many deaths,
how many deaths and loves lost, lost forever-

The sun sets; a man is making a movie of it
(this is hard to believe, but true)
and directly opposite
the full moon rises, covered with tears
It can't stop crying now but will, eventually,
one supposes, and look clearly composedly down,
composedly, on all the earthly dew

Change is what hurts worst; change alone can kill.
It kills us, finally - but not these earthly things.
One hates this immutability finally,
Finally one hates immutability.
Finally one hates the Florida one knows,
the Florida one knows

Oh palms, oh birds, & over- sunsets
oh full and weeping moon
- oh unendurable

And the dead black bird, or the breast of one,
lying just at the foam's edge
that proved to be a piece of charred wood - just like feathers..

Just at the water's edge
a dead, black bird, or the breast of one,
coal-black, glistening, each wet fetaher distinct
that turned out to be a charred wood,
feather-light, feather marked
but not a bird at all - dead, delicately graven, dead wood
light as the breast of a bird in the hand -
feathers ///

(Florida Revisited)?

I took it for a bird—
Just at the water's edge
a dead, black bird, or the breast of one,
coal-black, glistening, each wet feather distinct
that turned out to be a piece of [charred] wood,
feather-light, feather marked
but not a bird at all—dead, delicately graven, dead wood
light as the breast of a bird in the hand—
feathers

I picked it up—not a bird
It was light,
too light to be a bird,
weightless—
a surprise like
missing a step

The coconut palms still clatter;
the pelicans still waddle, soar, and dive.
Tall, sickly-looking willets pick at their food.
The sunset doesn't color the sea; it stains
the glaze of wet receding waves instead.
At night the "giant dews" drip on the roof
and the grass grows wet and the hibiscus drops blossom
folded, sad and wet, in the morning
[And it] still goes on and on, more or less the same.
It has, now apparently, for over half my life-time—:
Gone on after, or over, how many deaths,
how many deaths by now, [and] love lost, lost forever.

many deaths by cancer,
& suicides—
friendship & love
lost, lost forever—

The sun sets, & a man is making a movie of it
(this is hard to believe, but true)
and directly opposite
a full moon [rises], covered with tears.
The moon can't stop crying now but, one supposes—
it will eventually,

& look down
clearly & composedly
        bravely—
day & /bright/, on all
this earthly dew—
                Oh now, stop crying—

Change is what hurts worst; change alone can kill.
Change kills us, finally—not these earthly things.
One hates all this immutability.
Finally one hates the Florida one knows,
the Florida one knew.

Oh palms, oh birds, and over-exaggerated sunsets—
oh full and weeping moon   why do you weep?
—oh unendurable [world]   Well, loneliness is always
                                                        an excuse.

Sammy

Most comical of all in death,
Sammy, dear Uncle Sam,
dead these fifteen years, . . .
Sammy, my dear toucan. . .
I killed you! I didn't mean to,
of course; I cried & cried—
It *was* all my fault,
Sammy, dear Uncle Sam.

neon-bright blue eyes
looking at me, sidewise,
and I cried & cried full of wickedness

The cook made gingerbread
(I'd taught her how)
to try to cheer me up . . .
But—still I miss you;
I could cry all over again.
You cheered me up.
You were so funny, Sam.

You loved shiny things, bright things
(I think birds do see colors)
and anything bright red.
I was afraid your life was boring.
Remember I bought you
a pair of ten-cent-store, Carnival
big earrings
and hung them in your cage for you
to play with

I loved you, and I caged you.

Mr. and Mrs. Carlyle

The mail from Liverpool was fifteen minutes early
   at the Swan with Two Necks.
No sign of Mr. Carlyle, so Mrs. Carlyle
   put her "luggage on the backs

of two porters, walked to Cheapside,
   took a Chelsea omnibus"
and got inside it with her headache,
   hoping this would save a lot of fuss.

He was living only for his book
   these days, and she lived not to vex
Mr. Carlyle, who meanwhile had set out on foot
   to meet her at the Swan with Two Necks.

Her trunks went up on top.
   She would be at home now soon.
She was feeling perfectly wretched.
   It was a hot September afternoon.

One flesh and two heads
   engaged in kisses or in pecks.
Oh white seething marriage!
   Oh Swan with Two Necks!

Appendix

Mechanics of Pretence: Remarks on W. H. Auden *(1934–35)*

Much can be done by means of pretence. Children pretend to speak a foreign language or inscribe its imitation alphabet in their school books, and inspired by the same motives, grow up to become linguists, grammarians, and travellers. Lord Byron, looking in the mirror, pretended to be the Byronic man, and the Byronic man, with his curls and collars, came into existence by the hundred. The growth of the small nation into the empire contains infinities of such pretence, gradually turning to the infinite realities of empire.

In his earlier stages the poet is the verbal actor. One of the causes of poetry must be, we suppose, the feeling that the contemporary language is not equivalent to the contemporary fact; there is something out of proportion between them, and what is being said in words is not at all what is being said in "things." To connect this disproportion a pretence is at first necessary. By "pretending" the existence of a language appropriate and comparable to the "things" it must deal with, the language is forced into being. It is learned by one person, by a few, by all who can become interested in that poet's poetry.

But as this imaginary language is elaborated and is understood by more people, it begins to work two ways at once. "Things" gave rise to the language; now the language arouses an independent life in the "things," first dimly perceived in them only by the poet. To the initiate, the world actually manages to look like so-and-so's poems—the poems that he first carefully fitted to the "ways of the

"Mechanics of Pretence" is, according to Bishop's biographer Brett Millier, Bishop's first post-college "review essay," drafted in 1937 while she was living in New York at the Murray Hill Hotel. The uncorrected copy is included here in light of Bishop's discussion of William Empson's *Seven Types of Ambiguity* in the note on "It is marvellous to wake up together . . ." (p. 267).

world" himself. The play becomes a play on a stage dissolving to leave the ground underneath. The tendency, described by William Empson, of what a poet writes to become *real*; the tendency towards "prophecy"; obscurity, and "influence," are all [departments] of this original act of pretence.

The poems of W. H. Auden are an excellent example of the power of pretence at work, and from them it can be illustrated in several different ways. First, indirectly:

In his Journal, Gibbon, speaking of a military review, quotes from "A Treatise of Military Discipline," by Humphrey Bland. "The whole then attempted street-firings. . . . Note 'the firing will appeare [*sic*] more graceful when it is begun while the Regiment is in motion, than when it stands still. For as that which is performed in motion, carries a greater resemblance of real service than the other, it must therefore, by so lively a representation of action, raise the imagination to a higher pitch.' "

Many of Auden's first "Poems" are similar attempts to "raise the imagination to a higher pitch" by perfecting the pretence so that it resembles "real service."

> "We made all possible preparations,
> Drew up a list of firms,
> Constantly revised our calculations
> But allotted the farms,
>
> Issued all the orders expedient
> In this kind of case:
> Most, as was expected, were obedient,
> Though there were murmurs, of course. . . ."
>
> "Control of the passes, was, he saw, the key
> To this new district . . ."
>
> "And bravery is now
> Not in the dying breath
> But resisting temptations
> To skyline operations." etc.

The whole of the early play "Paid on Both Sides," and the terrible "plans" in "Journal of an Airman."

That his pretence has worked is proved by the mounting, uncalculated waves of influence. Auden is the founder of the "forsaken factory" school of literary landscape painting. (Not in his hands—trend toward romanticism—)

"It provides an emotional experience, and then, if we have the courage of our own feelings, it becomes a mine of practical truth."

Studies in Classic American Literature, D. H. Lawrence
N.Y. 1923, p. 2

Verdigris

The catalogues will tell you that they mean
the Chinese bronzes were like fresh-turned loam.
The time to watch for is when Time grows green.

Some like them green, some still prefer them clean,
as found in strange museums away from home.
The catalogues will tell you that they mean

it isn't any old phosphorescent sheen
confines them to the past; in polychrome
the time to watch for is when Time grows green.

The queer complexion of a former Queen,
Justice an upright leaf upon her Dome,
the catalogues will tell you that they mean

left in the earth, or out, it is foreseen
we get like that; also if lost in foam.
The time to watch for is when Time grows green.

"Verdigris" is included with reference to the prose fragment "Villanelle" because it is a villanelle. Bishop did not consider it successful, though. Katharine White, her *New Yorker* editor, returned the poem to Bishop on January 20, 1950, saying that it "drew a mixed vote but the no's won out in the end . . . it does seem to the majority to be obscure and not to have quite the simplicity and neatness that a villanelle should have." Bishop responded, "Please don't feel badly . . . It was just one of those hunches that I guess didn't work—& on studying it some more I think probably in order to make the meaning clear it will have to be turned into a *double* villanelle!"

Oh blue-green Seas of Greece, and in between,
the olive-groves and copper roofs of Rome!
The catalogues will tell you that they mean
the time to watch for is when Time grows green.

[1950]

Homesickness

It was October, 1899, and a cold heavy morning; but everywhere the scarlet and orange of the sugar-maple trees still threaded the sombre firs of the Nova Scotian woods. A horse named Nimble, pulling a faded red wagon, was climbing slowly along the road that ran up the side of a high bluff overlooking the Bay of Fundy, dipped down again, and then forked off into the woods, one road uphill, the other down. It was high tide; from the point of view of the travellers in the wagon, who saw it reflecting whatever light there was, the water looked metallic, a rose-gray-violet; but from another angle it would have looked like liquid terra cotta mud. The road was a damp, darker terra cotta, and narrow, winding among large granite boulders covered with gray and yellow lichens.

On the one seat of the wagon sat a man, a dog, and a young girl; a little boy sat on the wagon bed, facing backwards, his legs dangling over the let-down tail-board. The dog was a big hound bitch, her coat just a few shades darker than the earth of the road. She sat in the middle, smiling with pleasure at the ride, and looking from side to side. Occasionally she gave an excited lick in the direction of the faces of the man or his daughter, whose arm lay across her back; her tail, descending through the opening between the back of the seat and the seat, wagged slowly and steadily. Her name was Juno.

The man was John MacLaughlin and the girl his daughter Grace, about fourteen years old. He wore a gray tweed cap and a rather shiny blue serge suit, strained across his broad back more than usual because underneath it in place of his vest he was wearing

"*Homesickness*" is connected to the verse draft of the same title, presenting the story from a different perspective.

a gray cardigan buttoned to the throat. His eyes were very blue; his face broad and tanned, his enormous moustache almost white, with touches of blond at its overhanging corners. His face was remarkable for its cheerful benevolence and an expression of slightly, constantly resigning itself to the contingencies of the moment. Yet it was dreamy, and he looked around him in a pleased, dreamy way, as if somewhat surprised at the innocuous scenery. Grace was not dreamy; she sat up very straight and looked alert. She was sturdy, like her father, but very dark, with a fiercely determined round chin with a dimple in it. On her head she had a Scotch bonnet with streamers and a silver thistle pin set with a cairngorm, and she wore a maroon-colored woolen dress with black velvet collar and cuffs and a good many small jet buttons in rows here and there according to some vague design sprung from the fancy of the village dressmaker. She kept one hand on Juno, with two fingers through the brass ring on the dog's old collar; Juno had been known, when taken visiting, to decide to go hunting instead.

Under the seat there was a large osier basket, made by the Micmac Indians, trimmed [with] red and purple, filled with packages that looked like food and were wrapped in clean old sugar bags. Mr. MacLaughlin was on his way to see another daughter, Georgie, who had left home for the first time that autumn, to teach school, and he was taking her some presents.

The little brother, Amos, looked even dreamier than his father. His little blue cap, embroidered with a maple leaf and the word CANADA curved underneath it in yellow letters, was over one ear and his head hung forward on his chest. He wore a blue suit like his father's but with knee pants, streaked with lighter blue and stained, and a gray knitted muffler was tucked in solidly all around his neck, making him appear to be stuffed. One nostril ran and ran; he sniffed absent-mindedly, like slow clockwork, never taking his gaze off the left-hand rear wheel-track flattening out like a ribbon behind them, gleaming slightly from the pressure of the iron rim, straight, then taking little jerking changes of direction when the wagon lurched: a mysterious little road going along all by itself, imposing itself on the big road and all the other little wheel-roads, flat or crusted, darker or lighter, spinning itself out of itself, he thought, as if the wheel were a big spider. Amos held a whip in both hands, an old buggy-whip that had been covered with black glaze cloth, but it was worn gray, and the end was no longer tassled but frayed out. He dragged the tip gently back and forth over the wheel-track, making a slow, wavering line on top of the imprinted ribbon. He had completely hypnotized himself with this moving arabesque. Fine, red grains of earth kept rising a little way up the turning wheel-rims and falling back steadily, like thin little fountains.

No one spoke, but the old wagon shifted and creaked and the harness creaked and squeaked in a different key. As they started up the steeper branch of the road Nimble broke wind gently several times and a comfortable warm odor of manure hung for a moment in the air. The fir trees looked wet, and the few enormous old blackening, rotting toadstools and mushrooms, the last of the season, standing beneath them contributed occasional sharp whiffs of decay.

Juno thought she saw something moving in the woods. She gave a sudden bark and a jump towards the road, but Grace held onto her collar and pushed her down again. Juno turned and kissed her good-naturedly, wagging her tail harder, seeming to find her own impulsiveness rather amusing. She was ten years old and there were many white hairs and whiskers around her mouth. She had had more puppies than anyone could well remember; when they looked like her, which they sometimes did, Mr. MacLaughlin called them "Juno's chocolate drops." She had been promiscuous, and yet there was something very settled and domestic in her manner; if she could have talked one could imagine her conversation: cheerful, practical, and tedious,—but a character to turn to with confidence in life's darker moments. Indeed, although she didn't know it, that was exactly why she was being taken on this trip, and among the cloth-wrapped packages under the seat was a large leg-bone with some meat on it, to be given her when they reached their destination.

[c. early 1950s]

True Confessions

Then for a while I went to a strange sort of institution we have here for people who are in the same fix. It was rather far away to the left and up, in a cold cloud. It was extremely mournful. The trees had grown up and up and up and showed no signs of stopping and were bored with it all, and beneath them their needles were getting too thick and silent. There were plenty of graves there, and a cat with one white eye. It was not a story by Poe. The people in the graves had not been people of the finest oversensibility. They had been owners of the stock exchange. They had had railroads and wheat and many heavy heavy burdens. They lay heaped under pine needles as under the weight of their sins and the wind soughed half-heartedly, not really giving a damn one way or the other. On the grave of the chief of the clan stood a beer can.

The soap was yellow hard as a rock and smelled like cheap tea. The whole place smelled like cheap tea. The water was harder than the soap and getting out of a bath was like stepping from a tight fitting grave into refreshing water.

There I fell for, I can't think why, an elderly little girl with little yellow eyes and slightly harlequin glasses. Just about at the point she was able to read Dickens as a child—say "Little Dorrit"—she and her doll had decided it would be better all round for them to change places. I don't know where the doll had gone—off being an unfaithful wife somewhere, probably—but the doll's looks were becoming in an unnatural way so that you looked twice at that tiny chin and dimpled cheeks, and the little laugh, open to have crumbs poked in by birds, maybe.

"True Confessions"—surviving only in this very rough draft—is referred to in the note on "Crossing the Equator."

But the character out of Dickens has its drawbacks these days and many were the frustrations the (child) doll suffered because of the (unmarried) wife. It was inclined to make her as hard as nails.

Well, there I misbehaved myself into fits and starts, and everything started overdoing—my finger & toenails, my hair, my dreams. The snow would occasionally come and make a clean breast of everything and terrify me with its glitter. Up out of it stuck skeletal brown weeds clutching diamonds of ice like something Cartier never thought of—And the best thing was a water fall moss and all frozen in a show-case—like the stained glass staircase at the old Bijou movie house in Boston with water tumbling under the steps—

I was born there, sort of in the middle but slightly to the left and rather inset—a tiny, almost invisible baby. I could see it under a magnifying glass—a tiny, almost invisible baby, a small dark haired mother upstairs in a tiny toy wooden apartment house painted gray. Years later, when it was visible to the naked eye, but still not very big, I saw it from a trolley car. Someone said, "That's where you were born" and I turned around to stare and saw briefly through its gray walls and a vague fierce picture of myself being born hanging on one of them and then it receded behind my shoulder & up a curve to the left, and vanished—

All kinds of awful things happened to me there. I lived only in the summers and hibernated for ten months at a time. One summer was famous for its sunsets; perhaps still is, I just haven't heard anyone mention them lately. One summer there were northern lights twice and brighter than any ever seen in the winter. We were roused from our beds and stood ankle deep in the cooling sand, clutching each other's shoulders, to lean backwards and watch. Long blood red banners stretched and flew and sagged.

Clouds.

(Has to be short)

Then I dropped down to another place, dropped, dropped, as far as I could go, like a spider on its thread—it gives me a sinking feeling in my stomach—no almost a feeling of pulling at the tips of my toes even to think of that place now. I was lowered down through the lowest clouds I ever saw through the most fantastic waters and there I lived delighted, believe me, for some time and constantly taking photographs of banana trees in blossom—upside down like myself—

It was what they call the "Rum Latitudes" and everyone drank this beverage in the form of something they called "Scoundrels" the variation on this was "Rascals" (look up) all the time—"Down there" sounds dark. This Down There was almost too bright. The juke box songs were fearful beyond belief. "You made me love you I didn't want to do it I didn't want to do it"

[c. 1953]

Suicide of a (Moderate) Dictator—
A Report in Verse & Prose

The crowd stood, apparently, on two or three small side streets—not very compactly then; dazedly, some looking into the camera, a woman or two only, all the rest men, as is usual here with crowds getting closer together all the time. The tall, enormously tall, thin palms dreamed up behind them, a hot hazy day, as if they were rapidly growing. Open shirts, sweat, everything grayish. Two or three neat soldiers with tin helmets and tommy guns. A white ambulance smokes by and turns a corner, between hedges. What on earth has its fat red cross to do with any of this. The next shots—an hour or so later—from inside the yard apparently—the Important People arriving, black and concerned, with hornrimmed glasses or black glasses and black suits or khaki-poplin-uniforms—moving in. Aranha very handsome and tall, white hair. Then later the coffin scene, briefly—G. jammed into it tightly—at least according to our N. Am. idea of such things—none of our puffed silk, pillows, etc.—his head pushing against the top of the box, tightly framed in glass,—as if it were lined with paper—a tight squeeze, all in all . . . Lines going by fairly fast on either side, peeking in or smearing the glass with a kiss, carrying a long calla lily or a flash bulb camera (One has seen chiefly by now up the President's dead large nostrils with cotton in them.) It—the box, comes out the door—heaves out the door—heaves is the word from now on. Bolted all around the top—not very big. A shot of a large Cadillac with the really cartoon-like son, enormously gross,

"Suicide of a (Moderate) Dictator" is connected to the poem of the same title. Bishop evidently entertained the idea of publishing them together, the poem first and the prose account "to follow." "G." is Getúlio Vargas. The uncorrected copy is presented as Bishop left it. The handful of legible revised phrases have been incorporated.

smoking a cigarette, and rapidly shoving a woman in a black skirt and white blouse, and the black glasses, into it ahead of him, settling in, and whisking rapidly off with his arm around the back of the seat, not looking at the camera.

The coffin is carried off, apparently by the crowd, like a log tossing on a flooded river, but always with the head-end tilted upwards. Thousands and thousands of people surging rapidly, always, along the avenue by the waterfront to the airport—the coffin apparently on a small bier of some sort—how they kept it on it one cannot see or imagine. Thousands of soldiers by this time, too, but no "disorder" just surging surging, and cries and shrieks—weeping men and women—sobbing, howling men and women, clutching their limp long stemmed lilies—like the palm trees that shoot up languidly but rapidly occasionally in the backgrounds—A long long look deep into the eyes of a Negro girl, glistening blankly. Women sobbing in each other's arms. Then the women start fainting. Then the Wreath makes its appearance—an enormous circle of lilies and greens mysteriously floating along, too, bobbing along, like a gigantic frilled life-preserver—first here then there—where & how—Up it goes—sidewise it slips—it can never reach quite the side of the floating up-ended mystic black feather that the President has become, but it seems struggling to reach his side and never catches up. But those are people underneath. And underneath the people are the flowers. The avenue is littered with them now. Motorcycles, soldiers, push along too—like a released dam—a flash flood. How fast the coffin goes!

At the airport things start getting rough. Will they let the feather join the mystic bird or not? The soldiers start using their clubs. Ambulances close in and women are tossed on stretchers right and left. And there's the Wreath. How did *it* get here? Now it's over at the right—no, it's fallen behind—no there it is, tipping up up on a crest. But it never never tips over. It is a patented life-preserver. It is as buoyant as the coffin. The coffin reaches the plane door—the worst moment—tipping and swaying, almost writhing, push and pull, they get it in somehow—the camera heaves a sigh.

We see the wife, supported by two very plain female relatives—black glasses—her mouth twisted with a look of extreme self-pity. Hands try to reach her—a girl kisses her wrist—she murmurs something. Back to the plane, that makes a neat quick take-off through the bright haze, past the water and the hills of Guanabara Bay—Off and up and off—oh assumption! Where is your Wreath?

Newsreel I saw Sept 1st or 2nd—
The suicide took place the morning of the 24th.

[1954]

Mrs. Sullivan Downstairs

I lived with my aunt, [M?? Maggie], my mother's eldest sister, and her husband, Uncle Ned. They lived in the upstairs apartment of a two-family house on the outskirts of an old but hideously ugly city north of Boston. The house had been built, I suppose, around 1905 or 10; it was clapboard, painted a dirty yellow, with white trim, a concave roof the tar of which smelt right through in very hot weather, small bay windows front and side, and on the back two wooden "piazzas" as they were called: open staircases and palings, clumsy wooden cages. The rooms in these apartments were small, but living in the top one, we at least had three bedrooms instead of two; a front bedroom fitted over the impractically large space cut out of the lower apt. for our tall, dim, varnished front hall and staircase. The rent was never probably more than $25 or $30 a month, in fact I believe I remember its being raised to $30 when I was about ten years old. . . . I could draw the floor plan now: you went up the long staircase that was always cool—in the winter freezing—made a sharp right turn and entered the narrow hallway. To the right the front bedroom where my aunt & uncle slept, to the right front the doorway to the tiny living room. [Straight in front] of [one] the doorway to the tiny dining room, and off it a small bedroom with one window. To the left the kitchen where we did so much of our living, taken up by a blackish green [stove] (its name was Magee Ideal) and

The memoir "Mrs. Sullivan Downstairs" includes many details reflected in the drafts for "Dicky and Sister." Bishop made handwritten revisions only on the first page of seven and the legible changes have been incorporated here. I have restored her original phrasing in brackets in cases where the revisions are illegible or partial, obscuring the thrust of the original. This copy represents the slapdash punctuation, repetition, and syntax of the draft, as well.

two “set tubs” covered with a big hood with a great deal of brass pipe (my job to polish). Two windows, and hanging in them the canaries Dicky and Sweetie. Off that another small bedroom, mine. [Out from the end of the] kitchen another narrow dark hall, this one going onto the “piazza” and just having space enough for a small refrigerator. The narrow back staircase with two turns in it descended past Mrs. Sullivan’s back door.

It was a medium-poor section of a very poor town; most of the houses were of this type, or of four apartments instead of two, or sometimes three stories high. But there were scattered vacant lots between almost every house and its neighbor. Trees had been left at random, some of them quite big and old. We had one rock on our vacant lot. It was big enough for two or three children to climb up and sit on the top of, and it came in very handy. The streets were steep, [and] unpaved and there were no sidewalks, [either]—dried riverbeds, of gravel, [are all I remember, and] iron streetlamps, and ashcans [waiting to be collected.] Here there [was] a really old house, perhaps what once had been an old farmhouse, but they were very run down. A few of the younger & more energetic men, like my uncle, did have vegetable gardens,—but no attempts were made to brighten up the front of these houses and tenements. They all gave immediately on the [street], anyway—& perhaps it was too hopeless. Our street [ran] between two other larger streets that were paved, or at least they had sidewalks. So one could go either down the hill to roller skate, or up.

We had a “view.” That is, from the dining room bay window or the living room bay window you could pull back the white net curtains and see across a valley filled with other ugly houses, hit or miss, and vacant lots, onto two or three rolling hills that always seemed to be brown, although they must have been green at times—on top of the highest was the wire fencing of the “reservoir.” If we had been just a bit higher we could have seen the top of the Custom’s House tower, then the landmark of Boston, as it was we had to walk up the hill to the higher street to get the real “view.” This view that we did have, however, seemed to be awfully important, I noticed—my uncle always showed it to visitors and seemed quite proud of it. I think for a long time I thought that a “view” was any hill one could see without too much obstruction, or perhaps just living on any top floor—it certainly had nothing whatever to do with nature or esthetics.

There were gas lamps that I was afraid of and that surely did give an ominous cold bluish light. I can remember the awe with which I watched my aunt light up every night the one lamp that was kept burning—it had a "mantle"—and that I could make jump up into full awful glare by pulling a small balled chain—There was a hot air furnace that kept us all scorching underfoot and dried out furniture skin and all, all winter long—The furnace must have been a horror—I remember my poor aunt with her hair done up in a printed cloth and wearing old gloves of my uncle's scrupulously but complainingly shaking all the ashes in a stifling cloud of ash dust, saving all the odd bits of coal throwing away the "clinkers" and picking out all the unburnt pieces of coal. They were poor and thrifty. We also had, on the "piazza" at times large hard newspaper balls—made by soaking old papers in water and squeezing them into balls—when dry these started the fires and saved on kindling wood. The kitchen stove was a coal stove too, but it also had two gas burners on the back MAGEE IDEAL I read and read for years and made a rubbing of it and its cast-iron flowers once in a while when it was cold.

That's really about all there was to it although I remember every stick of furniture and almost every dish. We had our favorites my aunt and I, and planned wistfully to replace this or that awful thing with something we dreamed of or had seen in the Boston papers. Even the canaries wanted to improve their circumstances—or Sister [*sic*] did. Dickie had a better cage, older solider, bigger with fine brass screening around the bottom. Every time they were allowed out for baths or to fly around—almost every day—Sweetie would usurp Dickie's cage and hold on to his perch for dear life, finally to be chased out, squawking, by my aunt. We had another female for several years, too, "Sister" who was younger and gayer—I believe she was supposed to be a bride for Dickie but somehow the longed-for eggs never appeared either—like so many things in our lives—Sister had spells of rage, frustration or so perhaps despair in which she shrieked over and over at Dickie or at us—and my aunt would say firmly, "If you don't stop, Sister, you are going in the closet." Sister shrieked right at her, and was whisked off to the shelf in the closet in the dark for an hour. She emerged sulky but quiet; however, she cheered up almost immediately.

We also had a good many house-plants known to us as intimately as the canaries were—geraniums, palagon pelargoniums, ferns, and in the winter and spring dishes of bulbs—I had a large bowl of goldfish, too, bulging Japanese fantails. Quite often the canaries fell in among the fish and had to be rescued. Dickie fought them gallantly, or thought he did, they merely floated towards him goggling and gulping and stared solemnly as he pecked furiously attacked their round glass fortress—

Many poor Italians lived around us, and some not so poor. Mrs. Constantina owned the biggest wooden tenement house, across the street, and spoke no English at all. She also owned the biggest vacant lot to our right and farmed it; in fact all these Italians, except for the one rich Cameo family down the street who were bootleggers and had their vacant lot filled with paths of marble chips, cement park benches, bird baths, etc., our neighbors mostly lived as if they were still peasants in their old Sicilian villages. Hens, goats, grapevines, wine-making, tomato raising filled the days of the women and there were always a few out digging up dandelion greens in their lots. Their goats stood on top of our rock; sometimes to my aunt's despair, they stood on front steps and baa-aad at callers—or butted them. One dramatic week was when Mr. Constantina died of pneumonia. He was delirious for some time and once escaped from the family and rushed down the stairs out into a snowstorm in his night shirt, his daughter and two sons screaming after him. I happened to see this and thought at first they were abusing the dark hairy little man with a huge moustache. However, he disappeared inside again, my aunt explained it all, shaking with indignation and trying, as always, to smooth everything over for me and make it all seem natural and pleasant—and three days later we heard that Mr. Constantina had died, then a great mourning went up through the falling snow from the gray run-down big ark of a building.

The bootleggers' children's tricycles had thick rubber tires, the fattest ever seen, while those of the other children—those who had tricycles at all—the wheels either ground and bumped over the rocky sidewalks on iron rims, or had the merest layer of hard rubber and always falling off, at that—

Mrs. Constantina looked like a witch, very bent, dark, snaggled hair—She was reported to be a miser, she certainly had a bad temper. We could hear that across the street, even if we knew no Italian. Once every spring a man came with a horse & plow to plow up her vacant lots and then Mrs. C went to work and planted the whole thing all by herself. She set out rows and rows of green pepper plants and tomato plants. Once I was walking by and stopped to watch her—bent, filthy, several layers of petticoats and long soiled aprons, black, blue, or dirt-streaked white, one over the other. Suddenly she straightened up, said something unintelligible to me, and came towards me with a tomato plant in a lily cup in one hand and her trowel in the other. I was as afraid as all the other children of "Old lady Constantina" but suddenly I realized she was *smiling* at me. It was like a fairy tale. Mrs. C turned into the *good* fairy under my eyes and very formally presented me with the tomato plant and several pats on the cheek with her muddy hand. My aunt could scarcely believe this; but there was the tomato plant to prove it. We added it to our own collection. Every spring at a certain time we went to a place called "The Pansy Farm" and bought our own tomato and green pepper plants and also enough pansy plants to fill two large wooden boxes we kept on the "piazza." My aunt and I both adored these pansies and each and every face was studied, criticized, and they were never quite as big as they should be. My aunt liked the big dark ones best and I favored the pure bright yellows and most of all and rather scarce an occasional pale pure gray-blue.

Across the street lived Barb'runt, whose name of course was really Barbara Hunt and who was probably, I realized much later, a bastard. She lived in one of the old houses, high, three-storied, narrow, set on the side of the hill, somewhat Gothic with stained glass set in around the long dark front door, and two flights of long dismal stairs with black bannisters and handrails going up through the gloom. I don't know whose child she was. Mrs. Hunt was a terror and obviously not her mother. She called her "Cousin Helen" or Miss Helen. Mr. Hunt was small, reddish, silent, hen-pecked, with button boots. He was often drunk, but silently so. He would sit at their kitchen table drinking bottles of home brew without a word of apology, indeed without a word. If you stared long enough he'd wink and pretend to offer you some; that was all. There were two daughters, tall like their mother, one a red-head and one dark. They were both silent like Cousin Helen, too, and the house seemed to be a stormy one. I was not supposed to go in and rarely did. Mrs. Hunt had a disconcerting way of ignoring you one day, or even ordering you to go away, and the next being much too affectionate and almost fawning, and embarrassing. On those days she would give me a plant for my aunt, or an occasional jar of her own jelly—My aunt turned up her nose at this and said Mrs. H didn't know how to make jelly, and it was true, it was always like rubber and came out of the jar in strings instead of in a lovely shaky mold—but I rather liked chewy jelly.

But Barb'runt was a sort of standby for me when I got too lonely—and she would come and play with me, swing in the hammock on our "piazza" and we lent her books—she was bright and a great reader but had almost nothing of her own, poor child. She was also extremely long-legged and clumsy and every time she spent an afternoon with me something was bound to get broken. Once she fell into our best pansy-box and broke off or flattened out all my aunt's and my favorites of that year. My aunt actually shed tears over them. Perhaps because her own house was crowded, or because Cousin H wouldn't let her stay uninterrupted—she also used to use our bathroom when she came to play, and stay shut up in it for long stretches at a time. This drove my aunt wild. Although she was too polite to shout at her and tell her to come out she would gesture at the door or even shake her fist at it and roll her eyes at me—There were the two fighting sisters although the red-head was often away from home. B would say "They aren't speaking today." Then proudly, "They haven't spoken for 48 hours." There was also a lodger from time to time, "Mr.   from Weymouth." He seemed a slightly higher type and would sit on their bare porch rocking and reading a real book. He also brought Barb'runt a present each time he came, once even a new pink gingham dress. Almost always something to wear or he gave Mrs. H money for "my new Mary Janes." Several years later it occurred to me that perhaps he was her father. But could any of the females have been her mother? None of them showed even a trace of affection. None looked like her—A horrible strange grim unlovely cold family—Barb'runt was obviously the brightest member of it but I didn't even feel the mystery or romance of her sad situation then—we were both orphans, that is, almost fairy princesses and living here just temporarily—that was our great bond although we took it so much for granted we never once referred to it as far as I remember.

Their house smelled so different. Mrs. H made large sad flat cakes that she flavored with "Mapeline" and the house reeked of it.

My aunt was small, worried, nervous, shy. She was a clean housekeeper but not a very good one; things went undone often while she read a new magazine or a novel. The sewing-machine in the kitchen was piled high with old *National Geographics* always, as far as I remember it occasionally they were lifted off and deposited some other place while she made herself a dress. She did beautiful sewing. Or she'd sit down at the piano and we'd waste an afternoon singing World War I songs. She had "a beautiful alto voice" and we sang hymns in parts sometimes, too—While I polished the endless brass pipes in the kitchen and Dickie sang and sang the room smelled of coal gas and lighting gas, but it was warm and cozy—My aunt and I loved each other and told each other everything and for many years I saw nothing in her to criticize . . .

The street lamp on the steep hill just below us, below our vacant lot full of long brown tan weeds, crowned by our rock—There was a streetlamp that was still lit by a lamplighter every evening. It stood beneath a large [beech] tree. When I lay in bed at nights the light threw the shadows of the leaves uphill and greatly magnified on the tan painted walls—the white wall—The leaves looked gigantic—only a dozen or so—and on nights of strong wind, in the late summer, before they fell, or when some had fallen—their shadows would move agitatedly, frantically, wagging chop-chopping—I half-consciously frightened myself watching them. I looked at them and saw a group in lively conversation or in an argument, threatening each other, [menacing], interrupting, insulting, roaring—and all in silence—Horrible wide opening mouths, waving hands, gnashing jaws, thrown back heads, contemptuous laughs . . . I watched and watched and terrified myself—what were they talking about? Would they fight? Used to violence in the neighbors and a certain amount threatened even in my own apartment—

But what I really But

The Italians outnumbered the Irish; we were Canadians, but had no friends at all. There was one other Canadian woman two streets over but we didn't know her—I suppose my aunt despised everyone a little. It is true she was a cut above them—and she probably was intensely unhappy in our

No doubt aunt despised everyone a little.

The Italians outnumbered the Irish. They went to different Catholic churches—All these people were violent, drunken,

Catholic, "dirty" I was told although I didn't notice that so much. I liked their names. I occasionally talked to a small very dark little girl with long black hair and one torn pink dress. She had come from Naples at "two months"—Naples meant nothing to me except Vesuvius—and the pictures in the corner candy store, owned by her uncle. Her name was Emma Emilia Acquaviva and she said if she were American it would be "Drinkwater." Another little girl appeared with her once in a while, fat, curly headed, smelling of garlic and urine, but with an even more ravishing name: Philomena Barbaroni. The Cameos—the Reillies—

But it is Mrs. Sullivan I want to think about after all these years. I am sure she is living somewhere surrounded by grandchildren and I hope it is in Ireland, that her brute of a husband, Pat, has died long ago and left her well off and that somewhere right this minute Mary Sullivan is enjoying life—

We were almost all aliens, aliens, dreamers, drunkards. Everyone talked about "taking out their first papers"; few had actually reached full U.S. citizenship and probably many never bothered to at all. The Italians made their own wine some of them, or bought it from each other. We could look into one upper apartment and see Mr. and Mrs.   treading wine in a wooden bucket that almost filled their kitchen, side by side and up and down; their two smallest boys (they had six) lay sidewise on an old army cot and watched them, their heads almost in the bucket, too—One occasionally found masses of purple thrown out on the vacant lots, smelling fermenting headily, covered with flies. The Italians had their wine and occasionally their parties grew loud and musical, but the Irish did the real drinking. Where they got it no one seemed to know exactly, but they got it.

The original old New Englanders had almost vanished. A few hung on here and there in the older small old houses, but only one I remember as being of "original stock." She was an ardent Christian Scientist, about 70. Her husband had died and, my aunt said, to "save him" she had married his much younger brother who was a policeman. Not a bad job for that neighborhood but certainly a comedown for the "healer" and "reader"—a heavy set man at least twenty years younger, silent, stupid, "not all there" we said, who also drank—not drunk, but he smelled of it. His elderly wife treated him brightly and sweetly like a disappointing son. She would order him about, "George—take off your helmet in my kitchen." "George, will you hang up these clothes for me, now." He would say, "Yes, Leila. Anything you say, Leila—by God that's what I married you for."

Later on he was rumored to have a "girl friend," the children told me this mysterious and thrilling bit of news and I'd watch him come home from doing his beat, heavy, lumbering, red-faced under the high helmet like an English bobby's—but he always looked exactly the same, girlfriend or no girlfriend.

My aunt Maggie was fond of Mrs.   but firmly resisted all her attempts to come and pray for me when I had asthma, and that put a strain on one of the very few friends she made in the neighborhood . . .

When I arrived, Mr. and Mrs. Pat Sullivan had recently moved in, too. And they had just had their first baby, Elizabeth. I fell in love immediately with anyone with red hair in those days, and Mrs. Sullivan's hair was flaming red. She was very pretty, too—even I could see that—although already much too fat; she was twenty-one years old and had married Pat at 19, and he had sulked for a year and a half because she had been so slow about producing Elizabeth. "An ugly cuss" said Uncle Ned. He had come from Cork. He was a butcher in east Boston somewhere, and was about 30—heavy, blue eyed, thick black hair, a big jaw, built like a heavy weight boxer "Map of Ireland all over his face" said Uncle Ned who despised him but was not above taking a drink with him once in a while or sitting out on a Sunday morning leaning on the rock of a sunny Sunday morning smoking a pipe with him. To me he looked just the way a butcher should look—

Mrs. S red hair, green eyes, a lovely skin with too many freckles —and a wonderful brogue, new to me and fascinating. I wanted to listen to her talk all day long. I could listen to her talk all day long. She also sang as she worked—or didn't work—the housework she did wasn't much—and I loved that although Aunt Nellie [*sic*] would get impatient and wish that she'd shut up and give us some peace . . . She spoke Gaelic still, spoke it to her husband and children (Francis came along fairly soon after I got there) although Pat "didn't have much of the Gaelic, being a city man . . ." She made a lot of noise but was gentle with her children. Pat was sullen and a brute.

I learned her story from Aunt Nellie [*sic*] and from Mrs. Sullivan herself by bits over several years. I wasn't too small for her to talk to and although my aunt didn't like me to, I used to call on her in the mornings—The kitchen was a mess. It smelled of cabbage and urine, one combined smell, and often a large white china pot stood unemptied on the floor at eleven o'clock. Mrs. S would be sitting in the squalor, Elizabeth crawling about on the floor filthy dirty but with a blue ribbon off a chocolate box tied in her beautiful shiny red curls, a much darker red than her mother's, almost black—

[c. early 1960s]

"Writing poetry is an unnatural act . . ."

Writing poetry is an unnatural act. It takes great skill to make it seem natural. Most of the poet's energies are really directed towards this goal: to convince himself (perhaps, with luck, eventually some readers) that what he's up to and what he's saying is really an inevitable, *only* natural way of behaving under the circumstances.

Coleridge, in *Biographia Literaria,* in his discussion of Wordsworth, has a famous sentence. It says: "the characteristic fault of our elder poets is the reverse of that which distinguishes too many of our recent versifiers; the one conveying the most fantastic thoughts in the most correct and natural language, the other in the most fantastic language conveying the most trivial thoughts." He then goes on to quote some of George Herbert:

VIRTUE

"Sweet day, so cool, so calm, so bright,
The bridal of the earth and sky:
The dew must weep thy fall tonight;
For thou must die!"

LOVE UNKNOWN

that begins

" 'Writing poetry is an unnatural act . . .' " is referred to in the introduction. The quotations of poetry here were set down, I believe, by heart and without reference to texts, and are reproduced as Bishop typed them.

"Dear friend, sit down, the tale is long and sad:
And in my faintings, I presume, your love
Will more comply than help. A Lord I had . . ."

Another Herbert: LOVE

"Love bade me welcome, but my soul drew back,
Guiltie of dust and sinne."

and ends

"You must sit down," sayes Love, "and taste my meat.
So I did sit and eat."

This, I later discovered in *Waiting for God*, was Simone Weil's favorite; she translated it and knew it by heart.

The three qualities I admire in the poetry I like best are: *Accuracy, Spontaneity, Mystery.* My three "favorite" poets—not the best poets, whom we all admire, but favorite in the sense of one's "best friends," etc. are Herbert, Hopkins, and Baudelaire.

THE CHURCHE-FLOORE

"Hither sometimes Sinne steals, and stains
The marbles neat and curious veins: . . .
Sometimes Death, puffing at the doore,
Blows all the dust about the floore . . ."

His magnificent poem, THE SACRIFICE

"Arise, arise, they come. Look how they runne!
Alas! What haste they make to be undone!
How with their lanterns they do seek the sunne!
Was ever grief like mine!"

He has spontaneity, mystery, and accuracy, in that order?

Hopkins, WRECK OF THE DEUTSCHLAND

"Ah, touched in your bower of bone
Are you! turned for an exquisite smart,
Have you! make words break from here all alone,
Do you!—"

THE GRANDEUR OF GOD "it will flame out like *shining from shook foil . . .*"

"I am all at once what Christ is, / since he was what I am, and
This Jack, joke, poor potsherd, patch, matchwood, immortal diamond,
Is immortal diamond."

Auden's B [Baudelaire] here—

"Altogether elsewhere, vast
herds of reindeer move across
miles—miles of golden moss
silently and very fast."

It's accurate, like something seen in a documentary movie. It is spontaneous, natural sounding—helped considerably by the break between adjective and noun in the first two lines. And it is mysterious.

The first lines of D. Thomas's "Refusal to Mourn":

"Never,

Miss Moore's—["Plagued by the Nightingale":]

Frost's—

[Wordsworth, Shakespeare's "Prithee undo this button"—everyone is moved to tears by it; it certainly is the height of spontaneity, and yet it is so mysterious they are still arguing as to whether it's his own button or his daughter's button . . .]

Burns:—lacks mystery, maybe—but—weaker in the mystery—

"No matter what theories one may have, I doubt that they are in one's mind at the moment of writing a poem or that there is even a physical possibility that they could be. Theories can only be based on interpretations of other people's poems, or one's own in retrospect, or wishful thinking." [See note on p. 212.]

I'm not a critic. Critics can't rest easy until they have put poets in descending orders of merit; they change the lists every night before they go to bed. The poet doesn't have to be consistent.

Marianne Moore, MARRIAGE, that begins:

> "This institution,
> perhaps one should say enterprise . . ."

> NEW YORK
> "the savage's romance,
> accreted where we need the space for commerce—
> the center of the wholesale fur trade . . ."

accuracy: from A GRAVE

> "The firs stand in procession, each with an emerald turkey-foot
> at the top . . ."
> skeleton

FROST: the ghost that "carried itself like a pile of dishes."

ending of "Stopping by Woods on a Snowy Evening"

Auden here—

a single word does it all

ROBERT LOWELL:

> "Remember, seamen, Salem fishermen
> Once hung their nimble fleets on the Great Banks."

hung suggests the immensity, the depths of the cold stormy water and the tininess, the activity of the small "nimble" ships—and yet it's the simplest sort of natural verb to use—

THE DEAD IN EUROPE

"After the planes unloaded, we fell down
Buried together, unmarried men and women . . ."

"O Mary, marry earth, sea, air and fire;
Our sacred earth in our day is our curse."

DYLAN THOMAS:

"Pale rain over the dwindling harbour
And over the sea wet church the size of a snail
With its horns through mist and the castle
Brown as owls . . ."

A REFUSAL TO MOURN

"Never until the mankind making
Bird beast and flower
Fathering and all humbling darkness
Tells with silence the last light breaking
And the still hour
Is come of the sea tumbling in harness . . ."

Baudelaire: "Les soirs illumines par l'ardeur du charbon . . ." where *charbon* is the telling word—surprising, accurate, *dating* the poem, yet making it real, yet making it mysterious—

Spontaneity—Marianne's "Marriage," "N.Y."—

Herbert's EASTER

"Rise, heart; the Lord is risen."

Hopkins' "Glory be to God for dappled things"—

My maternal grandmother had a glass eye. It fascinated me as a child, and the idea of it has fascinated me all my life. She was religious, in the Puritanical Protestant sense and didn't believe in looking into mirrors very much. Quite often the glass eye looked heavenward, or off at an angle, while the real eye looked at you.

> "Him whose happie birth
> Taught me to live here so, that still one eye
> Should aim and shoot at that which is on high."

Off and on I have written out a poem called "Grandmother's Glass Eye" which should be about the problem of writing poetry. The situation of my grandmother strikes me as rather like the situation of the poet: the difficulty of combining the real with the decidedly un-real; the natural with the unnatural; the curious effect a poem produces of being as normal as *sight* and yet as synthetic, as artificial, as a *glass eye.*

(call the piece "Grandmother's Glass Eye"???)

spontaneity occurs in a good *attack,* a rapid line, *tight* rhythm—

Brazilian Poetry: I am reading B.P. I began naturally with the living poets & I intended to work backwards into Brazilian and Portuguese poetry. I've found many good things, but I feel that I don't know the language well enough, or the body of poets. To say anything about it at present would be an impertinence.

[c. late 1950s–early 1960s]

[Note: This quoted passage comes from an essay of her own, drafted in the summer of 1949, for John Ciardi's anthology *Mid-Century American Poets* (LM, pp. 217–18), but the passage addressing Brazilian poetry at the close persuades me that these notes were assembled much later in Brazil.

Bishop's remarks on the word *charbon*'s dating Baudelaire's poem summon up her appreciation of Empson's insights about word fashion quoted in the note for " 'It is marvellous to wake up together . . .' "]

Making the Wallpaper Come Off the Wall

"When I was a child . . . .
I had a funny way of using my eyes . . ."
—Sandra McPherson

In the long winter evenings after "tea" the sitting room hanging oil lamp—round table—Gammie in her rocker *tatting*—fast, taut, tiny white rings—with her one good eye—her one eye—Grandpa on the sofa asleep, a cat on his chest (Nanny?), Betsy at his feet—gray plaid wool slippers—boots on the floor. "Will—take those boots outside—I smell chicken dirt." Grandpa, sweetly—Ur-ugh-ur

I sat silent and made the wallpaper come off the wall. Small bouquets of red-gray roses, thin trellaces of golden wires, swayed, retreated and advanced, in space out from their background of wide white and faint silver stripes—up & down—Where a lot of wallpaper showed—between the parlor organ and a window full of house plants the gilt and rose skimpy summer house advanced as far as the lamplit blur of Gammie's white hair—Tatting, tatting—The lamp had a big base (hanging)—the kerosene was yellow—the wick wide two little horns dark blue—and occasional tiny sparks in the flame inside the flat flame—

[the marbles—another poem?]

My eyes must have looked funny—Grandpa went out to the dark kitchen to get another lamp
"Time for someone to go to bed"
Up the ladder-like narrow stairs—me behind my hands on a step two ahead of me—"Say your prayers" "Be sure she says her prayers"
Grandpa left my door ajar and the lamp turned low on the hall table

"Making the Wallpaper Come Off the Wall" is reproduced according to the single draft available at Vassar. It is referred to in the note to " 'A mother made of dress-goods . . .' "

or the sewing machine—He thought children were afraid of the dark.

I wasn't afraid of the dark.

That arbor, bower—summer house—I had no words for it—I didn't know where I'd go—where I'd be—anything—sealed between downstairs and upstairs dark, warm, smelling a little of dog, kerosene, geranium blooms—(the hen dirt once removed) indeed it had been strong—

and the pure white tatting, falling, falling slowly into Gammie's lap, little O's linked at their sides the black bobbin flew

[c. 1967]

The Fairy Toll-Taker

We drove back from Berkeley across the Bay Bridge about ten-thirty last night. A thin fog, more a mist, really. Thousands of small lights in lines, arcs, bows and isolated high ones mostly gold but many red and green and that long low line of very fine ones—I don't know what that is—it seems to extend across the bay like a railway line but I've never had a good look at it. The bridge towering above us—the buildings of S.F.—two or three tallest ones—with their heads in fog, pinkish. Sky blending two shades: pinkish and greenish. The one clock tower that always reminds me of a Klee—not the Ferry Landing tower, another one, dark, not all lit up, just the face which seems too big for the pointed tower and therefore childish. We went along in our slow cautious neck-turning way—not so many cars that time of night but those there are go extra-fast and the mammoth two-car trucks overtake like rapid buildings or over-sized freight trains with a new kind of heavy breathing mechanism—smooth and awful as fate.

The toll booths lit up inside rather dimly. Inside the one we stopped at just long enough

sentry sentinel of Sodom—

to hand over the quarter, I had one good glimpse of a strange small figure, like a dummy propped up there, really like a ventriloquist's doll, because he was chewing gum and his rather long jaw went up and down as if he were trying to speak but couldn't very well. Or was

"The Fairy Toll-Taker" is referred to in the note on " 'Far far away there, where I met . . .' " At the top, Bishop jotted "S.F.—1968?" There is a reference to the letters of Wallace Stevens tucked in this draft, "one feels (hears) the ground bass of MONEY . . . sense constantly—almost heard . . ."

speaking, without making any sounds. His face was rather large and flat and strangely pink & white, enamelled looking. His long eyes seemed to be either pale blue or green, but scarcely looked at us. He was wearing I suppose the pea jacket that is issued to toll-takers, a uniform, but it was much too big for him, and so was his navy blue peaked cap—low on his head with a space all around. At the sides were long thick wisps of bright straw-colored hair. A weird little figure, a lay figure? looking as if tossed into his glass box like a toy and forgotten there at night in the fog, at the beginning of the mighty bridge— An obvious homosexual. Perhaps he picks up men on his odd job?

Ungracious Poem

Why do Nurses talk?
Down all the corridors,
also in all the doorways
[at] crossroads, too, no doubt.
They are standing and talking and talking—
Why are these long life stories   *nevertheless*
so much less convincing than ours

Why do they talk? scream, rather
In general, we're not deaf.   (really)
And why are Nurses big?
Bigger than you or me.
[Poor] white giants, talking
long and long and loud,
[Their] eyes are bigger and flatter   proportionately
than any seen before (except a few

very tiny species. Look out for them
They're worse than the [normal ones].   stylish-stouts   out out-
size

Why do Nurses talk?
What do they talk about?
From what one can make out
of temple-rites, head-gear,   fake finger nails
breast pins, sacrifices,   [artificial talons]
blood that ran nicely now
down the newly constructed gutters.

"Ungracious Poem" is referred to in the note for "On the 'Prince of Fundy.' " I could not determine where to place it chronologically in the volume proper. Under this rough draft, the second of two in the archive, Bishop wrote "7 more stanzas."

Nurses never stop.
Sometimes we barely manage
perhaps in a gasp for breath   when they gasp for breath
to get born in between,   in between say one word or any
and some[one], one supposes,
dies the same way, in between.

Sometimes Nurses carry
a doll-size lily cup
(Their own dolls long ago   failed to communicate & were too small
gave up the ghost; they couldn't get a word in)
with a pill in it that falls out
No one can go *scrambling*, after all,
for an unknown pill, so it, too
Gives up its ghost on [the battleship] linoleum floor.
Nurses call them "Pinkies," or "Floosies," things like that
God knows what they are—or what
they'll do to the gray linoleum—

Sometimes, just at twilight,
a few birds start up outside,   [before the lamps are lit—]
small-voiced [plans for evening]   thoughts of evening, /
of when to perch-etc.—
calling, calling, faintly / / /

The Nurses talk louder and louder.
They don't get away with it.
Nurses have set all the elm trees
strung   strung up
with trip-cords of number 2 bandage—   rigged all the

The ELEGY poem - make it in sections, some anecdotal, somelyrical
different lngth - never more than two short pages -

Your style, your elegancies elegance Y?
My small dandaical
small & dandaical
Love of order) reticene - and pride
reticence and pride
the understandable snobbery & superiority
the temper and the "differences"
heroism, brave & young - the heroic apperance at the Yacht Club, country lucb, etc.
Convents, sadnesses, realization (a la Auden)
graons and howls when inuured
small hans, small feet the Beardsley sillhoute-
the Pierrot cotume - the English underdarwers and littlesokc -
the 1st communion -
the chip-on-the h shoulder - the of God, the books - the books -
athesit, pride, pride pride -

the beautiful colored skin - the gestures (which yo said you didn't have)
the ability to tease - to shout and scare and then a minute later
everyone was laughing

the sdoor slamming, plaster-falling - the cok and I laughing helplessly
ont the other side of the door
An d oh the dream - te house, tehe desire - Bonniers - Museums -
and oh the contry's ingtatirud e- misnuderstanding - WASTE

Nevrtheless: the family pride, the anecdotes - the wierd relations -
When societty broke up - the innocent snobbery -
Remarks I remember always - Lulu - bossiness - ruling class attitudes - a f
a landed aristocracy - (a bit Chekovian)

and courag e courage to the last, or almost to the last -

Regret and guilt, the nighttime horros (Lorca)

The three facsimile pages of notes for "The Elegy poem" about Lota de Macedo Soares connect to Bishop's first attempt at the poem, "Aubade and Elegy" (see p. 149). As late in her life as 1977, in her application for a Guggenheim Fellowship, she described her project as a new volume to be called *Grandmother's Glass Eye,* the title mentioned in her uncompleted lecture " 'Writing poetry is an unnatural act . . .' " and a book-length poem called *Elegy.* The lines in Spanish on the third page are from "Elegy for Ramón Sijé" by the Spanish poet Miguel Hernández (1910–1942).

Perhaps for the tenth time the tenth time ~~today~~ early
and still early morning I wake it's like waking
wake and go under the wave the black wave ~~of your death~~

~~-It's-a-beautiful-morning-but-you-are-not-here--to-adm~~ire it

The beautiful light of morning touches the grasses
the field of diamonded pink outside your window
-the mato has started to turn ~~son~~ it will be red soon
little
and that tree-full of blue metallic/~~steel-blue~~/birds ~~is~~/~~t~~/ who come
to eat the bitter ~~little~~/red fruits they are there   the're there
and the seven lines of mountains ~~gently~~/shouldering each other

away from the sun gently away from the sun, one by one

white like a bowl of milk

No your life slowed ~~first~~ then to that of the lichens
~~then/of/the/~~ circles, then of the rocks

Not there. And not there! I see only small hands in the dirt
transplanting Sweet Williams, tamping them down
dirt on the ~~dirt~~ hands, the rings, no more than that
small
No revolution can catch your attention.
You are bored with us all. It is true we are boring.

the poor cats come for our breakfast
They hesitate at your door the Siamese gives a faint howl
they run and jump onto my bed

the smell of the earth, the smell of the black-roasted coffee
as fine as fine humus as black

no coffee can wake you no coffee can wake you no coffee can wake you

No coffee

they hesitate at your door; they look back at me, big-eyed
the Siamese gives a faint howl; they rush to jump on my bed.

I want the mint to be weeping   Yo quiero ser llorando el hortelano
of the land you occupy (?) and   de la tierra que ocupas y estercolas,
companion of the soul, so temprano -

Nourishing rains, shells
and organos my grief without instrument
a las desalentadas amapolas

y siento mas tu muerte que mi vida.

for perhaps thetenth time the tenth time today
I go under the wave the bkack wave of your death
and put only your hands in th e dirt -

and trace the umbrella ants back to their nests -the hill

the seven lines of hills shouldering each other

the beautiful light of morning on the grasses
the field of diamonded pink weed outside your window

and the tree full of metallic steel blue birds eating the bt
bitter red fruits

no- your life slowed to that of the rock first the lichen then the rocks

no coffe can wake you no coffee can wake you no revolution catch your attention
bored with us all?/~~oh yes we were boring~~//- it is true we were boring.

(..& the flowers you abandoned, and the pets,
and the small children you made laugh so hard

the shelves of china you loved, the copper pans
the colored linens

the top drwaer
the 42 pairs of small shoes, the boots
the yellow hat, oh god, the yellow hat

Drafts of "One Art"

In a book devoted largely to unfinished work, it seemed a good idea to provide drafts of a finished poem, and "One Art" is the natural choice, as so many of the drafts exist. Victoria Harrison, author of *Elizabeth Bishop's Poetics of Intimacy*, which includes a detailed analysis of the poem, disagrees with the sequence established by the Vassar College Library, Department of Special Collections, and supported by Brett Millier in her discussion of the poem both in her biography of Bishop and in her article "Elusive Mastery: The Drafts of Elizabeth Bishop's 'One Art.' " Harrison numbers drafts one through nine differently, and concludes, "There is a possibility of error in either case, of course, since Bishop did not number them."

Bishop wrote the poem quickly, and it was completed to her satisfaction within months. ("I couldn't believe it," she said, "it was like writing a letter.") The last typewritten copy represented here is the version as set in type at the offices of *The New Yorker* on November 4, 1975. In Bishop's last letter to Katharine White, January 16, 1976, she wrote, "I am having a poem in your magazine fairly soon, I think—the one and only villanelle of my life. It is very SAD—it makes everyone weep, so I think it must be rather good, in its awful way, and I hope you will like it." The poem ran in the magazine's issue of April 26, 1976.

HOW TO LOSE THINGS /? / THE GIFT OF LOSING THINGS?

lost cont

[Draft 1]

One might begin by losing one's reading glasses
oh 2 or 3 times a day - or one's favorite pen.

THE ART OF LOSING THINGS

The thing to do is to begin by "mislaying".

Mostly, one begins by "mislaying":
keys, reading-glasses, fountain pens
- these are almost too easy to be mentioned,
and "mislaying" means that they usually turn up
in the most obvious place, although when one
is making progress, the places grow more unlikely
- This is by way of introduction. I really
want to introduce myself - I am such a
fantastic lly good at losing things
I think everyone shd. profit from my experiences.

You may find it hard to believe, but I have actually lost
I mean lost, and forever two whole houses,
one a very big one. A third house, also big, is
at present, I think, "mislaid" - but
maybe it's lost, too. I won't know for sure for some time.
I have lost one/long peninsula and one island.
I have lost - it can never be has never been found -
a small-sized town on that same island.
I've lost smaller bits of geography, like and many smaller bits of geography or scenery
a splendid beach , and a good-sized bay.
Two whole cities, two of the
world's biggest cities (two of the most beautiful
although that's beside the point)
A piece of one continent -
and one entire continent. All gone, gone forever and ever.

One might think this would have prepared me
for losing one average-sized not ~~especially~~------- exceptionally
beautiful or dazzlingly intelligent person
(except for blue eyes) (only the eyes were exceptionally beautiful and
But it doesn't seem to have, at all... the hands looked intelligent)
the fine hands

a good piece of one continent
and another continent - the whole damned thing!
He who loseth his life, etc. - but he who
loses his love - neever, no never never never again -

A
×
B

a
b
a

excellent
intelligent

[Draft 2]

The art of losing isn't hard to master:
so many things seem ~~really~~ to be meant
to be lost that their loss is no disaster.

Start out with ~~keys~~ ~~[illegible]~~.
~~Begin with little things~~,
~~[illegible]~~. ~~Lose~~ never wonder where they went.
The art of losing isn't hard to master.

minutes

Then practice bigger losses, lose them faster,
~~forget the names [illegible]~~ ~~[illegible]~~;
The mastered art of losing's no disaster.

Look! ~~[illegible]~~ ~~[illegible]~~ I've lost ten houses and my last, or
~~Look!~~ — ~~ten houses~~ and my last, or
next-to-last, ~~[illegible]~~ ~~[illegible]~~
Well, ~~the art~~ of losing's not hard to master —
And ~~also~~, ~~[illegible]~~, ~~(~~ ~~[illegible]~~ ~~)~~ and
~~And the~~ I lost two cities, ~~[illegible]~~, the rivers,
~~[illegible]~~, ~~[illegible]~~ a ~~[illegible]~~ continent ...
~~[illegible]~~ a ~~[illegible]~~ continent ...
~~And~~ Still there ~~[illegible]~~ ~~[illegible]~~ disaster.
~~[illegible]~~ — a ~~[illegible]~~, a continent —

question
protests
attests
ister

protests
boaster attests foster
faster

instead ~~[illegible]~~ evident
false

(I said I said
The art of losing's ... not to master
And losing it is ...)
disaster

The art of losing isn't hard to master
~~[illegible]~~,
Or ~~so I said~~. ~~But you [illegible] disaster~~ —
I ~~[illegible]~~ ~~[illegible]~~ ~~of losing [illegible]~~ the.
I ~~[illegible]~~ it's losing

possibly you will
avoid disaster

[Draft 3]

The art of losing isn't hard to master:
so many things seem almost to be meant
to be lost. ~~(the results)~~ their ~~loss~~ is no disaster.

Begin with reading-glasses, car-keys, ~~your tarots~~
~~(change of letters)~~ – & ~~don't~~ never wonder where they went.
The art of losing isn't hard to master.

Then practice bigger losses, lose them faster,
~~I keep you and~~. You'll find your time well spent,
~~and~~ the mastered art of loss is no disaster.

I ~~wish I'd given up the house~~ – last, or

The art of losing wasn't hard to master,

~~Two~~ Two major cities, (beautiful) the santa,
~~towns~~, a pipe, of one, & one whole continent,
And disaster

(azure water)

The art of losing isn't hard to master
~~of art~~. disaster

[Draft 4]

The art of losing isn't hard to master.
So many things ~~seem~~ ~~actually~~ ~~really~~ seem really to be meant
to get lost, that their loss is no disaster,—

and as you practice & keep losing faster
you'll [illegible] [illegible] time will upset
and in ~~the way~~ ~~by any step you~~ [illegible] ~~losing~~ mastery —

you [illegible] [illegible] lost, or
[illegible]

The art of losing isn't hard to master:
so many ~~objects~~ things seem really to be meant
~~[illegible]~~ to get lost, that their loss is no disaster.
to get lost, that is no disaster.

Begin ~~[illegible]~~ watches, reading-glasses, car-keys, or your houses
& then don't Change plates ~~[illegible]~~ [illegible] question [illegible] the [illegible] —
The art of losing isn't hard to master.

Then Practice ~~[illegible]~~ ~~losses~~; [illegible] lose them faster —
time will be well spent
[illegible] seem a disaster.

[Draft 5]

The art of losing isn't hard to master   isn't

spent
and possibly   disasters.

really glasses —

faults
went
masters.

lost, or
~~[illegible]~~
disasters.

Calmly [illegible] [illegible] [illegible] masters;
A ~~country, fruit~~, cont. ~~&~~ then a ~~spot~~ continent. ~~[illegible]~~ —
The art of losing isn't hard to master.

~~disasters~~

~~continent~~
~~disasters~~

— aster ?
least
The art of losing ~~'clearly'~~ isn't too hard to master
~~But now it helps~~ [illegible] Think of all the disasters
No — I am lying —

[Draft 6]

5,

The art of losing isn't so hard to master
& losing it may prove ~~the~~ the well expert,
just practicing your ~~possibly~~ ironic about disaster

As you go on, you lose things and a road & facts
you ~~[illegible]~~ learn to recall when they went.
The art of losing isn't so hard to master.

~~the~~ last, or
the next to last, you brought —
a practice for an even disaster.

The art of losing isn't so hard to master —

plasters

I practiced till I
a piece of or one whole continent!:
disaster —

lost one

intelligent
The art of losing is not so hard to master
until the point I lose it
faults & no disaster —

~~fasters~~
pilasters
(~~tasters~~)
~~[illegible]~~
~~[illegible]~~

fasters
vasts
last, or

[Draft 7]

The art of losing isn't hard to master:
so many things seem really to be meant
to be lost that their loss is no disaster.

~~Start slowly with your some keys, a fan, a gesture~~
~~Start with a glance~~ your glasses, ~~a posture~~ gesture
Start with ~~your reading glasses, keys, or~~
Reading-glasses, car-keys, you can master
innumerable easy things. You wonder where they went
The art of losing isn't hard to master.

Then practice bigger losses, lose the faster,
forget the faster — money, fame, intent —
The mastered art of losing's no disaster.

Look! I myself have ~~I have lost~~ lost ~~the~~ my ~~dog~~ lost, or
most I lost, a heart, however and

~~Begin with easy ones~~ ~~anyone can~~
~~reading glasses, car keys,~~
~~Even two major cities~~
And then two cities vaster
losses — a cup, a continent —
nothing is ~~lost, at all~~ a terrible disaster —

[Draft 8]

The art of losing isn't hard to master
practicing it my person you [illegible] will [illegible]
and possibly you will avoid disaster.

faster
ent
master.

last, or
ent
disaster

vaster
ent
master

. ster
ent
disaster

aster
all the exiles—ent

The art of losing [illegible] to master—
just while well
The [illegible] all I said — [illegible]
For never. The disaster—

[Draft 9]

The art of losing isn't hard tp master:
innumerable thing seem really to be meant   so many things
to be lost, so their loss is no disaster.   that

Lose something everyday. Oh you can muster   a list might muster
the usual list: car-keys,   keys, reading-glases, mortgages unsent -
The art of losing isn't hard to master.

Then practice losing bigger, losing faster,
forgetting fatter 0   & losing faster:
Then practice losing big, forgetting faster
places and names and where it was you meant
to go - None of them spells disastedisaster

Lose/~~sometim~~/ something every day. Oh, you can muster
the usual list:

Lose something eevery day. Lose every day. Oh ayone can muster
the   the packages un sent

mother's watch
Look! I have lost my ~~last~~/ two houmyslasd my last, or
next-to-last ~~of~~f my three houses. Where they went   beloved houses.
~~Was/ceased~~d   much less a disaster.
isn't a problem, much less a disaster.

I've lost two citiies, loveley ones,
Two cities vanished, loveley ones, and vaster
losses   a cape, a continent.
You won't believe the losses I can master.

Look°! I have lost my mother's watch, my last, or
next-to last of three beloved houses. WANDe they went

Look! I have lost my mother's watch; my last, or
next-to-last of t~~hree~~ loved houses went
off into nowhere away s~~omewhe~~re, bund they weren't a disaster.

Two cities, lovely ones. And on, to vaster
a~~nd/vaster/~~loss, a ~~cape//a/con~~ an entire continent.
The art of losing isn't hard to master.

geographical loss - a continent.
The artof losing isn't too hard to master.   The art of losing isn't hard to mas

gesture ?
All that I write is false, it's evident
The art of losing isn't hard to master.
oh no.
anythng at all anything but one's love. (Say it: disaster.)

[Draft 10]

with one exception. (Write it here)
(Why not just write "disaster"?)

The art of losing isn't hard to master:
so many things semm really to be meant
to be lost that their loss is no disaster.

Lose something every day. A list might muster — an hour's
keys, reading glasses, money, good intent — /one/ one nights good inent
The art of losing is't hard to master/

Then practise losing bigger, losing faster:
places, and names, and where it was you meant
to go - and none will spell disaster.

Look! I have lost my mother's watch, My last, or
next-to-last of three loved houses. They went.
off into nowhere, but they weren't disaster. But nothing just so serious as disaster

I've lost two cities, lovely ones. Then vaster
things, rivers/ a cape, an entire continent. — thing: island/ a cape, a continent
The art of losing isn't so hard to master. — of geography - a continent -

But, losing you (eyes of the Azure Aster)
But you if I lose you (eyes of azure aster)---
all that I write is false/. It's evident — lies, now. I'm writing lies now. It's
tha rt of losing isn't hard to master — quite evicent
of say/it/-
I've written lies above. It's evident
the art of losing isn't hard to master
with one exception..(Say it.) That's disaster.
with one exception. (Write it!)
(Say it - yes, disaster.)

[Draft 11]

The art of losing isn't hard to master:
so many things ~~se/ em/~~ seem really to be meant
to be lost that their loss is no disaster.

Lose something every day. Accept the fluster

Lose ~~something every day. Grow comfortable with fluster~~
of lost keys, ~~lost~~/keys, ~~of~~ glasses, ~~the~~ hour's intent.
The art of losing isn't hard to master.

lost glasses, keys, or

Then practise losing bigger, losing faster:
places, and names, and ~~where~~ it was you meant
to go. ~~But~~ none will spell disaster.

Look! I have lost my mother's watch. My last, or
next-to-last of three loved houses went.
But ~~nothing quite so serious as disaster~~.

And

I lost two cities, lovely ones. ~~Then~~ vaster
And ~~then~~ segments of geography; a continent.
The art of losing's not so hard to master.

But, losing you [eyes of the small wild aster)]
above's all lies now. It's quite evident
the art of losing wasn't ~~hard~~ to master
~~with one exception~~
except for (Say it! Say it!) that disaster.

I've written lies above. It's evident

the art of losing wasn't hard to master
in gnereal, but (Say it!)
with one exception, ~~which~~
but one exception is

The art of losing wasn't hard to master
All losing hasn't been too hard to master
~~but losing you~~

My losses haven't been too hard to master
~~with//with~~ but th
with this exception (Say it!) this disaster.

~~I've written lies~~. I wrote a lot of lies. It's evident
the art of losing ~~wasn't~~ isn't hard to master
with one exception. (Write it!) Write "disaster."

[Draft 12]

The art of losing isn't hard to master:
so many things seem really to be meant
to be lost that their loss is no disaster.

Try losing every day. Accept the fluster
of ~~the~~ lost glasses, keys, ~~the hour's [illegible] intent~~. [illegible] an hour badly spent.
The art of losing isn't hard to master.

Then practice losing further, losing faster:
places, and names, and where it was you meant
to go. ~~And~~ none will spell disaster.

I lost my mother's watch. And, look! my last, or
next-to-last of three loved houses went
~~off into nowhere~~. ~~That was not disaster~~. [illegible]
[illegible] the art of losing isn't hard to master —

I lost two cities, lovely ones. And, vaster,
two rivers, of my geography; a continent.
~~The art of losing's not so hard to master~~.
~~two rivers, then a cape~~; a continent.
--- ~~of geography~~: a cape, a continent.
I miss them, but it wasn't any disaster. [illegible]

But losing you (even a a gesture)
above's all lies now. It is evident
the art of losing ~~isn't~~ wasn't hard to master
~~with this exception~~. (Write it!)
~~but there~~
~~with~~
~~generally-speaking~~-
above's not lies, but it is evident

But, losing you (even to or gesture)
~~above's not lies - it's only evident~~
the art of losing ~~isn't~~ hard to master wasn't too
with this exception. ~~(Should I write?)~~
(Write it!) this disaster.
~~except this loss (Oh, write it!) this~~ disaster.

but this ~~loss is~~ (Go on, write it!) ~~is~~ seems disaster.

~~But~~ losing you (~~even~~ gesture)
I ~~haven't lied above~~. It is evident
The art of losing ~~wasn't too hard~~ to master
~~in general, but his (Oh, write it!)~~ seems
~~in general~~, , but this (Oh go on! ~~Write it!~~) looks like disaster.
~~but this~~ (Oh go on! Write it!) ~~seems disaster~~.

[Draft 13]

The art of losing isn't hard to master:
so many things seem really to be meant
to be lost that their loss is no disaster.

Lose something ever day. Accept the fluster
of lost door-keys, an hour badly spent.
The art of losing isn't hard to master.

Then practice losing further, losing faster:
places, and names, and where it was you meant
to go. ~~And~~ none will spell disaster.

I lost my mother's watch. And look! my last, or
next-to-last of three loved houses went~~,~~
~~[illegible]~~The art to lose them wasn't ~~too~~ hard ~~t~~ master~~.~~

I lost two cities, lovely ones. And,vaster,
~~small realms, two rivers, then a continent~~.
I miss them, but ~~I would not say disaster~~.
I'd never say disaster.

some realms of mine, [two] rivers, a continent.

joking one
(that/~~funny~~ voice; ~~that~~ gesture)

~~And losing~~ you ~~now-(a-special-voice,-a-gesture)~~--
doesn't mean I've lied. It's evident
the loss of love is possible to master,
even if this looks like (Write it!) like disaster.

(funny voice; one gesture)

In losing you ~~I~~ I haven't lied above. It's evident
do~~es not mean that I'[illegible]I'm lying. It's evident~~
the loss~~ of love is something one must maste~~r
even wh~~ich~~ it looks like (Write it!) like disaster.

[Draft 14]

The art of losing isn't hard to master:
so many things seem really to be meant
to be lost that their loss is no disaster.

Lose something every day. Accept the fluster
of lost door-keys, the hour badly spent.
The art of losing isn't hard to master.

Then practice losing further, losing faster:
places, and names, and where it was you meant
to travel. None of these will bring disaster.

I lost my mother's watch. And look! my last, or
next-to-last of three loved houses went.
The art of losing isn't hard to master.

I lost two cities, lovely ones. And, vaster,
some realms of mine, two rivers, a continent. × I owned,
I miss them, but it wasn't a disaster.

Even
In losing you (a joking voice, a gesture
I love), ~~I haven't lied~~. It's evident
the art of losing's not too hard to master
~~even when it looks (Oh, write it!) like disaster~~.

These are not lies.

though it may look like (Write it!) like disaster.

[Draft 15]

ONE ART

The art of losing isn't hard to master:
so many things seem r~~eally to be meant~~ ~~intent~~ filled with the intent
to be lost that their loss is no disaster.

Lose something every day. Accept the fluster
of lost door-keys, the hour badly spent.
The art of losing isn't hard to master.

Then practice losing farther, losing faster:
places, and names, and where it was you meant
to travel. None of these will bring disaster.

I lost my mother's watch. And look! my last, or
next-to-last of three loved houses went.
The art of losing isn't hard to master.

I lost two cities, lovely ones. And, vaster,
some realms I owned, two rivers, a continent.
I miss them, but it wasn't a disaster.

– Even losing you (a joking voice, a gesture
I love), these ~~were~~ not lies, it's evident
the art of losing's not too hard to master
though it may look like (Write it!) like disaster.

– Even losing you (the joking voice, a ~~the~~ gesture
I loved, ~~may not~~ . It's evident

(Even ~~So~~ losing you (the joking voice, a gesture
I loved, I ~~still do~~ ~~write~~ wasn't lie. It's evident

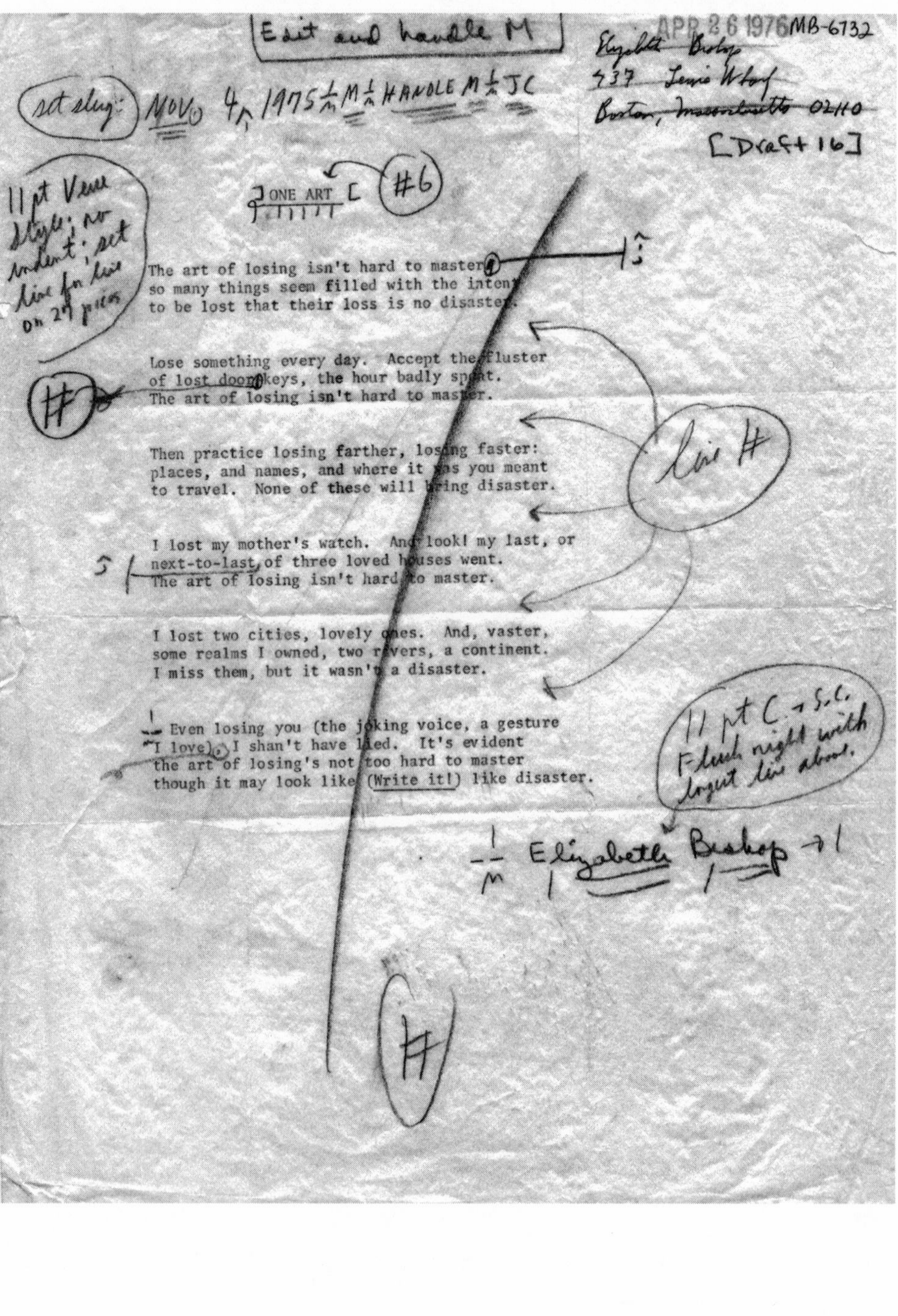

Edit and handle M

APR 26 1976 MB-6732

Elizabeth Bishop
437 Lewis Wharf
Boston, Massachusetts 02110

[Draft 16]

set slug: NOV 4, 1975 — M — HANDLE M — JC

#6

ONE ART

The art of losing isn't hard to master;
so many things seem filled with the intent
to be lost that their loss is no disaster.

Lose something every day. Accept the fluster
of lost door keys, the hour badly spent.
The art of losing isn't hard to master.

Then practice losing farther, losing faster:
places, and names, and where it was you meant
to travel. None of these will bring disaster.

I lost my mother's watch. And look! my last, or
next-to-last, of three loved houses went.
The art of losing isn't hard to master.

I lost two cities, lovely ones. And, vaster,
some realms I owned, two rivers, a continent.
I miss them, but it wasn't a disaster.

— Even losing you (the joking voice, a gesture
I love) I shan't have lied. It's evident
the art of losing's not too hard to master
though it may look like (Write it!) like disaster.

Elizabeth Bishop

Notes

Bibliography

Acknowledgments

Index of Titles and First Lines

Notes

Abbreviations Used in Notes

Numerical references are to folders of material housed at the Department of Special Collections, Vassar College Libraries.

AH MacArthur, Marit J. "Abandoning the House: Landscape and Meditation in Twentieth-Century American Poetry." Dissertation. University of California, Davis, 2005.

BP Goldensohn, Lorrie. *Elizabeth Bishop: The Biography of a Poetry.* New York: Columbia University Press, 1992.

CEB Monteiro, George, ed. *Conversations with Elizabeth Bishop.* Jackson: University Press of Mississippi, 1996.

CP Bishop, Elizabeth. *The Collected Prose.* Edited and with an introduction by Robert Giroux. New York: Farrar, Straus and Giroux, 1984.

EB/NY Biele, Joelle. *The Correspondence of Elizabeth Bishop and her* New Yorker *Editors.* New York: Farrar, Straus and Giroux, forthcoming.

EB/RL Lowell, Robert. *The Letters of Elizabeth Bishop and Robert Lowell.* Edited by Thomas Travisano. New York: Farrar, Straus and Giroux, forthcoming.

LAS Letters to Anne Stevenson; and Anne Stevenson letters to Elizabeth Bishop. The Elizabeth Bishop Papers, Washington University Library Special Collections. St. Louis, Mo. Quotations from materials in this collection are used with permission from the library and Alice Methfessel, executor of the literary estate of Elizabeth Bishop.

LIKB Letters to Ilse and Kit Barker. Manuscripts Division, Department of Rare Books and Special Collections, Princeton University Library. Princeton, N.J.

LM Millier, Brett C. *Elizabeth Bishop: Life and the Memory of It.* Berkeley and Los Angeles: University of California Press, 1993.

LMM Margaret Miller letters to Elizabeth Bishop. Special Collections, Vassar College Libraries. Poughkeepsie, N.Y.

LMS Letters to May Swenson; and May Swenson letters to Elizabeth Bishop. The May Swenson Papers. Washington University Library Special Collections. St. Louis, Mo. Quotations from materials in this collection are used with permission from the library and the literary estate of

May Swenson, and Alice Methfessel, executor of the literary estate of Elizabeth Bishop.

LRL Lowell, Robert. *The Letters of Robert Lowell.* Edited by Saskia Hamilton. New York: Farrar, Straus and Giroux, 2005.

OA Bishop, Elizabeth. *One Art: Letters.* Selected and edited, with an introduction, by Robert Giroux. New York: Farrar, Straus and Giroux, 1994.

OB Fountain, Gary, and Peter Brazeau. *Remembering Elizabeth Bishop: An Oral Biography.* Amherst: University of Massachusetts Press, 1994.

PI Harrison, Victoria. *Elizabeth Bishop's Poetics of Intimacy.* New York: Cambridge University Press, 1993.

VCSC The Elizabeth Bishop papers. Special Collections, Vassar College Libraries. Poughkeepsie, N.Y.

I. Poems from Youth

3 " 'I introduce Penelope Gwin . . . ' ": Single copy (VCSC 64.1). Tentatively dated "late 20s?" by the Vassar archive, the poem was most likely written at Walnut Hill. It's possible that it's one of the "two or three comic poems" Bishop refers to in a letter dated January 22, 1975, to her lifelong friend Frani Blough Muser, who attended the same summer camp in adolescence, the same boarding school, and the same college as Bishop:

> Judy Flynn [evidently a Walnut Hill classmate] . . . sent me a very nice note and a whole batch of *Blue Pencils,* 1928–29 [student magazine at Walnut Hill School], also two or three "comic" poems I'd apparently sent her a bit later. I haven't re-read them all yet—in fact I seemed to remember everything in them all too well after one glance. Ye Gods! what awful poetry I wrote then. (I hope to god I'm not deceiving myself if I think I've improved.) . . . I don't think you were nearly as corny as I was. We were very strong on sonnets. My "comic" poems are a lot better—couplets—but I haven't the faintest recollection of having written them . . . (OA, p. 594)

The heroine of this poem makes a lively drama out of two imperatives: avoiding her aunts ("My aunts I loathe with all my heart / Especially when they take up Art") and forswearing marriage ("One glimpse at my rejected suitor— / He was a handsome German tutor. / But no! I would be no man's wife, / The stark reality of life / For me"). *Gouine* is French slang for lesbian. The term may well have derived from the tuxedo-style attire fashionable among gay women in the 1920s and '30s, leading to the association with the penguin or *pingouin,* which the sophisticated young Bishop playfully explores. Perhaps she's also punning on the word "pen" as she pens her poem.

Following the death of her father in Worcester, Massachusetts, in 1911, when she was eight months old, Bishop and her mother lived at her maternal grandparents' house in Great Village, Nova Scotia, where she started school—see her memoir *Primer Class*—and where her mother's mental health deteriorated.

Bishop wrote to Anne Stevenson, author of the first book on her poetry, "It has always been said that what set off my mother's insanity was the shock of my father's death at such an early age, and when they'd only been married three years. (She was 29. He was 39.) It is the only case of insanity in the family, as far as we know" (LAS).

Bishop's mother was committed to a sanitorium in Dartmouth, N.S., in 1916, when Bishop was five, and a short time afterward her Bishop relatives made a pilgrimage to Great Village to collect their granddaughter. This is how Bishop describes that terrible interlude to Anne Stevenson in an undated letter, answering questions posed by Stevenson in a March 6, 1964, letter to her: "The B's were horrified to see the only child of their eldest son running about the village in bare feet, eating at the table with the grown-ups and drinking *tea*, and so I was carried off (by train) to Worcester for the one awful winter that was almost the end of me. 1917–18" (LAS). See also Bishop's 1961 memoir "The Country Mouse" (CP).

After that, from 1918 to 1927, she lived with her mother's older sister, Maud Shepherdson (married but childless), in Revere, Massachusetts, and subsequently in Cliftondale, another suburb of Boston, where her aunt Grace, one of her mother's younger sisters and Elizabeth's favorite relative, also occasionally took care of her.

In "Mrs. Sullivan Downstairs," an unpublished memoir written in Brazil in the 1960s (see appendix for the full text), Bishop writes of Maud and those early years: "My aunt and I loved each other and told each other everything and for many years I saw nothing in her to criticize" (VCSC 54.9).

On the subject of aunts and art: George Hutchinson, Bishop's great-uncle on her mother's side, studied painting in London and returned to Great Village, Nova Scotia, to set up a studio in the 1890s. Both Maud and Grace studied with him—with Maud, in particular, showing a talent for oils and watercolors.

In an interview with Ashley Brown in 1966, Bishop said, "All my life I've been interested in painting. Some of my relatives painted. As a child I was dragged round the Boston Museum of Fine Arts and Mrs. Gardner's museum and the Fogg. I'd love to be a painter" (CEB, p. 24). Her own significant gifts as a painter are reflected in *Exchanging Hats*, a fine book of her fetching watercolors and paintings, edited by William Benton and published in 1996 by Farrar, Straus and Giroux.

When Bishop first settled in Key West in 1938, she lived in a boarding house run by a Mrs. Pindar at 529 Whitehead Street, just a few blocks from her aunt Maud and Maud's husband, Uncle George, with whom she dined each night (EB to Frani Blough, Feb. 7, 1938, OA, p. 69). She remained close to her aunt until her death in 1940 and for years struggled to write the elegy variously titled "For M.B.S., buried in Nova Scotia," "Aunt M.," and "My Dear Aunt." One of the drafts appears here, on page 98.

In a notebook dating from her primary Key West years, 1937–48, an entry about her aunt Maud reflects Bishop's gift for mimicry. I quote just a fraction of the amusing passage:

> What form of punctuation to use for Aunt M's conversation—"manner of speech, which was inclined to drift gently to and fro in the subconscious."
>
> He was a man; he was a man; not a young man: along in years; well, like Uncle and me; along in years; well, along in years. He was a man; well, George, didn't he say he was from Boston? Well, a *nice* man, you know; a *nice type* of man; I wish you could meet him; well there was something sort of refined; not a young man; I mean he was just a nice *man*; better than Mabel Raite and *that* crowd; and oh the things he said about her! (VCSC 75.4b, pp. 116–17)

A journal entry dated January 2, 1938, from New York: "I had a letter from Aunt Maud mostly about cutting her toe-nails. It is very hard to do it while wearing bi-focal glasses, but she managed to finish seven before Uncle arrived home for lunch" (VCSC 77.2, p. 51).

Bishop closes a letter to Robert Lowell, dated December 16, 1958: "I am burbling like my poor dear Aunt Maud" (EB/RL).

On April 22, 1958, she wrote to her friends Ilse and Kit Barker from Brazil, mentioning her aunt Maud's devotion: "Children really seem to be much easier to take care of, and to be much healthier and happier in general than they used to be. It may be just a matter of being fed—However, love's the main thing always—I'm sure what saved me from being a complete wreck forever was my one aunt who loved me so much" (LIKB).

From the undated letter to Anne Stevenson quoted above, replying to questions posed by Stevenson in a March 6, 1964, letter that urged Bishop "to be a little more precise about people and exact places":

> On my mother's side I had three aunts: Maud, Grace, and Mary . . . I lived with Maud and was—and am—fondest of Grace. Mary is only 12 years older than I am . . . These last two are both living, in Canada; Aunt Maud died about 1942—I'm not sure. She and her husband stayed near me for two or three winters, or parts of winters, in Key West . . .
>
> Mary played the piano, quite well—all the aunts played some—and I think that and the hymns were how I came to love music from the beginning . . .
>
> I began writing poetry at about 8 and when I was 11 or so I remember Aunt Grace giving me some good advice about listening to criticism, not getting one's feelings hurt, etc. I went to school off and on, but remember chiefly lying in bed wheezing and reading—and my dear aunt Maud going out to buy me more books. When I was 13 I was well enough, summers, to go to camp, and it wasn't until then, briefly, and then at Walnut Hill, that I met girls who were as clever, or cleverer, than I was, and made friends, and began to cheer up a bit. (LAS)

Bishop's Worcester aunt Florence, on her father's side, figures prominently in the last scene of her memoir "The Country Mouse." She's called

"Aunt Jenny," and it is her dental appointment that prompts the drama recalled in the poem "In the Waiting Room," with its echo of Lewis Carroll's Alice puzzling over the sudden shift in her identity in "The Pool of Tears" chapter of *Alice's Adventures in Wonderland*, a book Bishop read in childhood and loved.

From a letter dated May 21, 1956, to her friend Pearl Kazin, after Bishop won the Pulitzer Prize: "My elderly Aunt Florence gave an interview to the Worcester newspaper, and with true family ambivalence announced that I would have made a great piano player (I don't believe she ever heard me play the piano once) and that 'lots & lots of people don't like her poetry, of course,' and that she was my 'closest living relative,' thereby insulting two perfectly good live aunts on the other side of the family . . ." (OA, p. 318).

On the subject of marriage: In 1930, Barbara Chesney, a classmate and friend of Bishop's from Walnut Hill, introduced Bishop to a former boyfriend, Robert Seaver, a handsome young graduate from Hamilton College who was partially crippled as a result of having contracted polio in his youth. Seaver loved literature and was a great reader, and at the time of their meeting he was teaching history at a boarding school in Massachusetts. He and Bishop dated during her years at Vassar, and he had hopes of marrying her. The summer after she graduated, in 1934, they traveled together to the little island of Cuttyhunk, off the coast of New Bedford, Massachusetts. Bishop copied some of his remarks in her notebook, among them: "Bob said at Nantucket once the water, where the waves come in on a coarse, rolling gravel, that it sound[ed] like hot fat sputtering in a pan. The water behind Mrs. Crane's house [mother of her college friend, Louise Crane], coming in in short, sliding waves on sand, he said sounded like someone shovelling snow" (VCSC 72A.3, p. 1). This is just the kind of observation that Bishop relished most.

Seaver proposed to her a year later, and she turned him down. His sister, Elizabeth Seaver Helfman, is quoted in Gary Fountain and Peter Brazeau's oral biography of Bishop: "I think that her relationship with my brother worried her because she did care so much about him. That's my theory. In a way she never really wanted to get involved. She said she was never going to marry anyone, and she never did" (OB, p. 68). Seaver subsequently committed suicide in 1936, after mailing Bishop a postcard with the message "Elizabeth, Go to hell," which she received after his death (OB, p. 68).

In Bishop's Penelope Gwin poem, "Our Heroine" is also emphatic on the subject of family: " 'This family life is not for me. / I find it leads to deep depression / And *I* was born for self-expression.' "

In the post-college notebook in which Bishop records Seaver's impressions at Nantucket, she reports a conversation with Margaret Miller, her senior-year roommate at Vassar, whom she loved deeply (see also the note for "Villanelle"): "Margaret was as sweet as a sherbet in her pink blouse today. Her face had that soft look about it, as if she had slept an extra hour or two, and her eyes a clear, original color that they blend for themselves out of several colors never in eyes before hers. We sat in the funeral-parlor rooms of Luchow's and had ice-cream. I said that families seemed to me like 'concentration camps'—where people actually let out their sadistic natures" (July 1 or 2, 1935, VCSC 72A.3, p. 29).

Balloons figure in several of Bishop's journals. One such entry dates from a stay in the American hospital in Paris, in October 1937, when Bishop endured a bad attack of asthma while traveling: "An 'old-fashioned' balloon went by this afternoon. Parachute-jumpers suit the Russian air, but in the pale, pearl-blue, Parisian air balloons go better. The balloon did not seem to be blown completely taut, it was a little puckered & limp. In the late afternoon light it bore a cheek of silver-gilt. The cords and the very small basket were pure white. I could distinguish no passengers, but a faint humming noise followed it through the air" (VCSC 77.2, pp. 23–24).

With further reference to "My aunts I loathe with all my heart / Especially when they take up Art," in August 1948, Bishop wrote to Carley Dawson, whom she had met through Robert Lowell when Dawson and Lowell were involved that year. She told Dawson that she had commissioned Lowell to find her "a rich husband in Washington. I think a nice comfy Oriental would do—one with lots of diamonds and absolutely no interest in the arts . . ." (OA, p. 165).

5 " 'Once on a hill I met a man . . .' ": Single copy VCSC 64.1. In her dissertation, "Abandoning the House: Landscape and Meditation in Twentieth-Century American Poetry," Marit J. MacArthur focuses on several of Bishop's earliest poems in a chapter entitled "Elizabeth Bishop: Incarnations of the 'Crypto-Dream-House,' " from which I quote: "By the time Bishop moved in with her aunt Maud, she had already begun to read Hans Christian Andersen and the Brothers Grimm, and seemed to identify with the many orphan characters in fairytales, who are often secretly of noble blood or have otherwise romantic histories and fates" (AH, pp. 14–15).

About this poem, MacArthur writes that it

> seems to refer to "Hansel and Gretel," evoking a prison-like house that is reminiscent of the witch's house and stable in the fairytale and perhaps of the Bishops' Worcester house. . . . In the poem, the speaker is apparently kidnapped by a sort of wizard who resembles "The Pied Piper" and also her grandfather Bishop, as described in "The Country Mouse": he had "thick silver hair and [a] short silver beard [which] glittered . . . a powerful but aging Poseidon." . . . We might read this poem as a reimagining of Bishop's involuntary move from Great Village to Worcester, which the child-narrator of "The Country Mouse" perceives as a kidnapping. . . . The poem ends not with a happy return home to the family cottage, as in the fairytale, but with a hopeless, ominous sense of the futility and danger of escape. (AH, pp. 15–17)

See the notes for "A Lovely Finish" and "Three Poems," with reference to "Hansel and Gretel."

Is it far-fetched to imagine that Bishop may have had Keats's "I stood tip-toe upon a little hill" in the back of her mind when she wrote the opening lines? In December 1927, she published an astute essay in *The Blue Pen-*

cil about her methodical summer reading of Shelley's poetry alongside a biography of the poet, and throughout her life she mentioned her early passion for the poems and letters of Keats.

In 1981, Wesley Wehr, one of Bishop's students at the University of Washington in Seattle in 1966, published a piece in the *Antioch Review* based on his class notes and conversations with the poet, quoting her thus:

> Everyone in this class likes Shakespeare, and after that, Dylan Thomas. But what about the seventeenth- and eighteenth-century poets? And the nineteenth century? I was shocked yesterday when you didn't spot those quotations from Keats, Tennyson, and Swinburne. We had a whole year of Wordsworth, Keats, and Shelley when I was in high school. The romantics are still awfully good poets. . . . You should have your head filled with poems all the time, until they almost get in your way. . . . I would suggest you read one poet—*all* of his poems, his letters, his biographies, everything *but* the criticisms on him. (CEB, pp. 39–40)

When Bishop was a child in Nova Scotia, her mother and the two aunts who cared for her later in Massachusetts (and who were scrupulous about providing her with good books and a great deal of poetry) belonged to a fortnightly reading group, described in the Brazeau and Fountain book: "Each winter was devoted to the study of a single writer, Keats, Ruskin, the Brownings, Milton, Shakespeare, Dante, and Tennyson among them" (OB, p. 7).

In a letter dated May 28, 1975, and addressed to "Miss Pierson," who had written to the poet seeking advice, Bishop counsels:

> Read a lot of poetry—all the time—and *not* 20th century poetry. Read Campion, Herbert, Pope, Tennyson, Coleridge—anything at all almost that's any good, from the past—until you find out what you really like, by yourself. Even if you try to imitate it exactly—it will come out quite different. Then the great poets of our own century—Marianne Moore, Auden, Wallace Stevens—and not just 2 or 3 poems each, in anthologies—read ALL of somebody. Then read his or her life, and letters, and so on. (And by all means read Keats's Letters.) Then see what happens. (OA, pp. 595–96)

II. 1929–1936: College, New York, Europe, Florida

11 " 'A lovely finish I have seen . . .' ": One of several nearly identical drafts (VCSC 75.4b, p. 223). Bishop copied this rather mysterious poem several times in different notebooks. She affixed the year 1929 on this copy in one of two notebooks dating from, roughly, 1938 to 1948, but a few lines of it also appear in another notebook she carried with her while traveling in France with Hallie Tompkins and Louise Crane (July 1935–June 1936).

That notebook contains (among many other items) early lines from "Love Lies Sleeping"; fragments attached to the title "Relatives"; a draft of a story called "The Death of the Marshmallow"; and early drafts of a masque she worked on titled variously "His Proper Tear," "The Proper Tear," and "The Proper Tears."

Underneath the few lines from this poem in the 1934–36 notebook are others referring to Hansel and Gretel (see the notes for "Once on a hill I met a man . . ." and "Three Poems"):

I looked for the kiss all night
It shone all night through the forest
(Those thoughts recumbent in the daytime stand up at night
and make a forest.)
Like the white crumbs or pebbles the foresters' children
followed home from the heart of the forest.

This morning I found it in my mouth (VCSC 72A.2, p. 13)

Opening lines from the poem and a version identical to this one—with a single variant in line two of the second stanza: "but waited for my teeth to touch"—can be found on pages 79 and 165, respectively, of the Key West notebook (75.4a). It seems clear that the poem was emotionally important to Bishop.

13 "Good-Bye—": Single copy (VCSC 64.3). Dated by Vassar 1931–1934, this draft exists on a single somewhat water-blurred page, making several words impossible to decipher. An entry from the 1934–36 notebook quoted above: "dirtier & dirtier If we had wept all the tears we had we / could not have washed off all the dirt. / Again tugging us around a curve—the drudgery of our flight" (VCSC 72A.2, p. 9).

14 "For a Pair of Eyebrows—": Single copy (VCSC 65.18). Bishop was intensely interested in allegory, as her notebooks from this time reflect: "Last night I had a very strange, pretty dream. I was seeing what I told myself was an 'Allegory' taking place" (July 1, 1935, VCSC 72A.3, p. 29). Earlier in the same notebook, in the fall of 1934, she writes, "Eyebrows (at least this is true of my own, and the 2 or 3 other pairs of human eyebrows I have happened to touch) have a sort of ridge pole in them, a raised core down the middle only noticeable to touch" (VCSC 72A.3, p. 13).

From entries in the 1934–36 notebook, it's evident that Bishop is either reading a book that attempts to outline what the features of the face reveal or conceal, or she has been conducting her own survey (VCSC 72A.2, p. 20):

forehead—circumstance
eyebrows—levels
eyes—intuition
nose—pride
mouth—ego
lips—form of, or, concealment of, ego
chin—attitude

Forehead, betray the circumstance,
But brows, be levels on the thought

An additional note at the top of the notebook page is helpful in the interpretation of the line about brows: "But brows, be levels [laid on thoughts, / The marker on the tape]."

A passage from July 1935, referring to a visit to her friend Margaret Miller's mother, provides another meditation on eyebrows:

> The other day I took Mrs. Miller a bunch of tiger-lilies, small ones, all freckled, striped, fringed, etc. Yesterday I sat opposite a young lady on the subway who had very odd eyebrows. Apparently she had disliked the shape of them, and had shaved them all off, except for the first half inch, or even less. From then on, she had drawn a very fine, almost straight line of brownish-red with eyebrow pencil. The width of this line didn't match the width of her own eyebrow—the curve wasn't the same—It gave her a half-wild look, & made me think of something, I couldn't remember what. It came to me after I got off the subway—the eyebrows were *exactly* like the things inside the lilies I had taken to Mrs. Miller—the same color, size, uncertain effect—all alike except that the eyebrows were a little bigger and not quite so unsteady. (VCSC 72A.3, pp. 31–32)

15 "Apologia": Single copy (VCSC 75.2, removed from notebook in VCSC 75.4). An undated poem to Margaret Miller that was located in the notebooks Bishop kept during her Key West years. The diction and high spirits give the poem the air of something written not long after graduation from college.

16 "A Warning to Salesmen": The most complete of several drafts of this poem (VCSC 72A.1, p. 6). From the 1935 notebook with the parenthetical tag "(some 1934–36)," dating from Bishop's early days in New York living in Greenwich Village at 16 Charles Street and her trip to France with Hallie Tompkins in July 1935. This notebook also contains early drafts of "The Map," which Bishop's biographer, Brett Millier, says she began composing on New Year's eve 1934.

Lines scribbled at the top of the page to the right of the title: "Let us, in confused, but common, voice / Congratulate th' occasion, and rejoice, rejoice, rejoice / The thing love shies at / And the time when love shows confidence." To the right at the bottom of the draft, Bishop writes, "OK," but the whole poem is crossed out. And below, on the left: "My Love / Wonderful is this machine. / One gesture started it."

Versions of the opening lines of "A Warning to Salesmen" are scattered throughout Bishop's papers. It becomes increasingly clear that these are addressed to Margaret Miller, Bishop's college roommate, who intended to be an artist, and to a lost time of innocence before a car accident in France in July 1937, in which Miller was radically injured, with her right hand and forearm severed from her body. (See the note for "Villanelle" for the story of the accident.) A fragment entitled "City Stars" has a similar opening:

Perishable, adorable friends
each sometime ends.

no rhyme to it at all
& not less of reason.
the miles of dirty air—
it's dim, but one is there
and there's another, fairly bright.
white, or is it a jet?
They're there they're there (VCSC 65.11)

From the Key West notebook, an address that appears to echo that of this draft:

No words could be formal enough (have ever been formalized
enough—)
You, my most beautiful friend

(that hollow sensation—dripping
tears
clinical hell

like a train going through a rural station at night
sulphurous
elegiac

If I wrote in the dark
If I wrote on the thinnest shelf of ice . . . (VCSC 75.4b, p. 150)

Near a page noting "V-Day, August 14th, 1945," Bishop is still turning this address over in her mind, "Perishable, dear friend," "M. / (an exceptionally beautiful woman) / Dearest, most perishable friend, / One would say, one would say / Just for the way you look— / And how . . . ," and "Most perishable, most adorable friend" (VCSC 75.4b, pp. 68–69). Another entry:

some beauty has to act itself out
that face had (has) to live itself out-
screen of the verandah of the
summer cottage
(Salter's Point, etc)
where one lay in a slightly damp bed
in the dark

headlights of cars

over wrist & temple
play

it used to be disproportionate
Once it was " "   " ",   not now
Then " " " " " "   ,

This last must refer to Margaret Miller, and the antecedent to "it" is evidently "beauty."

17 "Washington as a Surveyor": (VCSC 72A.1, p. 12). An alternative to the last phrase in the single extant draft is "but no inhabitant is there." The draft is from Bishop's notebook doubly dated "1934–36" and "1935." Her journal notes from the time indicate that she had in mind a series of poems:

American Characters—with Arguments—

Washington as a Surveyor
Susan Warner
Mather?
Poe?

For *Washington*—the deer—a miniature autumn landscape seen
through a sparse
snowfall
  the deer, whose sides look as if he had been painted by a snowfall

18 "Three Poems": From the 1935 ("some 1934–36") notebook. Only a handwritten copy of poem I survives. Poem II survives in nearly identical handwritten and typescript versions. Poem III is typed on a page with Poem II, with a handwritten notation to the left: "Tone all wrong" (VCSC 72A.1).

With respect to the amusement park reference and imagery in poem II: After college, Bishop spent time on Coney Island, inviting along Marianne Moore in June 1934, to accompany her and Louise Crane because Bishop and Crane had discovered a pretty merry-go-round there. (See also the note for "Naples, Fla.—'36.")

Following the publication of her first book, *North & South*, in the summer of 1946, and an emotionally charged visit to Nova Scotia, her first in twenty years, an entry in her notebook bearing the title "Half Moon Hotel, Coney Island, September 28th" records both some of her feelings about the place and also a scene of sand-sieving that recalls Edwin Boomer in her 1937 story "The Sea & Its Shore":

From my window I have a view of the gas tanks, which are now rising slowly like loaves of bread. Pale blue-gray unhealthy bread, full of gas. Tenements, tenements, & thousands of little brick villas. The distances seem tremendous, the light is semi-clear, pinkish, & gentle. There are even a few tall trees & the leaves left on their tops blink, a pale olive color . . .

. . . I ate some awful food somewhere & felt like Hansel &

Gretel that I'd been nibbling off bits of the decoration on the façades of roller coasters. The "Parachute Jump" is an immense steel tower, /raying/ out at the top in twelve petals—very dimly lit last night it did look like a monster flower-skeleton.

Two men, one is lame & they have a very dirty pet dog, are sieving the sand on the beach very slowly & thoroughly, a little strip about 2 ft. wide & 10 ft. long, at a time. [I'd love to know what they're finding.] The beach is almost deserted. An attempt to clean it up seems to be being made but it still is littered with papers & looks very tired. It is hard to believe that really *is* the ocean, there—blue, but not bright, a little tired too—supporting as if with an effort large stiffly swinging red bell-buoys at regular intervals. ("Buoy 18" "Buoy 19" etc.) cartographer effect

This morning the airplanes look like splinters of glass—very dangerous. (VCSC 75.3b, pp. 123–25)

The reference to fortune-telling cards in the last stanza of poem III summons up "the radio-singers" of love songs in Bishop's Key West poem "Late Air": "like a fortune-teller's / their marrow-piercing guesses are whatever you believe." Here the heart itself "in dreams seeking his fortune, / Sees travel, and turns up strange face-cards."

20 "Song—for the Clavichord": Single copy, handwritten (VCSC 72A.1). As is well known, Bishop played the piano and studied music at Vassar. In the year after college, she took clavichord lessons with a maestro of the instrument, Ralph Kirkpatrick, and in April of 1935 she ordered a custom-made clavichord from Arnold Dolmetsch.

In a letter to her college friend Frani Blough, dated January 30, 1935, Bishop quotes Ezra Pound, who wrote an essay on the Dolmetsches: "You don't think much of the clavichord, as I remember, but it's quite suited to my needs. Then, as Ezra Pound says somewhere, 'The further poetry departs from music, the more decadent it gets,' etc., and I want to learn whatever I can about the periods when it hadn't yet departed—which is approximately up to the end of the clavichord days" (OA, p. 31).

This draft of "Song—for the Clavichord" is on page 21 of the 1935 ("some 1934–36") notebook near a draft of a poem alternately titled "People Who Can't Remember Dreams" and, as it appeared in the "Uncollected Work" section of *The Complete Poems, 1927–1979*, "Dreams They Forgot." Under the draft in this notebook, Bishop writes (in capital letters), "TERRIBLE."

21 "In the Tower" is located on the same notebook page as "Song—for the Clavichord." Single copy, all crossed out (VCSC 72A.1).

22 "Valentine V": Single handwritten draft crossed out on p. 29 of the 1935 ("some 1934–36") notebook. Entry in the Cuttyhunk notebook, July 1934 (VCSC 72A.3, p. 1): "*Valentine V*—the minute when the man cut the sword off the sword fish."

In a letter to Moore, dated August 21, 1936, Bishop mentions having gone "swordfishing with the men" when she visited the island of Cuttyhunk in July 1934, and adds, "I think it must be the most exciting industry there is" (OA, p. 44).

"Valentine I" and "Valentine II" were first published in the *Vassar Review* and reprinted with a third valentine, introduced by Marianne Moore, in *Trial Balances: An Anthology of New Poetry,* in 1935.

"Three Valentines" (parts I, II, III), dated 1934, was published in the section "Poems Written in Youth," in *The Complete Poems, 1927–1979* (New York: Farrar, Straus and Giroux, 1979).

23 " 'The past . . .' ": Bishop wrote "(Poem from 1935)" at the top of the single available draft of this poem (VCSC 64.5). In her biography of Bishop, *Elizabeth Bishop: Life and the Memory of It,* Brett Millier speculates that the poem may have been written on New Year's Eve 1934, when Bishop wrote much of a draft of "The Map" (LM, p. 78). In a footnote in the dissertation chapter quoted in the note to " 'Once on a hill I met a man . . . ,' " Marit J. MacArthur writes, "In the unpublished 'Poem from 1935,' the past lies low for the moment, but seems threatening" (AH).

24 " 'We went to the dark cave of the street-corner . . .' ": This is from a notebook with drafts of several other poems Bishop worked on in Europe. The year 1935 is scrawled and circled at the top of the page followed by "36?" (VCSC 72A.2, p. 50).

27 "Luxembourg Gardens": Single handwritten draft (VCSC 72A.2, p. 59). In September 1935, Louise Crane joined Bishop in Douarnenez, in Brittany, and from there they proceeded to Paris to stay at the apartment of friends of Mrs. Crane's, the Comte and Comtesse de Chambrun, at 58 rue de Vaugirard. On October 20, 1935, Bishop wrote to her friend Frani Blough, who was then staying at Bishop's Charles Street apartment in New York:

> Comtesse de Chambrun (who's supposed to be a great authority on Shakespeare, I think—a homely, horse-faced, blunt woman, the bossy type, with all kinds of decorations in her lapels) is our landlady, and this apartment is furnished with her wedding presents, I guess—though it isn't so bad. . . . We have three bedrooms. The house is right at the corner of the Luxembourg Gardens, where we walk and look at the fountains and dahlias and babies—and the violent croquet matches going on among cabdrivers and professors of the Sorbonne, I think, from appearances. The trees are all yellow now, and the effect is too antique for comfort, but very pretty nevertheless. (OA, p. 37)

28 "In a Room" is dated by Bishop "Seville, 1936." Fragments of this poem appear elsewhere, but this typed and dated version revised by hand is the most intact and complete (VCSC 64.6).

On her 1935 trip to Brittany, Bishop wrote the following in her notebook: "A stain on the plaster of the ceiling looks like a cloud. In it sits a small black fly twiddling his front legs, like a negro angel playing on his harp" (VCSC 72A.3, p. 37).

Brett Millier remarks that this becomes the central image of "Sleeping on the Ceiling" (LM, p. 90). The stain and the flies figure even more prominently in this draft.

Bishop sent the poem to Marianne Moore, along with drafts of "The Weed" and "Paris, 7 A.M.," and she accepted some of the suggestions outlined by Moore in her reply. Moore writes:

"IN A ROOM is very accurate but the rhetoric does not please me entirely by comparison with the others.

> "hobgoblin" contributes meaning but I seem to resist an adjective in the phrase, "of its own accord."
> "for no reason at all" is somehow a little concessive.
> "The most bad dreams of my life" would sound like broken German, but I question "remarkably."
> Page 2: I think "they both went back and forwards" was right as you had it.

Perhaps you would let me see some other things? Also prose? (VCSC 64.6)

In an unpublished dissertation chapter, "Elizabeth Bishop: Incarnations of the 'Crypto-Dream-House,' " Marit J. MacArthur contextualizes this draft:

> On a visit to Spain in April and May of 1936, Bishop experienced the destruction of war firsthand, particularly the burning of churches, as skirmishes leading up to the outbreak of the Spanish Civil War forced her to return to the U.S. earlier than she had planned. . . . In Seville, Bishop was quite ill with stomach troubles, and may have begun the poem while confined to bed. . . . Outside the room is conflict, audible within the room: the couple fighting, writing, and drinking. The droning flies continue to hold their "dance" like a coven of witches, and talk of Revelations, heaven, and hell—they might also be compared to the average Spanish citizen, who had little hope of influencing the course of the war. They seem to be rehearsing the same "hopeless conversation" whose themes the speaker roughly understands, much as Bishop might have heard and not fully understood serious discussions of the state of war in Spain, in which everything was at stake, and both utopian (heaven) and destructive (hell) outcomes were imagined by fascists, republicans, communists, anarchists, and others. The flies, along with the sounds of the fighting neighbors, are the speaker's only company, as the bed becomes almost a world in itself, with its pillows "a range of mountains." (AH, pp. 25–27)

30 "Naples, Fla—'36": (VCSC 68.1). According to Brett Millier, following the suicide of Robert Seaver on November 2, 1936, Bishop "escaped New York with Louise Crane for the Keewaydin [fishing] camp in Naples, Florida, on December 18" (LM, p. 112). From there, she wrote to Moore on January 5, 1937: "At Naples, a long pier runs out in the water and the entire village seems to spend its time fishing off it. The pelicans gather there, too, and wait to take the fish off the hook before you can pull it in. They are very tame—on the beach you can walk right up to them, and then they just *walk* away" (OA, p. 53).

In a letter to her college friend Frani Blough, written on May 27,

1934, Bishop writes that she is reading a "Psysiologus," a bestiary popular in the Middle Ages, "trying to find some wise things to say about Marianne Moore," and she quotes: "It is written, 'As a turtle-dove did I chatter, and as a dove did I mourn.' 'So is this bird like to Christ our very wise and talkative turtle-dove.' 'The Centaurs have the upper part as of a man, and from the breast down the form of a horse. So has every man two souls, and is unstable in his ways.' It is all very edifying and quite nice. I notice particularly that every time they direct you to take a medicine they say to take it in wine" (OA, pp. 23–24).

A few weeks later she wrote in her notebook, "The best thing about the merry-go-round is the way the children appear to be sunk into the animals up to their waists like infant centaurs" (VCSC 72.A3, p. 8).

The following spring she invited Moore and her mother to join her and Louise Crane for supper at Coney Island: "We went down last Sunday, and it was really very nice, although a weekday is probably better. We thought we could start about four-thirty or five, which would give us time for a merry-go-round ride or two before supper. I have found a merry-go-round there which I hadn't noticed before, one with particularly pleasing horses, I think you might like" (April 27, 1935, OA, p. 33).

III. 1937–1950: Key West, Washington, D.C., Yaddo, Nova Scotia

The quotation on the part title page is from page 36 of the Key West notebook VCSC 75.4a. The notebooks designated in the Vassar archive as 75.3a and 3b and 75.4a and 4b, from which the majority of the poems in this part are drawn, were given by Bishop to her friend Linda Nemer, in Ouro Prêto, Brazil, in 1970–71. Nemer sold them to Vassar on June 24, 1986.

Bishop rarely dated entries in the two notebooks and must have used the books interchangeably. Both appear to contain drafts from the late forties, but one of them (VCSC 75.4a and 75.4b) would seem to date from December 1936, because it begins with entries on Wallace Stevens's *Owl's Clover*, a book Bishop discusses in the same terms in a letter to Marianne Moore posted from the Hotel Chelsea, New York City, on December 5, 1936. In that notebook can be found everything in this book's table of contents from " 'What would be worst of all . . . ' " to "Edgar Allan Poe & The Juke-Box."

The other notebook contains a few dates and also descriptions of travels that can be dated by other means. A passage about Lockeport Beach, for instance, clearly stems from the summer of 1946, when Bishop traveled from New York to New Hampshire and Nova Scotia and received copies of her first book, *North & South*. In that notebook, she jotted: "V-Day, 1945," "New Year's 1947," and "Hotel Earle—June 9th?—1948." Here everything on this book's table of contents from " 'Don't you call me that word, honey . . . ' " to " 'In a cheap hotel . . . ' " can be found.

I have preserved the sequence in which the poems and drafts appear in each of the notebooks, presenting all the drafts from one notebook first, followed by eight poems in neither of the notebooks but that are dated from the late 1930s and early to mid-forties or that appear to be from that time (everything in the table of contents from the poem entitled "Key West" to "Little Thaw in January"), followed by all the drafts from the second notebook.

To avoid a morass of speculation, I did not disturb the order that the notebooks' page numbers provide, even if it's clear that this sequence can't be relied upon to date the drafts accurately. All that safely can be said is that all the drafts in this part date from 1936 or 1937 to the late 1940s.

33 " 'What would be worst of all . . .' ": Single copy (VCSC 75.4a, p. 9). Drafts of stanzas 1, 3, and 4 of "The Unbeliever," from *North & South*, appear on the notebook page opposite this fragment.

In her biography of Bishop, Brett Millier cites entries that appear near this draft in the notebook as dating from Bishop's two-month stay at the Keewaydin fishing camp in Naples, Florida, from December 1936 through February 1937. Among them is "Grandmother's Glass Eye: An Essay on Style," which Bishop brooded over on and off for many years and referred to in an undated four-page outline for a lecture about poetry, which can be found in the appendix under the heading "Writing poetry is an unnatural act . . ."

35 "Villanelle": Single copy (VCSC 75.4a, p. 48). On July 17, 1937, while traveling through Burgundy, Bishop and her college friends Margaret Miller and Louise Crane, who was driving, were in a car accident that resulted in Margaret's losing her right hand and forearm. This prose passage about Louise's dream, earmarked as a possible villanelle, refers to the upcoming trial in France in October of that year. (A fuller discussion of the accident and trial can be found in Brett Millier's biography and other books on Bishop.)

Miller had studied fine art at Vassar and had hopes of becoming a painter. Bishop's letters and notebook entries in the months following the accident reflect how this catastrophe affected her—among them: "Most intimate possible association with the 'material world' an artificial hand" (75.4a, p. 48); and

> The arm lay outstretched in the soft brown grass at the side of the road and spoke quietly to itself. At first all it could think of was the possibility of being quickly reunited to its body, without any more time elapsing than was absolutely necessary.
>
> "Oh my poor body! Oh my poor body! I cannot bear to give you up. Quick! Quick!"
>
> Then it fell silent while a series of ideas that had never occurred to it before swept rapidly over it. (VCSC 75.4a, p. 57)

Alongside this passage, running vertically up the notebook page, Bishop adds, "So this is what it means to be really 'alone in the world!' "

On the page opposite "Villanelle" in Bishop's notebook, the following lines expand upon a single phrase jotted below the rhyme scheme on the facsimile of "Villanelle," "When the sparrow fell again." [Note the line in "Belated Dedication," "and the dead birds fell (and nobody saw them fall)."] Ruby is the wife of Bishop's father's brother Jack. All the lines have been entirely crossed out:

I was not quick enough to catch you then;
Time out of mind the sparrow falls again
(and so the sparrow falls and falls again.)

I wasn't quick enough to catch you then
Although I saw the terror in your eyes,
And so the sparrow falls, and falls again.

Aunt Ruby launched the deadliest of her lies
I wasn't quick enough to catch you then
And so the sparrow fell, and fell again

And so the sparrow falls, & falls again. (VCSC 75.4a, p. 49)

Among the many biblical references to sparrows, see Matthew 10:29–30. Two notebook entries written above the lines sketched for the poem seem emotionally relevant to it: "The standing posture of one asleep the / position they would be in, if standing. / One side of her face slightly distorted by the / pillow it rested on Mutileé"; and "In order to give to a child an expensive breakable object, the child must be dearly loved—loved more than the object, that is. So the lord must love us after all" (VCSC 75.4a, p. 49).

The poet Frank Bidart, a close friend of Bishop's through the 1970s in Boston, expressed his understanding of Bishop's feeling for Margaret Miller: "The person Elizabeth was really in love with in those early years was Margaret Miller. They never had a physical relationship. Elizabeth felt that Margaret was not homosexual. She had been in love with Margaret since they were roommates at Vassar. Once she told me that, after years of being obsessed with Margaret, when she woke up one morning, the knot in her chest always present when she thought of Margaret simply was gone" (OB, p. 70).

Bishop's delight in Margaret is recorded over and over in the former's post-college notebook. From an entry dated February 7, 1935: "M. in her new coat & green hat is surely the prettiest and most refreshing thing in New York. She comes out like a whistle in a chorus of humanity" (VCSC 72A.3, p. 24).

Bidart wrote of the accident in France, "Margaret was rushed to the hospital; Louise stayed with her. Elizabeth stayed behind at the scene. She found the arm. She sat next to it and covered it with her dress. She waited for the police, or at least more help, to arrive. She told me she had always wanted to write a poem spoken by the arm, but couldn't."

On December 31, 1948, in a letter to Robert Lowell, Bishop refers to Margaret Miller as "my old friend who is at the Museum of Modern Art. I've always shown her everything I write, since we were in college." She goes on to quote with pleasure Miller's response to Lowell's *The Mills of the Kavanaghs*: " 'I have never read a word of R.L. and had suspected that at least a portion of your enthusiasm for the poetry could be laid to professional politeness. I was therefore unprepared for all that blacktongued piratical vigor. I can't read more than three or four poems at a sitting—it's a little like smelling salts—but they are remarkable and wonderful, though the rhymes seem a little *too* strong or crass on occasions' " (EB/RL).

Letters from Miller to Bishop reflect the former's astute appreciation of Bishop's poetry and her constant encouragement:

> *North and South* came in the morning mail and when I got home this evening I read it straight through as nearly as possible as if I had never read it before. I wish that I could properly describe the effect—the amazing effect of luxuriance and movement. It was rather like a concert of the most exacting animated music and long before I reached "The Fish" and the "Roosters" I began to wonder, as I sometimes do at a concert, how the pace and quality could be sustained. But it is right to the end. . . . I feel absolutely certain that the main poems will hold their own right in the center of the tradition of English poetry. (LMM, 1947–49, VCSC, 12.3)

A letter to Bishop at Yaddo, from August 1949, asks for "a few verses, sample stanzas, or even metaphors in progress" (LMM, VCSC, 12.3).

From an undated letter to Bishop about a new poem, "Brazil, January 1, 1502" (which was published in *The New Yorker* in its January 2, 1960, issue): "There is something about it that is completely unique, unlike any poem I have ever read. Now it is hard to say just what this is, but I believe it is the absolute clarity, the sharp focus of the image, the expanding size of the image, and best of all the surprising changes in scale. . . . It is an extraordinary feat of illusionism and I take my hat off to you" (LMM, VCSC, 12.5).

Letters in the Vassar archive testify to a painful but temporary breach in the friendship months earlier. In the belief that Miller was suffering from mental illness and was financially unable to pay for treatment, both Bishop and Louise Crane had offered her money, which she resolutely refused. In a letter dated November 28, 1959, Miller alludes to the accident of 1937: "Do you remember my saying sometime in April or May 1937 that I didn't want Louise to come to Europe, that I was afraid of her driving or rather of driving with her. You could not remember in 1939. But perhaps you did remember during analysis. I will forgive you whatever it is. But you must tell me the truth for my sake your own and the sake of your art" (LMM, 12.5).

In a letter written on October 28, 1979, from Paris—a letter that never reached Bishop because she had died earlier that month in Boston—Mary McCarthy defends herself against Bishop's suspicion that she and Lota had been used as characters in McCarthy's novel *The Group.* In the course of her denial, McCarthy mentions Margaret Miller: "I promise you that no thought of you, or of Lota, even grazed my mind when I was writing *The Group.* The character Lakey owed a little something to Margaret Miller but only in her appearance—the Indian eyes and the dark hair—and in her Fine Arts studies" (OA, p. 614).

After writing the poem "One Art," Bishop told Bidart that she'd wanted to write a villanelle all her life and that the new poem represented her only success with the form—a form she apparently instinctively associated with catastrophe. The poem was published in the April 26, 1976, issue of *The New Yorker*, and on June 2, Bishop wrote to May Swenson: "I'm pleased that you liked my one & only villanelle" (LMS).

In a letter to May Swenson from Brazil twenty years earlier, November 4, 1956, following a discussion of her "Sestina" (originally titled "Early Sorrow"), Bishop writes:

> I've tried for years to do a villanelle, I like them so much, but without much luck—like Thomas's—"*Do not go gentle into that good night.*" If you have time to do some reading now may I tactlessly suggest Sidney's *Arcadia?*—that's where I got "*A Miracle for Breakfast*" from—and it's full of wonderful things. I don't think one should stick to the old forms, of course, but just by having them in one's head they seem to start the machinery going—for me, anyway. And I think it makes it easier to get the effect one wants, perhaps—and also not to waste time doing what's been superbly done already. (Another of my ambitions is a *PANTOUM.*) (LMS)

An unpublished villanelle entitled "Verdigris," written when Bishop was Consultant to the Library of Congress in 1950, can be found in the appendix.

Brett Millier describes Bishop in the 1960s as embarking on "an ambitious villanelle about an aviary in the rain, with these unwieldy rhymes: fiduciary, subsidiary, sumptuary, beneficiary" (LM, pp. 346–47).

36 " 'Under such heavy clouds of love . . .' " A single page of Bishop's notebook contains a first draft followed by recopied lines, indicating slight revisions reflected in the draft as transcribed (VCSC 75.4a, p. 62). Following the page with " 'Under such heavy clouds of love . . .' " on the next page of the notebook, are the initial lines of "Florida," as well as these, crossed out: "Sunday morning / If Love can anything oh let him show / This morning in this small town a marigold face. / And then—as if by accident I'll go / Along the streets and choose the lucky place . . ." These are succeeded by lines including a "magic gray Ford" that will "Drive up and park in front / Leave the church-goers to their minister— / under the sour chimes / That ring out Dulce Carmen / Meet the beautiful tourists' eyes and smile" (VCSC 75.4a, p. 63).

37 "Dream—": What appears to be the first of three nearly identical drafts (75.4a, p. 65). Two others can be found in the Key West notebook under the title "Blue Postman." Above the draft on page 98 of the notebook, Bishop wrote "*for music*—a wistful, rather dreamy tune—J.S.?" This version contains the lines "with a letter in his hand / postmarked from another land." The version on the next page reads:

> I see the postman everywhere
> vanishing in thin blue air
> with the letter I await
> postmarked from a different state.
>
> The postman's uniform is blue.
> The letter is of course from you

& I'd be able to read, I hope,
my own name on the envelope

but he has trouble with this letter
which constantly grows bigger & better
& over & over in despair
he vanishes in blue blue air.

Blue postman, blue postman,
Please stop disappearing down the street ?

—But over & over in despair
he vanishes in blue blue air.

(VCSC 75.3a, p. 99)

References to letters abound in Bishop's papers. A notebook entry from 1934, when she was living in New York, reads, "Last night (Dec. 22nd) I went out to mail some letters in the corner mail box, at about 1 A.M. Three drunken men were coming along, leaning on each other, very happy and amiable indeed. They watched me putting my letters in the box with an affected silent surprise, then one of them said loudly 'Oh, I hope one's for me' " (VCSC 72A.3, p. 23).

From a notebook entry when Bishop was traveling in France in the summer of 1935 and situated for a time in the fishing village Douarnenez, on the coast of Brittany:

> I am always getting myself in situations where I depend on some cold-faced woman, some mean-jawed postman, for my pleasures—and they keep them from me deliberately. The postman stands and talks with the patronne—she flicks my letters carelessly against the door frame—she stands there fifteen minutes while I pretend to read my book wondering if I dare raise my voice and call to her in dreadful French to please bring me my letters. The poor little dog, who sits quietly on a bench, at a table, as if at any moment she might order, in a trembling voice, an aperitif, or a cup of café au lait, looks at me sympathetically. We look into each other's eyes now & then—she shivers a little and shakes her head "Oh!" & her eyes fill with tears. We are both wretched, around eleven o'clock in the mornings here. (VCSC 72A.3, p. 37)

And from the Key West notebook: "At night the crack under the bedroom door was like a luminous (golden?) letter being slid through" (VCSC 75.3a, p. 71).

38 "Florida": The most developed version of two (VCSC 75.4a, p. 65). On the previous page, an earlier, more fragmentary, and less legible draft, crossed out, suggests interesting leaps for this poem. Note the variation on the line Bishop jotted below "Villanelle" as well as lines from her poem "Cirque d'Hiver."

Look, look! all the old Lears upon the beach
And no gray beards, but grizzled hairs on their chests
Sandy, like sea-weed, blow

They have brought their Ophelia daughters to the sea
Time out of mind the sparrow falls
His mane and tail are straight from Chirico.
He has a formal, melancholy soul.
He feels her pink toes dangle towards his back
Transfixed by a   pole

(VCSC 75.4a, p. 64)

39 "Money": Single copy with the first two stanzas crossed out (VCSC 75.4a, p. 111). Bishop enclosed "Money" in a letter sent to Marianne Moore from Key West on January 20, 1938: "I am enclosing two poems and a sort of joke (made out of a sentence in Dostoevsky's *House of the Dead*: 'Money comes and goes like a bird')" (OA, p. 67). She copied several passages from the Dostoevsky novel in her notebook, among them: "I have never been able to look upon the mad calmly or with indifference. There was one who was kept three weeks in our room: we would have hidden ourselves, had there been any place to do it. When things were at the worst they brought in another" (VCSC 75.4a, p. 103).

From earlier in this notebook, an unattributed quotation: "Only the mad will never never come back" (VCSC 75.4a, p. 96).

Across from "Money," on the previous page of the notebook, Bishop writes, " 'society' is like drinking—it's too hard to stop at any particular point."

Across from copied passages from *The House of the Dead* and *The Idiot*, Bishop drew a rough sketch of what she had in mind for her poem "The Monument," and beneath the sketch, which she had introduced as "a *frottage* of this sea," she wrote the lines that are the kernel of the close of that poem: "This is the beginning of a painting / a piece of statuary, or a poem, / or the beginning of a monument. / Suddenly it will become something. / Suddenly it will become everything" (VCSC 75.4a, p. 100). In a letter to Anne Stevenson, Bishop elaborates:

> You are right about my admiring Klee very much—but as it happens, "The Monument" was written more under the influence of a set of *frottages* by Max Ernst I used to own, called *Histoire Nature* [*sic*]. I am passionately (I think I might say) fond of painting; in fact I'd much rather talk about painting than poetry, as a rule. I am equally fond of music—although I am rather behind with that, living in Brazil. Next time round I'd like to be a painter—or a composer—or a doctor—I seriously considered studying medicine for several years and still wish I had. (LAS)

40 "Valentine": Single copy (VCSC 75.4a, p. 114).

41 " 'We hadn't meant to spend so much time . . .' ": The first of two nearly identical drafts. The draft represented is crossed out but intact and clearer.

Revisions in the second copy include "see" for "stand" in line six, "the shadow" for "that shadow" in line seven, and "the clerk" for "Harlequin" in the last line, but that line and others are crossed out (VCSC 75.4b, p. 142).

In a letter to the young poet and critic T. C. Wilson, whom Bishop had met through Marianne Moore—Moore wrote to Ezra Pound in 1935 that Bishop's letters and Wilson's were "the best letters from young people that I have seen"—Bishop wrote from Key West on June 1, 1938, of the house at 624 White Street, which she and Louise Crane had just bought: "The house is beautiful inside and out—so cool and pure. I have most of my books here at last and stacks of old papers & note-books to destroy. In the back yard we have a lime-tree loaded with limes, which simplifies drink-making—also banana-trees, avocados, a mango, a *sour-sop*, and a grape-vine which bears one bunch of very wry-looking grapes" (EB to TCW, *The Yale Review*, October 2005, p. 19).

Bishop mentions the lime trees of Key West many times in her letters and journals: On May 5, 1938, in a letter to Marianne Moore, she writes, "It is spring here now and the Royal Poinciana trees are in bloom all along the streets—brilliant flame color or dark red. Also a large tree—Spanish lime?—that sheds in some places fine green powder all over the streets, very pretty" (OA, p. 73).

From her notebook: "In the icy shadow of the lime-tree. Is the shadow of a large tree colder than the shadow of a small one?" (VCSC 75.4b, p. 136). On page 158 of the same Key West notebook: "The lime tree, unexhausted by the bees" and "all in a sentimental rush the evening tries to make up for / the slighted yards & houses."

In another notebook dated by Bishop "March 6, 1938 Sept 25th 1942," she describes the cat, Baby, on the lawn of the house. The entry is undated but is preceded by one dated "Jan." (1939) and followed by a note about the visit of President Truman on February 17, the first time Bishop and Louise had the philosopher John Dewey and his daughter, Jane (who became a good friend), to dinner: "—Baby playing on the lawn, looking very small and bewildered. He lives in the shade of the lime tree, blinking at the white & yellow butterflies, and occasionally pouncing at a cricket or a lizard. If I call his name from an upstairs window he looks all around, but never *quite* high enough" (VCSC 77.3, p. 17).

From a notebook entry dated November 13, 1939, quoting one of the locals, possibly her housekeeper and friend, Mrs. Almyda, she writes, "The yard is full of little green birds—all over the lime tree, even lighting on the limes. 'We calls them Chip-Chips; no, they don't have no meats' " (VCSC 77.3, p. 23).

It seems evident that this poem is about her relationship to Louise, with whom she shared the home "in the shadow of the lime tree." Their life as a couple came to an end in 1940, although they remained friends. (Bishop finally sold the house in 1946.) In the Fountain and Brazeau oral biography, Mary Meigs, a lover of Louise's in the late forties and a great admirer of Bishop and her work, said, "From Louise Crane I heard about the difficulties of her breakup with Elizabeth, about Elizabeth's despair and her suicide threats. Louise was irresistible to women; she had very blue eyes, full, it seemed, of innocent candor and love of life" (OB, p. 86).

In the summer of 1934, just after college, Bishop wrote of her friend in her notebook: "Louise is the only person I've ever seen who has preserved the charm of the really charming, not sickening, baby, up into adulthood. It is, in the baby, a certain wisdom and sophistication of the round-faced sort (Round Faced versus Thin Faced Sophistication) plus a little boredom with being a baby, but willingness to let it go on if anyone gets any satisfaction out of it" (VCSC 72A.3, p. 6).

Two entries in her Key West notebook: "L. toddling across the gray, snap-shot colored sand, which was probably snap-shot colored anyway. The happy baby-expression which when one knows the adult well is so sad. For the story—"; and "(picture of L as a child) / the photograph colored sand / color left out (as love was from your life then)" (VCSC 75.4a).

For many years, Bishop contemplated writing something on the subject of "Tact & Embarrassment." In her notebook, she describes tact as "the most beautiful virtue going by a minor name because that is its nature" (VCSC 75.4a, p. 90). Another entry on the subject involves Louise: "*Examples of Tact*—L. at the Walgreen drugstore in Miami—when the woman overheard us saying we wished we had a comb & offering us hers—L. saying so quickly & so politely—'oh thank you. I *couldn't*—my hair is so dirty . . .' " (VCSC 75.4a, p. 124).

See the note for "The Salesman's Evening" for further reference to the subject.

42 " 'From the shallow night-long graves . . .' ": Single copy (VCSC 75.4b, p. 203). Another poem earmarked for "Bone Key," a sequence of poems about Key West and a title Bishop considered for her second collection. Another was "Hotels."

Bishop remarked on the soil of Key West in the following notebook entry, dated October 26, 1939: "Something inherent about the soil here—so shallow, & digging in it with a trowel I found a bottle neck, several bones, an old celluloid hairpin, lots of rocks, plaster, etc." (VCSC 77.3, p. 23).

43 "The Street by the Cemetery": Single copy, entirely crossed out (VCSC 75.4b, p. 227). Another poem earmarked for "Bone Key."

A forthcoming volume of Bishop's correspondence with her editors at *The New Yorker* from 1934 up through August 1979, the year of her death, contains a letter dated March 7, 1941, from Charles A. Pearce: "Dear Miss Bishop: Apparently 'The Street by the Cemetery' is one *The New Yorker* is unable to use. I am sorry the decision has turned this way. It's a good poem, I think, and I hope to be able to see it in print soon" (EB/NY).

The poem as represented here was published in *The New Yorker* in its February 21 and 28, 2000, issue.

From the 1938–42 notebook, dated November 23 (Thanksgiving), 1939, describing the scene of the poem in Key West:

> These people sitting on their porches in the moonlight—looking at the graveyard—like passengers on ship-board. Third class, steerage passengers who nevertheless, somehow or other, have been given deck-chairs. Not speaking to one another, or to the people on the porch of the next house, 3 ft. away—
>
> Very cold & brilliant moonlight. Windy. Nothing can look

> more hysterical than a palm tree in the wind—it is completely feminine, strident & abandoned.
>
> The branches of the long row of oleanders across the way at the barracks moved more slowly, the white blossoms showing up like the pieces of paper & garbage that float in clusters in a harbor.
>
> Unevenness of the sidewalks here; unevenness of the tombs. In the North they say the frost did it; here I don't know how they explain it. In the cemetery the tombs are every which way, laid that way to begin with on one level, and then broken up & cracked & tipped on edge on another. Probably it is just poor *cee*-ment work. (VCSC 77.3, p. 24)

Another entry from January 1941: "We have all suddenly taken a great fancy to the road by the graveyard although I always did like it very much—I can't get enough of walking it back & forth at night. I wouldn't even mind living in one of the little houses there, with my front yard full of decorated graves" (VCSC 77.3, p. 40).

And from late January/early February 1941 (the next dated entry is on Bishop's birthday, February 8):

> I was bicycling through the cemetery this evening when I saw this amazing spectacle: A tall man, pressed against the wall of one of the little white plaster mausoleums, in the sunset-light, holding a big, open Bible in one hand, and a banjo in the other. I got off the bicycle & looked around & discovered he was having his picture taken—another man & a woman & a girl were all taking it. They had a Brownie camera on top of a packing-box on top of a little table. When his picture had been taken, the woman posed with the banjo, alone, & with the girl, who carried a large concertina. I recognized the woman as Sister Mary, of the House of God, here—the most popular evangelist, & the man I suppose is her husband, with whom she lived as "brother & sister" until she got a divorce from her first husband. She was all dressed up in a blue silk dress. But why choose that background of white monuments & artificial flowers to have their pictures taken in? (VCSC 77.3, pp. 44–45)

In the Key West notebook, on a page with the phrase "The world's obsessive imagery—":

> The leaves of the house-plants on the verandah—slightly dirty underneath, like the cat's ears.
>
> The banana trees unfolding like green diplomas
> Their blossoms hanging like
>   surveyors' plumbs—
>
> The ground that would dry their tears like
> blotting paper—in the cemetery—

or let it through, scarcely detaining
it, to join the sea below. (VCSC 75.3a, p. 14)

44 " 'It is marvellous to wake up together . . .' ": One of two copies. The facsimile reproduces the typed copy, which Bishop gave to her Brazilian friend Linda Nemer c. 1970. Bishop also entered the poem by hand in her Key West notebook, and there are just three small changes from one draft to the next. In the handwritten copy, the second to last line of the first stanza reads, "All over the roof rain hisses" without the article before "rain."

The seventh line of the second stanza has "That" instead of "How," but the word is crossed out. And in the fourth line of the last stanza, "must be" is crossed out and replaced by "are": "Since always to warn us there are these black" (VCSC 75.4b, p. 229).

Besides giving Nemer the typed poem, Bishop entrusted her with the Key West notebooks, from which so many of the poems in the third section of this book (and so much of the quoted material in this book) are drawn. Nemer shared these notebooks with Lorrie Goldensohn when Goldensohn visited her in Belo Horizonte, Brazil, in the spring of 1986. As Goldensohn describes the moment in her book *Elizabeth Bishop: The Biography of a Poetry* (New York: Columbia University Press, 1992): ". . . Pulling a piece of folded onionskin from one of the notebooks, [Linda] opens it carefully and hands it to me. Linda reads no English. She has questions about what she is giving me. It is a typescript of a rather remarkable poem, no erasures, a doodle in the corner that looks a bit like a fourposter bed" (p. 23).

Bishop's biographer Brett C. Millier believes that this poem is probably about Marjorie Stevens, and its placement in notebooks that span the years 1941–46 when Bishop was living with Stevens in Key West confirms that likelihood. However, it may have been written earlier, in the late 1930s, years in which Bishop was with Louise Crane. While I have sequenced the drafts according to their placement in the notebooks, there is no certainty about the order of their actual composition.

Bishop has numerous entries in her notebooks about rain (see the note for "After the Rain"). This one, written on November 11, 1938, includes the word "marvellous": "L.'s [Louise Crane's] birthday. Marvellous showers of rain on and off all day—I went out early to do errands and got caught in one" (VCSC 77.3, p. 12).

Bishop singles out Auden's use of the word "marvellous" in a journal passage about William Empson's *Seven Types of Ambiguity: A Study of Its Effects in English Verse*, published in England in 1930 and in the United States by New Directions in 1947. She takes issue with John Crowe Ransom's view of the book in his piece "Mr. Empson's Muddles," and explores her sense of what Empson was after in his discussion of word fashions.

> E. *isn't* showing what the poet *intended*—but clearing up the poet's associations because of place, time, vocabulary, etc., etc. with the words he uses. It isn't that he *intended* a pun here or a reference to this or that personage or event there—E. tries to get

the *feeling in the air* about the words (the switch say inside 3 yrs. of from "nice" to "ravishing" for the same thing—Auden's use of "marvellous"—the word fashion which is so much more subtle, even, than clothes fashions. Cecil Beaton's "infinitely beautiful" in 25 yrs. will sound like the "a capitol treat" of 1880.) . . . A sensitive reader, I think, familiar with the work of a poet, can *feel* what words are fashion-words, used ironically, "waked up," etc. etc., *but* they tend to fall back, I believe, to the previous use—I mean A's "marvellous" will lose its slight tint of mystery-Oxbridge-naiveté and become anyone's "marvellous." (D. H. Lawrence & "manly," etc.) (VCSC 75.4b, p. 131)

Bishop makes a note about Lawrence a few pages earlier: "What seemed *fresh* begins to blend so rapidly—'he had a strong *manly* energy—' D. H. Lawrence.—6 years ago his use of the word *manly* seemed to indicate something—now I've forgotten what it was & it seems the same word employed by Matthew Arnold—or Kipling.

—So Auden begins already to sound more & more like Tennyson—or Kipling" (VCSC 75.4b, p. 123).

(See, in the appendix, "Mechanics of Pretence: Remarks on W. H. Auden" for further reference to Empson.)

From Bishop's contribution to *The Harvard Advocate*'s Auden issue of 1975, entitled "A Brief Reminiscence and a Brief Tribute":

> When I was in college, and all through the thirties and forties, I and all my friends who were interested in poetry, read him constantly. We hurried to see his latest poem or book, and either wrote as much like him as possible, or tried hard not to. His then leftist politics, his ominous landscape, his intimations of betrayed loves, war on its way, disasters and death, matched exactly the mood of our late-depression and post-depression youth. We admired his apparent toughness, his sexual courage—actually more honest than Ginsberg's, say, is now, while still giving expression to technically dazzling poetry. (Lloyd Schwartz and Sybil P. Estess, eds., *Elizabeth Bishop and Her Art*, Ann Arbor: University of Michigan Press, 1983, p. 308)

When confronted by a young friend seeking advice on love, in 1966, Bishop replied, "If you really are concerned about that subject, I'd suggest that you go and read Auden. If *he* doesn't know something about love, I just don't know who else does" (CEB, p. 44).

In Bishop's poem "Rain Towards Morning," the conjunction of birdcage and bedroom occurs, too, along with "an unexpected kiss." In a diary entry from the Murray Hill Hotel on December 26, 1937, Bishop describes the birdcage effect of the wallpaper in her room:

> Came to N.Y. by train through a dreary, tangled-etching landscape. I have quite a nice room for $2.00 at the Murray Hill. It

> has a picture of a large mourning woman, with itsy-bitsy wings, in sepia, and an etching of a brook. Below the brook, on the mat of the picture, the artist has drawn a fish creel & a couple of dead fish, so that you'll get the idea. I also have a white china spittoon and a gas-log—3 logs with little worm-holes in them, where the gas comes up, I suppose.
>
> The shiny silver stripes of the wall-paper make it a bird-cage by lamplight. (VCSC 77.2, p. 51)

Her single entry the next day: "N.Y. Rt. back where I started from" (VCSC 77.2, p. 51).

Bishop also drew on the details of the Murray Hill hotel room for her story "In Prison," which won a *Partisan Review* one-hundred-dollar contest in 1938, a story she described to Marianne Moore as "another of these horrible 'fable' ideas that seem to obsess me":

> The room I now occupy is papered with a not unattractive wallpaper, the pattern of which consists of silver stripes about an inch and a half wide running up and down, the same distance from each other. They are placed over, that is, they appear to be inside of, a free design of flowering vines which runs all over the wall against a faded brown background. Now at night, when the lamp is turned on, these silver stripes catch the light and glisten and seem to stand out a little, or rather, in a little, from the vines and flowers, apparently shutting them off from me. I could almost imagine myself, if it would do any good, in a large silver bird cage! But that's a parody, a fantasy on my real hopes and ambitions. (CP, p. 182)

45 "Florida Deserta": Single copy (VCSC 75.4b, p. 231). "—for Bone Key."

46 "For A.B.": Single copy entirely crossed out (VCSC 75.4b, p. 233). The dedication is possibly to Dr. Anny Baumann, the physician who treated Bishop from 1947 until her death, and whom she met through Louise Crane in the late 1930s in New York. Above the dedication, which functions as a title, Bishop wrote and then crossed out "The pale child with the silver hair."

From the editors' commentary in Gary Fountain and Peter Brazeau's *Elizabeth Bishop: An Oral Biography*: "Bishop's most helpful confidante and ally was Dr. Anny Baumann. Louise Crane had introduced Bishop to Baumann in the thirties, and Baumann became throughout Bishop's life the mainstay in her struggle with both asthma and alcoholism. According to many of Baumann's patients, she was an acute diagnostician who possessed uncommon compassion and a strong authoritarian bearing" (OB, p. 96).

The New York architect Harold Leeds, friend both of Bishop and of Lota de Macedo Soares, Bishop's Brazilian companion from 1951 to 1967, described Baumann as "one of those old European doctors who believed in taking care of the whole person. Anny used to say, 'If I can see you once a year, I can keep you in good health.' . . . I think that she loved seeing her patients well. She loved going to Elizabeth's readings" (OB, p. 97).

On page 81 of the notebook, below a penultimate draft of "Late Air" (then titled "K. W."), Bishop wrote and then crossed out:

To take a walk in a dream

What was it the hands wanted
That stole my heart. Not the heart,
certainly, not a heart at all

I was startled by
your tears that fell past my eyes
like lightning
as we lay embraced

a wet kiss on my
ear, like an image
2 /   /, out of Andersen, lying
here in the dark talking nonsense   (VCSC 75.4a, p. 81)

From her post-college notebook "(1934–35)": "Sometimes a children's book—a fairy tale—might be made to hold things that could only be put into poetry in three life-times" (VCSC 72A.3, p. 6). From the same notebook: "woodcutters always have 2 children—" (VCSC 72A.3, p. 16). And in a notebook entry from New York, November 1941: "In the child there resides the synthesis and understanding that the parents could not reach" (VCSC 77.3, p. 59). See the note for "Once on a hill I met a man . . ." with its reference to Bishop's childhood reading of Hans Christian Andersen's tales.

From a letter to Robert Lowell from Rio de Janeiro, April 4, 1962: "I am so glad Dr. Baumann is in attendance and I do hope you are better and gaining weight. Please don't go into a 19th-century decline! Dr. B. always made me feel that everything was possible if I only did my duty, and that my duty was plain and simple, too. Of course it isn't, but it's a good way to feel sometimes" (OA, p. 405).

47 "The Salesman's Evening": The single extensive draft entirely crossed out (VCSC 75.4b, p. 237). Bishop began to sketch this scene earlier in the Key West notebook: "In the cheapest café the drinks were naturally much smaller. . . . The glasses resembled little pillars of crystal [with] little hollows in the tops of the capitols. . . . It was a hideous town and there was nothing in it he could take home as a souvenir to the person he loved—" (VCSC 75.4b, p. 47).

One of Bishop's many fascinating entries about embarrassment—she had long wanted to write a poem or piece of prose on the subjects of tact and embarrassment—can be found on the opposite page: "The man living in the advertisement knew *Embarrassment* to the ends of his soul. Other sensations have been used in this phase—but none are so suicidal. Self-consciousness because of the PRODUCT everyone took him for representing & which he did *not* represent" (VCSC 75.4b, p. 46).

Bishop originally wrote, "Why, that horse out there / is the only living creature." She revised that to read, "Why, that horse out there / is more alive than they are—"

49 "Edgar Allan Poe & The Juke-Box": Single draft with a note, "Neddy & bone-key," to the right of the title (VCSC 75.b, p. 239).

Neddy is the name Bishop gave to her alcoholic uncle Arthur, her mother's younger brother, in the loosely fictionalized "Memories of Uncle Neddy," published in 1977 but begun many years earlier in Brazil. (". . . after all these years, I realize only now that he represented 'the devil' for me, not a violent, active Devil, but a gentle black one, a devil of weakness, acquiescence . . .") (*cp*, p. 228). (I'm grateful to the Bishop scholar Barbara Page, who helped me to decipher the name "Neddy.")

Robert Giroux, Bishop's editor from 1956 until her death, told me that Bishop intended this poem to conclude her second volume. So it's likely that this is the poem she mentions in her July 28, 1953, letter to her editor at Houghton Mifflin, Paul Brooks: "I think the poems form a fairly unified book as they are now . . . There *is* one, however, a sort of farewell to Key West, that I should like to add to this one [a poem forthcoming in *Poetry*, which she enclosed with her letter], and trust I can in a few weeks" (OA, p. 268).

In December 1953, in a letter to Robert Lowell, she also mentions hoping to "get that last impossible poem off to H. Mifflin" (EB/RL).

The lines at the top right-hand side of this draft, "blue as gas / blue as the pupil / of a blind man's eye," invoke the narrator of Poe's "The Tell-Tale Heart" describing his blind neighbor: "He had the eye of a vulture—a pale blue eye, with a film over it. Whenever it fell upon me, my blood ran cold; and so by degrees—very gradually—I made up my mind to take the life of the old man, and thus rid myself of the eye forever" (*The Complete Poems and Stories of Edgar Allan Poe.* With selections from his critical writings. Edited by Arthur Hobson Quinn and Edward H. O'Neill. New York: Alfred A. Knopf, 1946, p. 445).

On May 2, 1938, Bishop wrote to her college (and Walnut Hill School) classmate Frani Blough from Key West about her immersion in Poe: "I begin to wish I weren't where I am, but I'm just going to stay here for a long, long time, I'm afraid. Lately I've been doing nothing much but reread Poe, and evolve from Poe—plus something of Sir Thomas Browne, etc.—a new Theory-of-the-Story-All-My-Own. It's the 'proliferal' style, I believe, and you will shortly see some of the results. There was an indication of it in the March *Partisan Review* [a reference to her prize-winning story 'In Prison']" (OA, p. 71).

Three days later, she wrote to Marianne Moore: "I was curious to hear what you thought of the story ['In Prison'], because it is the first conscious attempt at something according to a *theory* I've been thinking up down here out of a combination of Poe's theories and reading 17th century prose!" (OA, p. 73).

From her Key West notebook: "Poe's 'Each law of nature depends at all points on all the other laws'—Versus Pascal's 'Nature has made all her truths independent of one another—' etc." (VCSC 75.4b, p. 34).

Notes on this poem appear in the notebook some fifty pages before this draft: "pleasure is *exact,* though meretricious / & knows before *exactly* what it wants—" (VCSC 75.4b, p. 193). Above that entry is a significant note on her poetic aims: "some surrealist poetry terrifies me because of the sense of irresponsibility & *danger* it gives of the mind being 'broken down'—I want to produce the opposite effect."

Another start of this poem (the title missing the hyphen Bishop used for both the draft represented and her drawing) below the notes "the true course & nature of love—fall downward flight—":

> Edgar Allan Poe—& the Juke Box
>
> Glowing in the dark—the awful music falls
> so easily in the dark & the love that falls [as]
> easily as the hands fall under the table, everything
> descending, descending (descent of love from the
> eye = our idea of it, anyway) everything descends
> falls, falls, the drinks down the throat, one
> down   beat
>
> but not mechanical
>   alcohol
>
> oh no & [is the] horror here.
>   here.   (VCSC 75.4b, p. 194)

Notes on the next page, jotted below "To Edgar Allan Poe," refer to "the full and final degradation of our love" (VCSC 75.4b, p. 195). Bishop addresses Poe directly on the same page: "you said that poetry was *exact* / but so is pleasure." Earlier in the notebook: "and every fault will find its friend" (VCSC 75.4b, p. 59).

Elsewhere in her journals, Bishop jots: "Baudelaire . . . bad luck . . . Poe's moving around, etc." Bishop is referring to Baudelaire's famous essay of 1852, "Edgar Poe, His Life and Works," which begins:

> Recently there appeared in court an unfortunate man whose forehead was marked by a rare and strange tattoo: *No luck!* He bore thus above his eyes the inscription of his life, like the title of a book, and cross-examination showed that this bizarre label was cruelly true. In literary history there are similar destinies, real damnations—men who bear the words *bad luck* written in mysterious characters in the sinuous creases of their foreheads. The blind angel of expiation has seized upon them and whips them with all his might for the edification of others. (From *Baudelaire as a Literary Critic: Selected Essays,* trans. Lois Boe Hyslop, and Francis E. Hyslop, Jr., University Park: Pennsylvania State University Press, 1964, p. 91)

Bishop continued to reflect on the plight of an unlucky individual, as this entry from her notebook of 1948 attests: "Loved the wrong person all his life / lived in the wrong place / maybe even read the wrong books— / who could say—" (VCSC 72B.5, p. 5).

"Talk to an American about Poe," Baudelaire writes, "and he will perhaps admit his genius; perhaps he will even show himself proud of it. But, with a superior, sardonic tone, which smacks of practicality, he will speak to you of the irregular life of the poet, of his alcoholic breath that could have been set on fire with a candle, of his vagabond habits; he will tell you that Poe was an erratic and eccentric person, a stray planet, that he moved constantly from Baltimore to New York, from New York to Philadelphia, from Philadelphia to Boston, from Boston to Baltimore, from Baltimore to Richmond" (ibid., pp. 93–94).

Bishop's continual peregrinations and worry about the tyranny of alcohol evidently keep Poe, and Baudelaire's sympathetic essay on him, in the foreground at this moment. Another passage worth quoting: "Is it not a cause for astonishment that this simple idea does not flash into everyone's mind: that progress (insofar as there is progress) perfects sorrow to the same extent that it refines pleasure . . ." (ibid., "New Notes on Edgar Poe," p. 123).

Baudelaire's eloquent appreciation of Poe's poetics chimes with many of Bishop's reflections on the art in her early notebooks. Baudelaire exclaims of Poe: "The choice of means! he returns to that constantly, he insists with a learned eloquence upon the adjustment of means to effect, on the use of rhyme, on the perfecting of the refrain, on the adaptation of rhythm to feeling. He maintained that he who cannot seize the intangible is not a poet; that he alone is a poet who is master of his memory, the sovereign of words, the record book of his own feelings always open for examination" (ibid., p. 130).

In an early notebook entry, Bishop refers to rhyme as "mystical," and throughout her notebooks, her lists and lists of end rhyme words make it clear that she looked to rhyme to drive and refine her intuitive thinking on the basis of the unfettered associations that rhyme yielded up. With respect to Poe's conception of the poet as "master of memory," compare this entry from Bishop's post-college notebook from 1935:

> Anyone who can learn really to "face the facts," as they say, should have much more to write about, should have hundreds of fresh things to say. It is because you don't, can't, won't, admit many unpleasantnesses, recollect them or see them at present, that you occasionally feel that there is nothing to be said. Think: if you were to resurrect any one year or week of yourself at any past age and be quite honest with it—how awful you were, how awful all those people were, what things really looked like—there'd be enough there for many poems. This holds good for the *smallest* impression as well as "morals." That's where a foolish passion for order, getting everything to *fit,* would be all wrong for anyone who wants to write poetry. You're bound to have to fix things a little if you insist on order, just as "social *orders*" have to use "propaganda." (VCSC 72A.3, p. 25)

In "The Poetic Principle," Poe writes, "*That* pleasure which is at once the most pure, the most elevating, and the most intense, is derived, I maintain, from the contemplation of the Beautiful. In the contemplation of

Beauty we alone find it possible to attain that pleasurable elevation, or excitement *of the soul,* which we recognize as the Poetic Sentiment. . . . I make Beauty, therefore—using the word as inclusive of the sublime—I make Beauty the province of the poem . . ." (*The Complete Poems and Stories of Edgar Allan Poe,* p. 1027).

In "The Philosophy of Composition," he writes, "Regarding, then, Beauty as my province, my next question referred to the *tone* of its highest manifestation—and all experience has shown that this tone is one of *sadness.* Beauty of whatever kind, in its supreme development, invariably excites the sensitive soul to tears" (ibid., p. 981).

Bishop's college friend Harriet Tompkins Thomas recounts an upsetting dinner conversation in Paris in 1935, when Bishop felt she had to defend "the idea of beauty," which for her (in her friend's words) "was one of the eternal verities, the most important thing in life." Frustrated by the superior arguments of a "practiced debater," Bishop fled to the kitchen where Thomas found her ten minutes later "drinking a large glass of gin and weeping profusely" (OB, pp. 65–66).

On December 21, 1948, Bishop sent a postcard from Key West to her New York friends the painter Loren MacIver and her husband, Lloyd Frankenberg, a poet and critic: "Had the good luck to find a huge, wonderful apartment with my former landlady, Mrs. Pindar—upstairs, with the biggest Poinciana tree in Key West shading the screened porch. Don't know what I did to deserve it. . . . Jane [Dewey] and I went to the museums in Baltimore, and to Poe's grave in the pouring rain" (OA, p. 179).

In a letter to Robert Lowell (August 26–27, 1963), Bishop compares William Burroughs to Poe. Lowell had evidently been quoted on the jacket of *Naked Lunch*: "James says wonderful things about naturalism—the more natural just means the more art, etc.—but try to apply that to 'The Naked Lunch,' say . . . I derived a Polly-Anna-ish pleasure from that book. I'm so happy I'm not a drug addict. But it's really not very good. The notes and medical facts and omniscience remind me very much of Poe—he's probably very much like Poe, don't you think?" (LRL, p. 257).

51 "Key West": Single copy of part I and two copies of part II. (VCSC 66.2). The revised version of part II is represented.

From a letter to Marianne Moore from Key West, dated February 14, 1938: "We have a Carnival here now, set up on the vacant lot beside the burnt-out deserted cigar factory. It is quite a thorough little Carnival with a high-diving tower, a merry-go-round, trained apes, etc., and I hope to be able to make some photographs of it worth sending to you" (OA, pp. 69–70).

53 "Hannah A.": Alternately titled "Mrs. Almyda" (VCSC 66.6). Six pages of fairly legible handwritten drafts including the facsimile page, indicating that this was to be a six-part poem. Bishop crossed out much of the material on these loose pages and wrote "stiff" above a version of the opening stanza, but all the stanzas were copied out at least twice. Two pages, numbered one and two, present the first four stanzas in this order, and a separate page contains two crossed-out copies of the last stanza as reproduced. Between stanzas one and two as represented, the omission of the following is indicated by the short, horizontal line:

[which although weathered
still is deeply feathered]
where the dry claws slithered
[on the shale,]
of those who wore fur then,
or the inelegant pin—
feathers that marred the skin,
or dressed in scales,

On another draft, between stanzas four and five, Bishop wrote, "in the face of so much generalizing / to assert *one* thing, one person / myths?"

In the fall of 1938, Bishop hired Hannah Almyda as the housekeeper for the home she had purchased with Louise Crane at 624 White Street in Key West. In her biography of Bishop, Brett Millier describes their closeness: "The two women developed such an attachment for each other that she became Elizabeth's nurse, adviser, even a mother figure on whom she depended" (LM, p. 144).

A notebook entry from February 1939:

> The editor of the Key West "Citizen" has an agreement with the K. W. Women's Club that on every day that goes by without at least a minute of sunshine he is to give them $5.00. Mrs. A. told us this & said, "It's real nice of him to do that. I don't think he's given them anything for over two years." She said it without irony—the truth is that *original sin* is so completely lacking in Mrs. Almyda that she can't put things like that together. Neither can she understand puns, and if she tells a story that involves one she explains it so carefully & so many times that you realize it is still a mystery to her—like the Trinity. (VCSC 77.3, p. 18)

The note that lays out the foundation for this draft dates from January 1941:

> Mrs. Almyda as a Phoenix, a mythological bird of some sort . . . self-sacrificing, brooding on a nest. A phoenix that's forgotten how to set fire to itself & just waits—no, I guess the Pelican, self-sacrificing, tearing feathers from its breast to line its nest, is closest.
>
> Her exclamations of "Precious love!", "Pleasant hope!" etc., somehow add to the mythological character—no one else uses them, that I've heard. Her heaviness—clumsy hands, although she never breaks a dish—her heavy pats of affection, are like the clumsy Pelican taking off on one of her wonderful, powerful flights—once off the water she soars—Mrs. A's love is like that. (for a poem?)

Other stray notes running up the side of this page: "Love, heavy flight / (Insoluble) [Incredible] (astounding) migration, affection." And at the bottom of the page: "over gray water, long, slow, strong— /

incredibly strong, ignorant except in affection" (VCSC 77.3, p. 42). Bishop studied the science of the bird's flight and entered the following unattributed material on the next page of her journal: "reminiscent of the Pterodactyls . . . the Brown Pelican has retained through 100's of centuries the . . . form that we associate with the ancient flyers. . . . Although much flapping is required to lift their heavy bodies from the water, when once launched their flight is buoyant. They will often soar to great heights, & remain there for long periods before descending."—from 3,000–8,000 ft. 1 1/6 strokes a second—quite slow—" (VCSC 77.3, p. 43). Another stanza drafted by Bishop appears to incorporate a line from a letter by Mrs. Almyda. (See below for other quotations from letters Bishop received and saved.)

On coarse, absorbent, pale-
blue-lined writing paper
written in blue-black ink
and breathing love
the flame breathes in
the five-cent paper lantern
and makes it burn clear pink.

"your dear letter received."   (VCSC, 66.6)

Loose notebook pages grouped with drafts of this poem contain a poignant reference to Mrs. Almyda:

It is the middle of the beautiful month of June,
I am eating a green melon with a silver spoon.
It is late afternoon. The walls of the house are white.
The sun comes through the shutters in a way I like.

And the housekeeper whom I love more than precious jewels.

But there are more severe entries on the same page, including a directive to herself, possibly pertaining to alcohol or to her behavior as her relationship with Louise Crane was ending—"stop, and prove your strength"—followed by:

the moon, medieval monster with the round face—
has eaten away half your body
and trapped the bureau in a corner

But the nightmares
tramping down the stairs

                    the smell of gas
The oven is full of black smoke and the sink
                    is full of blood.

We're polite to each other along the accepted lines (VCSC 68.1)

From a letter to Moore, dated July 26, 1941, describing her move from 624 White Street to 623 Margaret, the home of Marjorie Stevens: "If only I could just hand you over Mrs. Almyda. The thought of all your packing, book problems, etc., makes me feel so unjustly pampered. She and I packed and moved everything in one day, not a safety pin left in a bureau drawer, and all the linen marked and counted and so on—and several little sit-down periods for limeade and conversation as well. Well, as I guess I've boasted before, I am trying to compose something about her, and then you'll see the full value of the personality, perhaps . . ." (OA, p. 102).

Bishop saved two letters from Hannah Almyda, sent to her in Brazil in 1961 and 1963, the first containing a recipe for "Cocoanut Pie" and news of Almyda's burgeoning family: "I often think of you and my prayers are also for you. Altho so far away you are often in my thoughts. I have not worked for 3½ years. I have a very nice apt. 3 rooms and bath which right now is about all I can take care of. The grandchildren that is Williams children, three of them are married only Clarence is at home. He will soon be 18 years. I now have two Greatgrand daughters Leroys children. So you see I am getting to be an old woman." In the second, Mrs. Almyda writes, "Truly hope you are well and happy where you are and enjoying your writing. You are often in my thoughts and trust I will see you again. Nothing like seeing the ones you love. I will always have a warm spot in my heart for you" (VCSC 1.3).

55 "After the Rain": One clear copy of the opening stanzas of a poem of which there are numerous drafts among Bishop's papers, including two with the beguiling title "Walk Around Here & Now." (The draft represented is dated 1942 in the archive, VCSC 64.8.) Bishop was working on this poem in Brazil in 1953 and evidently had large plans for it. On September 10, she wrote to Paul Brooks, her editor at Houghton Mifflin, suggesting that the poem would soon be ready for inclusion in her second collection: "I'll probably be able to mail you 'After the Rain' by next weekend. . . . It will be three or four pages in a book" (OA, p. 270).

Below the stanzas represented, Bishop alludes to what she envisioned as the title of her second book:

opens his geography
thinking "Bone Key,—

largo Hueso, key of bone."

the snow that he has never seen
"except in a photograph"

In a single draft of three pages, Bishop indicates her plan for eight stanzas, including the three represented and another three blank in the template. Sketched next to the number 4: "on to houses, plants etc.— / Everything so clear and quiet / & standing still the better to be seen / (like models) on purpose to be seen / (like models) for themselves / (helplessness)."

And number 6: "Between them / twirled around (over) the wires like vines / kites no bigger than this page, / and one of cellophane, / like a broken window-pane."

And an unnumbered set of lines: "The sea sucks on its coral reef. / The puddles, the sky-blue tessellations, / (all) gone; imaginary grace goes, too. / The children will burst out / of school & scream & shout" (VCSC 75.4b).

A quote from St. Teresa introduces a passage from Bishop's Key West notebook from early 1937, which precedes by a page her description of a dream dated February 4. The entry appears to describe a vision Bishop had while reading the saint's book.

> "For from this overflowing river spring many rivulets, some large, others small, while there are little pools for children." Immediately I was let into a country, like the background of a medieval painting, clear, clear, twilit, with an endless perspective of narrow and broad streams and pools, large, irregular, round, small; all reflecting the whiteness and the few clouds of the sky, the endless moist blue air. The nuns went easily in their grey robes from water to water—tall, narrow, silent. What? With the perfect reflections in the shining water, there was more heaven to the picture, than earth. The devil slunk about the edges of the scene—large, slender, rubbery, of bright blue and red with a smoky black face—his fins and folds and [ ] carefully arranged, smart as a fish.
>
> It was all there even as I read the words—I am not making it up. I am describing what I saw in that minute and you can bring *back* to mind but not add to. (VCSC 75.4a, p. 14)

A March 26, 1941, entry:

> A heavy rain-storm & now it seems as much like Spring as it can here. Up & down one little street were bright blue puddles, the gray houses looked clean & bleached, and the little white "orchid trees" were all in bloom—freshest, most beautiful big white flowers on very delicate ragged little trees. In front of one big old house are two cast-iron urns painted white, with the bases & handles faded red, filled with tall pale pink begonias.
>
> I want the garden here to be like the 18th century idea of "The Beautiful & the Useful."
>
> —the spirit in which the Key West people after a hurricane run out & stick the uprooted palm trees back in their holes again. (VCSC 77.3, p. 48)

From the Key West notebook: "The air after the rain as delicious as sherbet—or a drink with grains of ice floating in it" (VCSC 75.4b, p. 136).

Bishop's notebooks abound with descriptions of rain. In New York, July 25, 1934: "When it rained the neighbors all came to the windows & leaned out, absorbing the rain like a collection of plants. . . . The rain came down straight and hard and broke into white arrow heads at the tips—" (VCSC 72A.3, p. 5). In New York, June 1935: "The drops of rain were large and scattered loosely over the sidewalk, not enough to wet it all. They were shaped exactly like seals on legal documents—stylized suns, rather than stars" (VCSC 72A.3, p. 28). And from Key West, her last substantial entry in a notebook dated May 29, 1937–February 23, 1938:

> Tonight we are having the 1st real rain since I've been here. It is pouring. . . . I can see the moths fluttering across the illuminated face of the court-house clock. Under the street lamp the rain bounces off the road in sparks & the trees glisten like Christmas trees hung with tinsel. The cars kick up speed-boat wakes of spray. And what a wonderful noise—like a thousand bee-hives. I sat out on the porch for a while, hanging my arms over the rail into the rain—& Mrs. P. [Mrs. Pindar, landlady of the boarding house at 529 Whitehead Street] was moved to come out, too, in her night-gown & kimono, with her hair down her back. "Oh, I was glad to hear this," she said. Today we have sung in chorus
>
> "They all will sweetly obey His will,
> Peace, peace, be still," etc. (VCSC 77.2, p. 59)

57 "The Soldier and the Slot-Machine": Single typed copy (VCSC 75.4b, p. 175). The drawing on page 56, which refers directly to the slot machine described in this draft, incorporates both the horn of plenty and Bishop's "Twin Jack-Pot" and "Gold Award." Another slot machine, pictured in a watercolor titled *E. Bishop's Patented Slot-Machine,* can be found in the book of her art, *Exchanging Hats* (William Benton, ed., New York: Farrar, Straus and Giroux, 1996, p. 77).

On behalf of Katharine White and his fellow editors at *The New Yorker,* Charles A. Pearce wrote to Bishop on October 28, 1942,

> Dear Miss Bishop,
>
> I am sorry indeed to say that we cannot use this poem about the slot machine ("The Slot Machine")—at least, not in its present form. It doesn't seem quite precise enough (I believe this is the right word), just to use as light verse and also, as it stands, it is a bit too long, we feel. If you feel tempted to try a revision of this, and I hope you will, please let us have a chance to see the result, won't you? (EB/NY)

It's unclear whether Pearce was returning this poem or the one alluded to in Bishop's letter to Robert Lowell of December 11, 1964, answering his report of Marianne Moore's praise for Bishop's "The Burgler of Babylon," which had appeared in *The New Yorker* in November: "Marianne's saying the ballad was my 'best' makes me a bit uneasy! I think she likes the message: 'Crime does not pay' too well! . . . Once I wrote an ironic poem about a drunken sailor and a slot-machine—*not* a success—and the sailor said he was going to throw the machine into the sea, etc., and M congratulated me on being so morally courageous and outspoken" (EB/RL).

In her post-college notebook, in between entries dated "Nov 23rd" and "Dec. 22nd," 1934, Bishop writes, "Are the mirrors always attached to the slot-machines a fore-thought or an after-thought in advertising? Are you meant to look at them and say 'That face needs a penny piece of gum?' or regard yourself with the gum installed in the mouth and say 'Now I look better'?" (VCSC 72A.3, p. 20).

Early notes for this poem appear on pages 184–85 and 47, respectively, of the Key West notebooks 75.4b and 75.3a. In the latter, under the title "The Slot Machine" and below this parenthesis, "(C's candy vendors)":

It is hard to imagine
the world without women
that's going to be heaven—

a world where we all

being somewhat (how) male

without love without luck
        probability

no secrets   or surprises

59 "Full Moon, Key West": Two drafts. This one, dated "about 1943" by Bishop, includes the address of the apartment she often referred to as her "genuine garret" at "46 King Street, New York 14, N.Y." which she kept from the summer of 1944 until the building burned down in 1948. This dated draft presents two stanzas of twenty-two typewritten lines, with the addition of a new line—"Listen!"—handwritten and clearly positioned with an arrow under the line "click click." In the other draft, Bishop marks stanza breaks in two other places, following the line that ends "click click" and the line that ends "tick tick."

The other draft closes with these lines, revised in the draft represented: "a zither laid / on the glittering flood / of the moving Gulf."

"Full Moon, Key West" was returned to Bishop by Charles A. Pearce of *The New Yorker* on September 9, 1943, and then again, along with her poem "Argument," by her customary editor, Katharine White, on October 10, 1946. White spoke warmly of Bishop's just-published début collection, *North & South*, mentioning several reviews. (White had been one of the three judges who had selected the manuscript for publication by Houghton Mifflin from a pool of 833 manuscripts.) She wrote, "The sticking point for those who voted no on the Key West poem seemed to be the second stanza with its prolonged and slightly loose structure. Everyone liked the first stanza. The other more personal poem some thought was not so good for our purposes as your poems usually are. . . . Do be forgiving and send us something else soon" (EB/NY).

In her notebook of late January/early February 1941, Bishop describes an evening walk that may have prompted the clock imagery in this draft:

I walked by a little yellow house on Angela Street, by the cemetery—It was all shuttered up tight, except for the 1 upstairs window which was black & open, & from it, or from the whole house, came the tremendous ticking of an alarm clock—It made the house seem alive, as if it had a heart. (VCSC 77.3, p. 44)

61 " 'The walls went on for years & years . . .' ": Thirteen pages of closely related drafts (65.6). Alternately titled "Long Stay," "For a Long While," "Asylum," and, less explicably, "A Cousin," this handwritten draft is the most seamless. Not one word is crossed out, but I have no idea where the poem as represented fits on the spectrum of drafted material. Under this draft, Bishop wrote the word "robbed" as a possible replacement for "deprived" in the second to last line.

Early notes for this poem appear in the Key West notebook:

The walls went on for years & years
they went away
                    they traveled   (fast) (slow)
          through night & day

where I sometimes wrote significant words
          (with a piece of coal?)
people—the threes, & the Agent—

the view at 1 window—faded & sad, tried to look in, stole away
(VCSC 75.3a, p. 13)

On the same page, one of the most beautiful entries in the notebook describes Bishop's feeling for "the morning light" of this draft, "The morning light on the / / clapboards catches every splinter—rough as they are, Hope itself can not be fairer" (VCSC, 75.3a, p. 13).

On another page of the drafts, Bishop jotted subject categories to the left of sketched stanzas: "bricks & bals [for balconies]," "clothes," "view," "Clouds," and "robbed of all" (VCSC, 65.6).

A few lines that Bishop apparently aimed to incorporate in the poem were copied three times on one sheet with slight variations. The first version is the fullest:

and a pitcher of white enamel that
sat for some days on a window-sill
against the light. Some chipped spots
deceived one into thinking it was
a black-&-white cat—   (VCSC, 65.6)

65 "Stoves & Clocks": Seven pages of notes, and this one partially resolved draft (VCSC 67.13). Bishop evidently sent a draft to her friend Margaret Miller, who wrote to her on April 14, 1943: "In the future I trust that you will enclose more letters from away back as well as poems you have 'turned against.' . . . I liked the chorus from 'Clocks & Stoves' very very much.

[Miller is probably referring to this couplet, which Bishop copied several times in her notes: "The stoves more worry than the weather / the clocks more trouble than the time."] It seems flawless as it stands and I wish you had sent more of the poem. I know that feeling of not being able to finish anything, which you mention, and I would give anything to understand it" (VCSC 12.1).

In 1941, in a piece about a visit to Mercedes Hospital in Key West, Bishop uses the same language in this draft to describe the eyes of an old woman: "bright milky blue, like the flames of a gas burner when they have just been turned off and are about to sink back into the black pipes" (CP, p. 68).

Other lines on pages of drafts were holding out possibilities: "Leave the shop without a fear: / a secret's undiscovered there. / no secret's undiscovered there" and "no undiscovered secret here."

A few other notes: "rouged where it used to be red-hot"; "authoritative word 'Regulator' in gilt, Victorian lettering"; "desolate landscape"; "*exteriorizing*—always approximations anyway—" (VCSC 67.13).

Bishop jotted down a list of stove names—among them "Gem, Garnet, Empire, Mars, Orbit, Oriole, Economic, Triplex—"

A note—"call the stove 'Magee Ideal' "—connects this draft to that of "Dicky and Sister."

66 "Little Thaw in January": Several small pages of notes are represented as Bishop left them and in accordance with her numerical instructions for sequencing words and lines (VCSC 66.15).

68 " 'Don't you call me that word, honey . . .' ": Single fragment from the Key West notebook (VCSC 75.3a, p. 23). Bishop drew a line under this fragment and below it entered the following as a title, "Lullaby for a Dark Child." In the Vassar archive there are twenty-three pages of notes labeled "Blues, etc.—K.W. 1938? 39?" These include titles, lines, and refrains of some of Bishop's favorites—among them:

> EVIL HEARTED WOMAN by /   / Boy Fuller
>
> "You're a hard-hearted woman
> Don't mean me no good"
>
> KIDNAPPER'S BLUES by "Petie Wheatstraw-the Devil's Son-in-Law"
>
> "They kidnapped ma baby
> She was all I had"

along with a number of observations intended for an article, including these:

> "displacement of accent"
> care in giving the dates, names (use of "Mr.") etc.
> cliché of the white songs
> occasional poetic effects of N. songs
> "My baby's gone and left me
> Got a big bed all to myself."

general use of very simple statements . . . They're all "Blues" while the ballads are rather smug about the fate of the victims, etc. (VCSC 74.12)

From a letter to Anne Stevenson, March 20, 1963, from Brazil:

> I have always wanted—like many other poets, I think—to write some really "popular" songs, not "art" songs. One thing I like very much in Brazil is the popular music—the yearly sambas are, or were (too much U S influence now, I'm afraid), often superb spontaneous folk-music, and I want very much to write a piece about them—the collecting is very difficult here, however. There is also a living tradition, in the interior, of ballads—news events, old tales, etc.—not such good poetry as the sambas but rather wonderful all the same— (LAS).

69 "Current Dreams": One handwritten draft, entirely crossed out (VCSC 75.3a, pp. 31–32). On page 33 of the notebook, two stanzas are rewritten and then crossed out:

> the air turning
> to salt-water on the way,
> we descend some creaking stairs
> drawn by music of marimbas
> to the cellar-cabaret.
>
> When we get there, it is silent.
> Around us the impetalled fish
> swim seriously;
> this is not a cabaret at all.
> It is a wax-works, dimly lit
> where rows of lonely figures sit
> whose fresher tears naturally cannot fall.

In her journal entry of February 24, 1941, Bishop describes the dream that sparked this draft:

> Last night I had a horrible & beautiful dream—I was on the edge of a wild, dark coast, with breakers rolling in. The beach was all of dark rocks, like flint. There had just been a "bombardment," & wherever the piece of shell had fallen the flint was red-hot—large stains, under ten inches of clear black water—like stained glass. There were lots of little children trying to pick their way along the edge of the water, avoiding the stains in order not to burn their bare feet.
>
> The night before I dreamed that very early in a cold gray morning, M. said to me "What my life is coming to, I can't imagine" & then neither of us could think of anything further to say. (VCSC 77.3, pp. 45–46)

"M." is most likely Marjorie Stevens given that she is mentioned by name in the notebook just above the dream entry, on the page noting Bishop's birthday, February 8, 1941: "—I am thirty years old to-day—& nothing accomplished."

72 "The Museum": Two handwritten drafts (VCSC 75.3b, p. 105). The other draft seems more preliminary:

> Dear—please let's go back
> to [that] little provincial museum
> that stood so modestly on a side-street,
> neglected, small concave heaps
> of dust
> lay in the corners of the doorstep.
> Let's go through its galleries again,
> maybe reversing our order
> if we can remember what it was the first time,
> & take all the time we want
> even the whole day—
>
> The shades were mostly drawn
> a few worn but still solid slabs of sunlight
>
> or perishable round loaves of it,

Stray notes related to the draft appear on the page opposite:

> dust
> scattered birds
> something we missed, I think.
> you in your nice new suit
> went out into the full sun
> I want to go back again—
>
> meaning to go back
> but of course we never did
>
> saucers
> horrible little gods
> incomprehensible uses
>
> (Now that we're past the idea)
>
> & of course it will have moved.
>
> yr. Comments
>
> my sense of history (linked to) confined to an occasional
> shiver—
> If I concentrate on the horrors of the past
> does it seem real— (VCSC 75.3b, p. 106)

75 "The Traveller to Rome": One full handwritten draft and revisions of the first two stanzas incorporating the change of tense indicated in parentheses in

the earlier draft as well as the substitution of "grave" for "cold" in line twelve (VCSC 75.3b, pp. 133–37). Bishop evidently sent the poem to her friend Margaret Miller, who responded with her own version, "Reply for the Traveller to Rome," with a note scribbled beneath it: "Isn't the meter ravishing?"

Beneath the recopied stanzas, Bishop wrote: "(& so: with love at 1st sight) / faith / there is little to add to faith." The drafts can be found on pages 133–37 of the Key West notebook 75.3b, near fragmentary notes on page 131 for a poem "New Year's 1947," about children playing in a snowstorm in New York:

New Year's 1947

I only like the children banging dishpans
along [the] street   screams & sighs
far uptown the   & thousands sigh
far north the town sighs with
                    (the effort of NY /birth/)
fire engines race
the ships groan
the little brick street with children
banging pans calling each other's names
among the small hard mazy snow
flying every which way through the
    air

a /burning/ baby carriage
lit up the fire-escape
they wrote their names on the steps
& on the hoods of cars—
                                        string
the tangle of fire escapes   like
Christmas tinsel

In November 1937, following the trial that resulted from the accident in which Margaret Miller was maimed, Bishop and Louise Crane traveled from France to Italy. In her journal, Bishop described seeing the Alps for the first time ("for an hr. the peaks were in that brilliant pink stage-light that makes them look so un-concrete") and noted, as they crossed the border into Italy: "The car was flooded with men in several different kinds of uniforms—all very pleasant men. The passport collector, in navy blue & gold, was followed by 2 helpers in Robin Hood get-ups—the last of whom had nothing to do but *carry* the rubber stamps."

On the thirteenth, they arrived in Rome and settled in at the Hotel d'Angleterra: "The rooms are large, filled with pleasantly ancient furniture, and very cheap, so it is very nice, although a little on the English-old-maid side. We walked up the street from the Hotel and found the Piazza di Spagna [and] the flight of steps going up with the fountain below. Suddenly I recognized at the right the house where Keats died—without having seen the plaque. It was almost as bad as having found his body, and then I saw the wreath hanging on the side of the house" (VCSC 77.2, p. 27).

Of their trip to St. Peter's, Bishop writes that she had "expected the courtyard to be *flat*. . . . The statue of St. Peter was the nicest thing in it that I saw. I never had so clear an idea before of the vast commerce, the *tides of gold*, of the church, and I never disliked it so much—though the effect is usually supposed to be the other way, I think."

There are entries on the Colosseum and the many churches they visited, and this passage, often quoted with respect to their five-week Italian tour, which Bishop documents so extensively: "Every 3rd man is in uniform. Friends seem to find it a nuisance to give the salute and *then* shake hands. We see soldiers marching perpetually—this morning an old lady volunteered that one troupe was 'going to Spain.' . . . There are so many different uniforms, some very smart, but some like the 'Soldiers Chorus,' but worse. Today a Von Sternberg officer, monocled, corseted, with a cigar as thick as my little finger, and 10 inches long" (VCSC 77.2, pp. 26–29).

In a July 24, 1948, letter to Robert Lowell, Bishop writes, "I've always promised myself I'm going to spend my declining years just taking walks in Rome. Nothing could be more profitable, I think, for the last 20 years of one's life" (EB/RL).

77 "Dear Dr.—": Four copies with only slight variations (VCSC 75.3b, pp. 153–57). This is the fourth according to the page order in the notebook. In the spring of 1946, in the last painful stages of Bishop's relationship with Marjorie Stevens, the psychiatrist Ruth Foster was particularly helpful to her.

Above the draft of "Dear Dr.—", on page 153, Bishop writes, "from Halifax," where she stayed for two or three weeks in July of 1946, at a hotel that Brett Millier locates "across the bay from the hospital in Dartmouth where her mother had lived and died" (LM, p. 180).

In December 1947, Bishop wrote to Robert Lowell about his poem "Falling Asleep Over the Aeneid": "I am terribly impressed with the dream poem & I gather from it that when you dream you dream in colors all right—(a psychiatrist friend of mine is writing an article on color in dreams and I've heard quite a lot about it)" (EB/RL).

The version of this poem on page 153 of the notebook:

Dear Dr.,
yes dreams come in color
and memories come in color
though that of dreams is more remarkable,
particularized & brighter;
sometimes [when at its best] like that green light
suspended /here/ out there above the harbor
which must belong to a society

of similar lights somewhere, peaceful & clean,
but came to look at this one just for now unenviously.

Another draft opens, "[Dear Dr. Foster] come in."

And in another, Bishop describes the green light as "gregarious."

In a letter to Loren MacIver, written from Yaddo on July 19, 1949, Bishop writes, "If there is anything one gains from psychiatry at all it's the simple thing you kept saying yesterday and said for nothing, too—that one must be oneself" (OA, p. 190).

In an October 22, 1950, letter to Marianne Moore from Yaddo, Bishop speaks of Dr. Foster's death of the week or so before: "It was so sad—she was so nice—I wish you had met her, or maybe you did. . . . Dr. Foster was so good and kind, and certainly helped me more than anyone in the world" (OA, p. 206).

79 " 'I had a bad dream . . .' ": Several pages of notes and this one developed draft with the notation "Should rhyme" above the opening lines (75.3b, p. 167). The last lines of this draft share the phrase "loneliness like falling" with a fragment, "The Strike of Love," which follows it on the next page of the Key West notebook.

On a subsequent page (p. 169), the dream is an active protagonist:

The bad dream stepped in
toward morning, speaking
of you. You lay unconscious.
The dream said it was for
"twenty-four hours."
Wrapped in a khaki blanket
on a bed close to the floor

Other notes on the page: "The bad dream stepped in / toward morning, speaking, / in the dark, of you."

Another draft of this poem begins: "Towards the grave break of morning / a bad dream stepped in / speaking about you" (VCSC 75.3b, p. 171).

This is a terribly prescient poem when one considers the death of Bishop's companion of fifteen years, Lota de Macedo Soares, who died after lingering in a coma for five days after taking an overdose of pills while visiting Bishop in New York in September 1967.

In the notebooks from the twenties and thirties, Bishop explores the subject of love from a variety of angles. In May 1935, when she is twenty-four and living in New York, she writes: "People who love each other shouldn't promise faithfulness to each other, but each to himself: Each perpetually correcting and marking himself, not the other. In fact with love a certain indifference to recognized aspects of *character* in the other is best of all" (VCSC 72A.3, p. 25). And about Gertrude Stein (whose lectures she'd attended both at Vassar in 1934 and in Paris in 1935) this entry, entirely crossed out: "G. Stein's reason for 'concealment' of the 'automatic' nature of her writings = or, is another form of, her 'concealment' of the 'homosexual' nature of her life—False Scents we all give off" (VCSC 75.4a, pp. 2–3).

Her sense of one's helplessness in the face of "the strike of love" can be seen in the following fragment tucked in among the drafts of "Hannah A.":

Mulatto Cupid on the widow's walk
Shoots his last arrow over jungle town.
Downstairs there's card-playing & pleasant talk
"Mama" leans on the bar and hides a yawn.

It's not the   of night-spots—
Flavia combs out her hair,   Olivia acts
out a cockfight

Mama leans on the bar & yawns

Meanwhile, (how straight?) the poisoned arrow flies

                    and hits, straight in the heart,
The smallest taxi-driver at the bar,
The one who's always smoking a cigar

And in the Key West notebook: "Love is a wilderness of truths" (VCSC 75.4b, p. 133). And this, crossed out, too: "The correct system for conducting love-affairs is like the arranging of an aquarium—oh dear! They say they put in the most dangerous fish *first*—the fish that's put in 1st won't eat the fish that's put in second etc., but put a dangerous fish in afterwards & he'll eat them all" (VCSC 75.4b, p. 134); "& fought / love's battles in the moonlight" (VCSC 75.4b, p. 192); and "Love like money—the more carelessly concealed the less apt to be discovered" (VCSC 75.4b, p. 193). And entries which follow her notes for a poem "New Year's 1947," include: "Love that walked so long & got lost track of— / Love that walked so far & got lost track of—" (VCSC 75.3b, p. 141); and:

(whitewashed)

In the brightest sunshine I have ever seen
we made the night again with our mouths
at ten one morning
The darkness [flowed]
the fountain of night
misplaced dreams that overpowered
us ("mugging") from behind—

Imagine restoring the night intact
like that
It grew dark
& darker as we went upstairs
into the (brilliant) white room
with the palm trees swinging &
clashing like (taffeta) bright tin
outside, & the   nine blue-flowers
the darkness we were enabled to
a gift

come down like Thunbergia

displaced night (VCSC 75.3b, p. 143)

In this section of the notebook, other entries suggest that Bishop is feeling a tremendous sense of conflict and pressure: “the lowering world keeps threatening ‘now or never’ ” (VCSC 75.3b, p. 146); “My dearest, the only freedom that / we’ll ever know / No, not another’s age, my own” (VCSC 75.3b, p. 151).

80 “ ‘In the golden early morning . . .’ ”: This single draft was removed from one of the Key West notebooks and is undated (VCSC 75.1). “M.” would appear to refer to Marjorie Stevens, with whom Bishop was involved from early 1941 to 1946, the year *North & South* was published. In her biography of Bishop, Brett Millier describes their struggle, which seems reflected in this draft:

> Elizabeth spent the fall of 1945 in Key West with Marjorie at Margaret Street. She had a late-November deadline for new poems from Houghton Mifflin and set out to finish the elusive two or three. . . . She left Key West for New York in December, then returned in early January, only to leave again on the nineteenth. As she struggled to write, her relationship with Marjorie Stevens was ending. Marjorie’s letters to her in the spring of 1946 suggest that Elizabeth was drinking heavily, that her lifelong tendency to use the long-distance telephone when she was drunk had begun to irritate the recipients of her calls, and that she was wavering painfully in her decision to leave both Marjorie and Key West. Finally Marjorie, essentially out of kindness, forbade her to come back. “I don’t think you should consider it a possibility anymore, for as long as you do you obviously aren’t going to adjust yourself to anything else. . . . [We’ve been] trying to make something work that doesn’t.” When she came North, it was for more than a year, and when she returned in the winter of 1947, she lived for a time in Pauline Hemingway’s house at 907 Whitehead Street. (LM, pp. 179–80)

Pauline Hemingway may be the person addressed in this draft.

83 “ ‘In a cheap hotel . . .’ ”: Single copy (VCSC 75.3b, p. 199). In 1966, Bishop reworked an account (begun a decade or more before) of her short stint with a shady correspondence school in 1934, just after she had graduated from Vassar. An earlier draft was initially rejected by *The New Yorker* on October 19, 1956, but the revised piece, “The U.S.A. School of Writing”—as it appeared in *The Collected Prose*, edited by Robert Giroux—was published in the magazine on July 18, 1983, several years after Bishop died. In the piece, Bishop quotes from letters and stories by her correspondents at the “school.”

The draft of this poem summons up a passage not quoted in Bishop’s prose account but preserved in her notebook dating from November to December 1934:

> *A week at the U.S. School of Writing*
>
> *May Robley*—"Chained Love," story of Danny Hawn, chained to his bed-post for 25 yrs. by his mother to prevent him from going with a girl she disproved of. She wove him "slips" of linen, and all the sheets. In his spells of insanity he tore them up "as fine as rug filling." Drove another son to run away & then disinherited him. A wild section of country in Pennsylvania. (?). When the girl died, Danny was set free and spent the rest of his days sitting silently by the fireplace. A very sinister, Bronte-esque tale. (VCSC 72A.3, p. 20)

In college or shortly after college, in her notebook of 1934–36, Bishop sketched out a masque entitled, alternately, "The Proper Tear," "The Proper Tears," and "His Proper Tear," which also concerns a chained victim:

> ARGUMENT: The Doctor, or Magician, has captured & chained up the Hero, or Victim. Because he has no instruments which are capable of testing the genuineness of the Hero's emotion and sentiments, he is attempting to have produced by him a 'specimen' of the proper tear. In order to do this he must make him cry. He brings in one after the other the various citizens of modern life that prey on, play on, the sympathies: the Reporter, the Social Worker, the *Freak*, the Starving Artist, the Sole Survivor of a Horror, the War Veteran, etc., who tell their tales while the Hero is moved to tears. To off-set these is a group of four Tempters who represent at different times alcohol, flippancy, *refinement*, insanity, etc.—means of solving the distresses. The Hero cries easily enough, but the tears are not right. Finally he cries
>
> and the experiment succeeds all too well.
>
> Tempters: 1. flippancy, sophistication / 2. alcohol, dope / 3. refinement, neuroses, schizophrenia / 4. study and knowledge / 5 or 6 melancholy? and 7 *Sorrows*
>
> Look up: Anatomy of Tear Ducts, etc.
> Psychology of Weeping (VCSC 72A.2, pp. 31–32)

Other notes about the hero stipulate that he is "chained to the wall, arms & ankles, by massive chromium-plated chains. He wears ordinary clothes" (VCSC 72A.2, p. 4).

Also on page 4 is a stray note about "strangers in a waiting room," which is of interest, of course, because of Bishop's late poem "In the Waiting Room."

The poet Elizabeth Spires, who interviewed Bishop for *The Vassar Quarterly* in 1979—an interview that was later expanded and published in *The Paris Review*—conveyed to me her sense that the line "love chains me to the bed and he berates me" may reflect something of Bishop's abiding guilt over the suicide of Robert Seaver, the young man she dated in college. Brett Millier discusses this in her biography of Bishop:

> Later in her life in her most abject moments of guilt and self-recrimination, Elizabeth told the story of the death of Bob Seaver, the boyfriend of her college years, who committed suicide in Pittsfield, Massachusetts, on November 21, 1936. Seaver had wanted to marry Elizabeth, and she had told him that she felt she would never marry. On her return from Europe, she had been called on to make this point more emphatically. When Seaver shot himself, perhaps in frustration at his loneliness or his physical limitations [he was partially crippled], the only note he left was a postcard, which arrived in her mail a few days after his death. It said, "Go to hell, Elizabeth."
>
> Primed as she was to absorb this kind of guilt, Elizabeth felt until her own death that she had "ruined" Bob Seaver's life. Marrying him was impossible, but his death and his unanswerable condemnation of her were devastating blows. (LM, p. 112)

84 "To the Admirable Miss Moore": Single copy (VCSC 67.18). Bishop tentatively titled this draft "The World's Greatest Living Observer," the title she gave to an essay on the poet that was contributed, along with her poem "Invitation to Miss Marianne Moore," to a birthday tribute to Moore in the August 1948 issue of the *Quarterly Review of Literature.*

Bishop's long and profound respect for and attachment to Moore is well documented.

Her post-college notebook contains this appreciation:

> Miss Moore's "architectural" method of conversation, not seemingly so much for the sake of *what* she says as the way in which it is said; indifferent subject matter treated as a problem in accuracy, proportion, solidity, balance—If she speaks of a chair, you can practically sit in it when she has finished. It is still life, easel painting, as opposed to the common conversational fade-out." (VCSC 72A.3, p. 20)

In his commentary accompanying an interview with Bishop in Brazil in 1964, Léo Gilson Ribeiro writes that Bishop considered Robert Lowell and Marianne Moore "the most important U.S. poets of this century," and had said to him that "even T. S. Eliot would concur in this judgement." Gilson Ribeiro quotes Bishop (but I feel the label "poetess" must be his):

> It is difficult to define her contribution, so decisive it appears to me, but I am certain that she is our most original poetess, the one who has brought a brilliant precision to poetic language by means of a meticulous conservatism. . . . She has succeeded in introducing a great variety of poetic motives, maintaining the ancestral, "out-of-date" virtues of American culture—such as irony, a

subtle sense of humor, understatement—while keeping herself at the same time within the creative vanguard of poetry in the English language. (CEB, pp. 15–16)

In another interview from Rio in 1970, conducted by Regina Colônia, Bishop said, "There is a great flowering in contemporary poetry. Of the older generation, Robert Lowell and Marianne Moore stand out—the latter, in fact, I consider to have made the greatest and most original contributions to twentieth-century poetry" (ibid., p. 52).

In spite of her lifelong reverence for Moore and her work, a journal entry from New York, dated January 2, 1938, when Bishop was twenty-seven, reveals her delight in irreverently pondering her mentor: "I saw a very poor movie, but Mickey Rooney played in it & I find that he looks very much like Miss M.! His face is fuller and his hair blond instead of red, but it's the same type of Irish face. The eyelashes are light and give a powdery effect. The mouth is defiant—even Miss M's manner of talking & tone of voice is Mickey Rooney's Irish-toughey on a small scale. The area around the mouth is a little protuberant and lumpy. They both speak obliquely—and Miss M's laugh is perfect "Ha-ha—coarse and low" (VCSC 77.2, p. 51).

This entry from her Key West notebook also appears to describe Moore, who lived with her mother in Brooklyn at the time: "M.—I believe she often dreams of 'riches' / —the exaggerated affection for— / & the unnatural solicitude for —'s mother—" (VCSC 75.4b, p. 193).

From Bishop's notes on Moore's collection *What Are Years?*:

If I were reviewing it, I should call the review, "The Price of Originality."

In places she has not used the "light" rhyme carefully enough, so that in reading it casually one is apt to run the lines over and give them quite an ordinary iambic or trochaic meter with end-rhymes. The general effect of extreme *purity* & independence. (The independence of Miss /Wright?/—commanding natural respect without effort, & yet a little sad.)—but sometimes the dangerous purity that leaves one more vulnerable to disease, and the independence of the child that refuses to come to meals . . .

Coldness?—what is it—a slight rippling *chill*—a sense of draught.

Like bird songs—like the bird-songs here—the tonality and rhythm eludes us—slides away obliquely— (VCSC 75.4b, p. 215)

On June 30, 1948, Bishop wrote to Robert Lowell from Wiscasset, Maine, about her poem "Invitation to Miss Marianne Moore": "My best friend in N.Y. thought my poem about her was 'mean,' which I found rather upsetting because it wasn't meant to be & it is too late to do anything about it now, I'm afraid" (OA, pp. 159–60).

But apparently she needn't have feared. In her biography of Bishop, Brett Millier states, "For the rest of Moore's life, her letters would from time to time burst into appreciative reminiscence of the poem. In 1956, when it was reprinted in *A Cold Spring*, she wrote, 'Never could I deserve so lovely a thing. I shall always be trying to justify it' " (LM, p. 207).

By the time of this draft, Bishop was no longer sending her poems for Moore to critique—she hadn't done so since 1940—and she even allowed herself to indulge in a little *frisson* from time to time with respect to Moore. From a little notebook dated August 1948, the same summer that Bishop wrote the June 30, 1948, letter to Lowell—the summer when "Over 2,000 Illustrations and a Complete Concordance" was published in the *Partisan Review*: "Marianne these days: the slightest contact & she gives off a shower of moralistic sparks—or, more, like a talking-doll . . . The endless politenesses, thank-yous-for-thank-yous, etc., become like playing with a dog who likes to retrieve a little too well" (VCSC 72b.5, p. 24). Yet on the previous page, she writes, "M's wheelbarrow of guilt / The pigmentation of the air / save me against my will" (VCSC 72b.5, p. 23).

A couple of years later, when Bishop was feeling especially desperate and uncertain about her future, Moore recommended her for the inaugural Lucy Martin Donnelly Fellowship given by Moore's alma mater, Bryn Mawr College. The $2,500 Bishop received enabled her to board a freighter in November 1951 and embark on a trip that would transform her life. On the ship headed first for Brazil—where she unexpectedly fell in love and where she would stay, with brief interruptions, for the next fifteen years—she had Moore much in mind. She had pledged to review Moore's *Selected Poems* for the *New York Times*: "I don't know why I said I would," Bishop wrote to Lowell on August 19, 1951. "I'm hoping to be able to turn it into a sort of poem" (OA, p. 223).

Her journal entry from the "H.M. 'Bowplate' en route to Santos [Brazil]," dated between November 20 and "Thanksgiving Day, 22nd, 1951":

> I've been thinking about Marianne a lot—trying to finish that review before Santos. I don't think I've ever really given her enough credit for her *democracy*—being put off by the tediousness of her politenesses, etc. And yet that is one of her most admirable traits—that absolute refusal to differentiate between people at all—at least I've never seen her. If her manners are too ceremonious at least they are equally so for "Gladys", "Tom" (TSE), or the elevator man. I wish I could quote Pascal's remark exactly, about how all men are *not* created equal but it is spiritual death if we don't behave as if they were.
>
> I'd also like to get in something about the absolutely wild contrast between her form & her admiration of "spontaneity" . . . this *form* is seen in her manners & somehow hitches on to her *guilt*—but the spontaneity is seen in her wit, & in the laugh with which she greets others' witticisms.
>
> The Telephone-Stylist aspect, too—that final "good*bye*, Elizabeth"—gruff—I'm glad my name is what it is, because I get so

much more out of Marianne's style of speaking than a Mary or something like that. (VCSC 76.2)

In a letter to Anne Stevenson from Rio, dated February 16, 1964, Bishop comments on the work of her contemporaries: "[Karl] Shapiro, [Yvor] Winters, etc.—seem sad to me—the problem is how to be justly but *impersonally* bitter, isn't it—(Even Marianne Moore's disappointments show through too much sometimes, I think—but then she is very Irishly cagey and manages by avoiding a great deal . . . She's a wonder!)" (LAS).

87 "Homesickness": The only developed draft on several pages of material related to this poem (VCSC 54.3). Based on a reference, in letters to friends, to a story of the same title (see "Homesickness" in the appendix), this draft appears to date from 1948 to 1950. (Note that "the sloping bedroom ceiling" as well as a detail about wallpaper can be found in the draft of "A mother made of dress-goods . . . ") In this draft, "thumped" replaces "thwocked," as can be seen on the facsimile.

In her early years in Brazil, roughly 1951–1955, Bishop worked on a number of poems set in Nova Scotia—among them "For M.B.S., buried in Nova Scotia . . ."; " 'One afternoon my aunt and I . . .' "; "Syllables," " 'Where are the dolls who loved me so . . .' "; "A Short, Slow Life"; "Poem for a Child"; and "The Grandmothers." It's likely that she continued to work on this poem then, too. A later fragmentary draft that refers to the poet's birth and her mother's madness ("And this was how it all began?") can be found in a notebook of Bishop's from the 1970s that also contains the many pages of drafted material for the poem "Dicky and Sister":

Beside the bed, or on it—

or die,
        where later I was born, and I cried, too—?
        where later I was to be born & cry—
                                                    weep—

She cried but tried   to say her prayers
Frantic &   Juno licked her ears.
Concerned—frantic " " " " "
  And this was how it all began?
Or had it started earlier?
Beside a bed, or on one,   where we weep

or die where later   I was born   (VCSC 74.9)

Bishop's story of the same title, based on the same incident (see the draft, the most advanced of five in the archive, in the appendix) is referred to in a March 1964 letter to Anne Stevenson: "My mother went off to teach school at 16 (the way most of the enterprising young people did) and her first school was in lower Cape Breton somewhere—and the pupils spoke nothing much but Gaelic so she had a hard time of it at that school, or maybe one nearer home—she was so homesick she was taken the family dog to cheer her up. I have written both a story and a poem about this episode but neither satisfy me yet" (LAS).

At the top of what appears to be the first (although very partial) typed draft of the story, which includes handwritten dialogue penned below the three typed opening paragraphs, Bishop writes, "to work up to a point of tragically repressed hysteria—"

The closing lines of "Homesickness" are echoed in a fragment attached to draft pages of another story about children named Grace and Una: "It was too late, too late. She didn't know why that sad phrase seemed so conclusive. / The phrase sounded sad & conclusive, she didn't know why" (VCSP 68.5).

In another letter to Anne Stevenson, written on May 5, 1964, Bishop mentions the River Phillip of the poem: "My mother's father ran the tannery [in Great Village, Nova Scotia] for many years. His people were farmers from 'River Phillip' (wherever that is!—I just remember hearing that). One of his cousins, very rustic, used to appear once or twice a year when I was small, with gifts of bear meat and venison, in sacks in the back of the buggy" (LAS).

Bishop mentions starting this story and also working on her poem "The Prodigal Son" in a letter written to Lowell on July 11, 1948, the summer of so much correspondence between them, when she was in Maine and he was based in Washington, D.C., where he was serving as the Consultant in Poetry. A year and a half later, in October 1950, she wrote from Yaddo to her friend the artist Loren MacIver about illustrating the story: "I am writing so fast I expect to be rich before long. The story about Nova Scotia is coming along fine—the one with the dog in it—I think I told you? That's one, if I can sell it, and sell it to an illustrated magazine, I'd give anything to have you do some pictures for— . . . There are rocks with lichen on them & the wagon wheels go by them & the little boy trails the buggy whip—I should think you'd do that *beautifully*. A large hound dog is a very important character—can you draw a hound?" (OA, pp. 207–208).

In writing to Katharine White, her *New Yorker* editor, on November 23, 1952, Bishop addressed some reservations which White and her colleagues expressed about her story "In the Village," which they very much wanted to publish—it eventually appeared in the December 19, 1953, issue of the magazine—and in the same letter alluded to what must be "Homesickness": ". . . there is one more Nova Scotia one almost done, too, I think, laid around 1900." In a letter to White the following February, she mentioned it again, comparing it to "In the Village": "I have another one, the same people and locale, laid around 1900 (no me, of course!) and I think it is much more straightforward" (EB/NY).

In his book *Becoming a Poet: Elizabeth Bishop with Marianne Moore and Robert Lowell*, David Kalstone confidently asserts that Bishop was still working on the story fifteen years after she'd begun it, "never able to finish it." He elaborates on the effect of Bishop's trips to Nova Scotia and Cape Breton in the summers of 1947 and 1948: "We can judge the intensity of her feelings from the persistent recall of details that first turn up in letters of the 1940s and from their delayed slow absorption into her work. She saved these recollections for years, some of them not coming to the surface until her very last book, *Geography III* (1976): Great Village with its elms, the big farm collies, the Bay of Fundy with its salt marshes and long lavender-pink tides" (pp. 118–19).

At the bottom of the second of three typed and similarly developed versions of the story in the Vassar archive, Bishop drafted a moving letter to Lota de Macedo Soares, which she titled "Letter," dating the draft of the story, I feel, to the early years of their love affair. Only a handful of Bishop's letters to Soares survive because Lota's friends in Brazil, blaming Bishop for her suicide in 1967, burned those they found.

Bishop writes a few lines above and to the right of the letter, next to "San Paulo?" and just below the last typed lines of the story draft: "selfish, as all mothers are— / Mother of twenty-two— / (Craves Security)—house"

LETTER

> Now that you're away, I can write, I can falsify & exaggerate a little—not a lot—just enough to make it writing, L—; I think you understand the difference—Saying something & meeting your eye is one thing—writing something & reading it & re-reading it with vanity & satisfaction is another—but both are partly true—
>
> You got some mail while you were away—
> A love letter
> [Dear] Lota!—(if I may call you so—I confess to some difficulty with the letter "L") Come scratch me again!
>
> I am madly in love with you. My nature & training prohibits me from telling you (frank expression). I call to you every morning. Don't you hear me? It is from the heart. Why, oh *why*, do you never answer? & When I need you most?
>
> Forever yours, 5 AM
> oh god

To the left of the letter, she writes, "I feel like something caged!" (VCSC 54.3).

Bishop describes an acute attack of "homesickness" in her post-college notebook, written from the freighter *Königstein,* on which she traveled to Europe in July 1935 with her college friend Hallie Tompkins. In speaking of the trip years later, Tompkins said that the two of them hadn't realized until they boarded it that they'd booked passage on a Nazi ship: "I remember the scene as we pulled out of New York harbor, one mass of people on the dock raising up their arms in the light, and Bishop said, 'Oh, how horrible. It's like the dead' " (OB, p. 63).

From the ship, Bishop wrote in her journal:

> Twice now, both times at the table (which is natural-enough) I have been overtaken by an awful, awful feeling of deathly physical and mental *illness.*—something that seems "after" me. It is as if one were whirled off from all the world & the interests of the

world in a sort of cloud-dark, sulphurous grey, of melancholia. When this feeling comes I can't speak, swallow, scarcely breathe. I knew I had had it once before, years ago, & last night, on its 2nd occurrence I placed it as "*homesickness.*" I was homesick for 2 days once when I was nine years old; I wanted one of my aunts. Now I really have no right to homesickness at all. I suppose it is caused actually by the motion of the ship away from N.Y.—it may affect one's center of balance some way; the feeling seems to center in the middle of the chest. (VCSC 72A.3, p. 32)

91 "The Owl's Journey": The third of three drafts, dated 1949–50 by the archive (VCSC 64.10). Two lines handwritten at the bottom of this draft suggest that Bishop has somebody important to her in mind: "In the grand, the regal injustice of the heart / I suppose I can never forgive you for haunting my life—(days)." Bishop worked on this poem at Yaddo, giving it the title "Old Dream" on a notebook page dated November 3, 1950:

> Somewhere the owl rides on the rabbit's back
> Down the long slope, through the long dried grasses
> Through a half-moonlight, igniting everything
> To the coolest, ? specks of fire
>
> They made no sound, no shriek, no *Whoo!*
> Off on their long—forgotten—journey
>
> Where Adventure is so small, so ancient—
>
> Collaboration thought of by a child—
> But they obliged, & off they went together.
> The owl's claws locked in the rabbit's fur
> not hurting him, the owl—
> looking sidewise as if his mind were on something else—
> The rabbit's ears laid back, his eyes very bright—
>
> But the dream never got any further. (VCSC 77.4, p. 37)

Above the draft, she quotes remarks by Beaufort Delaney, whom she mentions along with May Swenson (who became a good friend) in a letter to Robert Lowell written a few days later on November 7, 1950, from Yaddo: "I have a suite in East House—very nice and plain and sunny. At first I shared the house with a rather elderly Negro painter whom I liked very much, but he's left now" (EB/RL).

The journal entry from Yaddo: "Beaufort: 'It's time to take up Pain when that's all you / can keep company with.' / 'If I have the mumps don't treat me for the measles.' / 'Have a sip of sherry?'—then when I'd accepted, he'd / toast me benignly & say 'You & me, Elizabeth, are / alike. We like *Fun*, & we like Alcohol' " (VCSC 77.4, p. 37). Bishop enclosed "The Owl's Journey" in a letter to Loren MacIver dated December 1950, remarking, "This scarcely counts, as poetry, but I thought you might like it.

Sonnets next time" (OA, pp. 214–15). During this stay at Yaddo, Bishop was often miserable and drinking heavily, but she completed her poem "The Prodigal," and Ilse Barker, a fiction writer she met there (who would, along with her husband, Kit, become a lifelong friend), described her satisfaction with it: "It was the first poem she had written for a long time. One of the lovely things about Elizabeth was that she was unself-consciously pleased with her poetry when it worked well. She showed us the poem with obvious pleasure" (OB, pp. 123–24).

On November 6, 1950, Bishop sent a version of "The Owl's Journey" to Katharine White at *The New Yorker*: "Here is an old old dream that doesn't seem to want to grow any longer." In a follow-up letter dated November 10, 1950, that begins, "I can't seem to stop writing you!" she made two changes reflected in this draft. And on November 14, White replied, "I might ask you, about that poem, whether a vague stirring of memory that three of us here seem to have has any basis in fact. Is there a picture, say, from Audubon, or from a nursery picture book, or from an old chromo, or even from Blake, that was the basis of your dream? If there was, it might be interesting and clarifying to put it in the subtitle. However, it may be purely a dream but I wish you'd write me about it. Perhaps this is something on the fringe of everybody's subconscious and not in an actual picture at all."

Bishop replied on November 16, 1950, with a tale involving her friend Margaret Miller, which describes the art in facsimile here: "The story about the owl is really rather strange and I guess I'll go ahead & bore you with it—I've never been able to see any way of getting it into the poem, though. A long, long time ago, when I was a child, I had that dream or maybe just imagined it—I had certainly never seen any such picture, never saw Blake or Audubon—to my conscious recollection, although as you say it might have been in a nursery book. At college I had a friend (now with the Museum of Modern Art) who drew & painted very well; and I told her about the owl & the rabbit and asked her if she'd make a picture of it. She tried and tried and did a lot of pen & ink drawings but somehow neither of us were ever satisfied with them. After graduation she had a scholarship in art at New York University, and one of her courses was illuminated manuscripts, with Meyer Shapiro. Well, I've forgotten exactly where & how she found it—I think in the British Museum, but I'm not sure, but she'd know—she came across, in the margin of a very early English manuscript—I think 12th century, but again I'm not sure—the exact picture I had had in mind all those years, and she was able to get me a tracing of it. Exactly the way I'd imagined it—the rabbit running diagonally to the left, the owl seated facing a little the other way, etc. It was just in simple outline drawing, although the MMS had painted illuminations in it. I was so pleased and mystified I decided to use it as a kind of seal, and I even had one of those gadgets made, at great expense, that make an impression in the paper. It's in storage now, or I'd give you a sample. As I write this it all sounds as if I were making it up—but I guess it really isn't the kind of thing one makes up.

"I can't seem to do any more with it than that brief poem. I suppose there might be a subtitle to the effect that it was an 'Early dream, later found in the margin of a—cent. English, or Saxon or whatever it was—I could find out—MMS.' But maybe that's stupid" (EB/NY).

Friends of Bishop's who were also friendly with Margaret Miller tell another story linking the two to the drawing.

From a 1984 interview with the architect Harold Leeds and the documentary filmmaker Wheaton Galentine:

> Harold Leeds: "Margaret was very special in many ways. She and Elizabeth had a very similar curiosity about things and words. . . . Margaret would talk about such things as the marble in the toilet stall [at college] and how she and Elizabeth would disagree about what the figuration in the marble [resembled]."
>
> Wheaton Galentine: "Elizabeth [did] a little drawing and made stationery embossed with a rabbit that had an owl riding on its back. The rabbit was galloping, and the owl was just sitting there enjoying it. This was a fossil they had fantasized on the toilet wall." (OB, p. 41)

In the same December 1950 letter to MacIver, Bishop describes two "weird dreams" she had had at Yaddo the night before. In one of them, "I dreamed up a poem—this was just about sunrise. I can't remember it very well, but it was about a couple, a man & wife, and the man was 'owless'—owl-less—that was the end of line b. It was a simple a b a b affair. I was frantic trying to find a rhyme for owl-less, and so finally I had the wife be cow-less. . . . What is all this about owls? It's beginning to get me. Of course they hoot a great deal in the night here, which may have had something to do with my dream—there seems to be a particularly frustrated one quite near me" (OA, pp. 214–15).

In her biography of Bishop, Brett Millier speculates on the poet's consideration of marriage to Tom Wanning, her close friend from New York who stayed with her in Stonington, Maine, in the summer of 1948. In her journal from this period, Bishop describes him: "T—sleepy baby-owl face—blond hair, but the heavy dark beard showing on the heavy jaw adds to the sleepy effect—grows in lighter bristles around the mouth" (VCSC 72B.5, p. 13).

92 "On the *Prince of Fundy*": Four pages of notes (VCSC 65.4). The draft represented is the clearest and most developed and contains her instruction to herself to arrange the poem in four-line stanzas. Notes on other pages suggest that Bishop envisioned something larger—for example:

> The Portuguese explorers came
> and found it looking much the same
>
> Something diffident, withdrawn . . .
> History has come and gone
>
> to [see] the famous autumn foliage
> the apple crop that breaks the trees

Lifting a veil of fog mist
so like a frontispiece engraving
History—or lifts
shifts drifts

We edge in gingerly bump
like a misplaced un-kiss

A version of the lines about "someone . . . tramping overhead" is followed by:

No sooner had our trip begun
than craps, roulette, and twenty-one

The Gift Shop has the usual

150 proof Lamb's Rum,
and that fake Nova Scotia plaid
in blue and yellow—

This draft dates from Bishop's August 1951 journey to Sable Island, about 180 miles off the coast of Nova Scotia, where she did some research for an article she hoped would interest *The New Yorker.* On July 11, 1951, she wrote to Robert Lowell about the upcoming trip: "I'm trying to get out to Sable Island, cheerfully known as 'the graveyard of the Atlantic' (my great-grandfather & his schooner and all hands were lost there, amongst hundreds of others) and if I am not fulfilling my destiny and get wrecked, too, I think I can turn it into an article and maybe a poem or two" (EB/RL).

On August 19, she wrote to Lowell describing her jaunt: "It was quite an interesting outing; I had to get permission from Ottawa to get taken out on a lighthouse tender, etc. The actual place is nothing much except sand-dunes like Cape Cod, but its history is spectacular, just the kind of thing I feel you might like. . . . Anyway I'm hoping to sell a travel piece about it and make some money. If I do I may take a trip of some sort, probably a long freighter one" (EB/RL).

Bishop's notebook for the trip begins with a description of clouds seen from above, during the airplane rides from New York to Boston and from Boston to Halifax. Upon her arrival in Nova Scotia, she is jolted by the sight of the insane asylum where her mother lived from 1916 until her death in 1934:

> We sailed among many more of the great soft white snow-heaps 11,000 ft-high—enough to follow the map of the coast easily, the Bay of Fundy, etc. N.S. looked lovely from the air—fresh dark greens, red outline, glittering lines of rivers—more animated than Maine had looked, & that amazing *cleanness* that strikes me every time. We landed in Dartmouth—a clearing in the fir woods—the taxi comes across on the little ferry—1st driving right by the Insane Asylum (I was quite unprepared for this.) A beauti-

> ful, dazzling day, & the unparalleled *dullness* of everything—I feel it in everything here, shop-windows, food,—the smallest trifles. Depression here must be worse than anywhere—only fortunately I'm not depressed. (VCSC 43.6)

At Yaddo nine months earlier, Bishop recorded a "ghastly nightmare about my mother—outside the closed door, 'they', beating, etc.—1st time in about 15 yrs., I think, & wonder why—" (November 14, 1950, VCSC 77.4, p. 40).

The plaintive interrogative in this draft of "On the *Prince of Fundy*,"—"Why are they walking around like that / and singing, too, at all hours of the night?"—echoes lines about nurses in a clinic in the draft called "Ungracious Poem" (see appendix for the poem) and anticipates the phrasing (so different in tone) in lines from "Filling Station," published in *The New Yorker* on December 10, 1955: "Why the extraneous plant? / Why the taboret? / Why, oh why, the doily?"

In a letter to her aunt Grace dated September 16, 1957, from New York, Bishop alludes to "the famous autumn foliage" that crops up in the notes for this poem: "I spent the morning at the dentist's and read the September *National Geographic*—a very silly piece about the Bay of Fundy, but I think I'll buy it just for the photographs. Some of them made me feel homesick, and I do wish I could get there now to see the colors of the maple trees" (OA, pp. 340–41).

IV. 1951–1967: Brazil, Seattle, New York

95 "Crossing the Equator": Four pages of drafts, with one titled "P.P.H." (VCSC 65.13 and 76.2). The dedicatee of this poem is Pauline Hemingway, Ernest Hemingway's second wife and a dear friend of Bishop's in Key West. Above an earlier draft with the same title, written in Bishop's notebook en route to Brazil in November 1951, a month after Pauline Hemingway's death, she wrote: "The nights when you were drunk, & funny, / The nights when everything went just too far— / The candles in the hurricane lamps / awfully / the rum scoundrels."

On July 13, 1953, in a letter from Brazil to Kit and Ilse Barker—who had met Bishop at Yaddo during her miserable stay there from October 1950 to March 1951—Bishop makes mention of a story she'd been typing that morning called "True Confessions" (see appendix for the full text) and says she found herself "putting in Yaddo—I never thought I could" (OA, pp. 266–67).

The story opens with a description of "a strange sort of institution we have here [for people] who are in the same fix," and it concludes with an account of the "Rum Latitudes," where the narrator finds herself surrounded by people drinking "this beverage in the form of something they called 'Scoundrels' the variation on this was 'Rascals' (look up) all the time—'Down there' sounds dark. This Down There was almost too bright. The juke box songs were fearful beyond belief. 'You made me love you I didn't want to do it I didn't want to do it.' "

Other versions of lines addressed to Pauline Hemingway on the notebook draft mentioned above: "directly / & characteristically you set off, [dear,] to the stars— / Tonight wit, wounding no longer, glitters with them."

As she ended her trip to Sable Island, Bishop jotted lines for this poem in her journal of August 1951:

> As we left S I Mr. Bolcan came up to me—I was hanging over the stern—& asked me what I thought of it now. I said it looked like a mistake & he thought that was very funny & said "You've got the right word for it!" It was gone by 12 miles on the "Cherub" log, twirling away in our wake.
>
> For quite a while before it went several of the higher, isolated dunes on the Eastern end looked exactly like distant pyramids. Just before that—I could make out the whole island—the lights on either end—a very slight obstacle to the horizon. A *catch*—a hesitation in the coastline—(then the horizon was again unbroken, the way it seems to want to be.)
>
> We imagine
the horizon
& so it hardens
>
> imagination   infinitely
definition   infinite
>
> The horizon illustrates imagination
hardened into definition
BUT—in & out
>
> & then the horizon was again
unbroken, the way it seems to want to be.
>
> Other things we can imagine
aren't obliging

She drafted lines for a poem titled "On Shipboard" and "On Board Ship" in that Sable Island notebook, and lines about geography in the notebook draft "P.P.H." appear first there:

> I like geography best
because it's easiest.
Economics & history
arithmetic—
>
> People I like too much—
>
> Geography simply states
how everything separates,

or separated once
& forever

No attempt could ever
fit these lands together
no theories could ever find
(cut the game to fit the cloth)

so geography suits (VCSC 43.6)

This draft of "Crossing the Equator" incorporates lines from "P.P.H.," located opposite it in the notebook Bishop used on the freighter bound for Brazil in November 1951, following her summer Sable Island jaunt.

Millier comments: "The poem is a conversation, presumably with the late Pauline Pfeiffer Hemingway, who had died suddenly in California on October 1, about death, hard choices, and the reasons for the trip. . . . The draft approaches the 'questions of travel' Elizabeth began to articulate over the next seven or eight years" (LM, pp. 236–37).

Did Bishop have Pauline Hemingway in mind when she began the poem on Sable Island the previous August? In any case, she incorporated her address to Pauline in subsequent drafts, and Millier states that she "talked about the poem for a long time after, as if she had meant to finish it."

The draft of "P.P.H.," from the voyage to South America (and following Pauline's death), begins

flying fish

like falling stars
or like a dream of skipping phantom sapphires

& so

you set off, [sweetie] (as you said), to the stars
[The] wit that wounds no longer, glitters with them.
(& so you set off to the stars—)
like a dream of skipping stones,
or skipping sapphires, rather.

Lines about the horizon are followed by these:

Do not blame me if
I choose geography,
perhaps just because it's easy—

Something I out of the atlas

manila folders, maps, & guidebooks—
disconnected notes & lists of letters
(light, etc.) unfinished poems, (VCSC 76.2, p. 4)

In her journal, she elaborates on the flying fish: "The flying fish remind me sometimes of falling stars—falling stars, flying stars—or a procession of meteors?—I think I just read a description of such somewhere, but where was it—a sort of flock of meteors progressing together, silently, then vanishing. Something unearthly about them—flying saucer-ish—phantom skipped stones—skipped stones in dreams" (VCSC 76.2).

And a note about crossing the equator, dated November 21: "We crossed the Equator sometime in the night. I sat out on deck between 3 & 4—quite rough, 1/2 a moon—masses of soft, oily-looking stars & a damp wind" (VCSC 76.2).

Bishop mentions Pauline Hemingway in a letter to Anne Stevenson dated January 8, 1964, from Brazil:

> I think snobbery governs a great deal of my taste. I have been very lucky in having had, most of my life, some witty friends,—and I mean real wit, quickness, wild fancies, remarks that make one cry with laughing. (I seem to notice a tendency in literary people at present to think that any unkind or heavily ironical criticism is "wit," and any old "ambiguity" is now considered "wit," too, but that's not what I mean.) The aunt I liked best was a very funny woman: most of my close friends have been funny people; Lota de Macedo Soares is funny. Pauline Hemingway (the 2nd Mrs H) a good friend until her death in 1951 was the wittiest person, man or woman, I've ever known. Marianne was very funny—Cummings, too, of course. Perhaps I need such people to cheer me up. They are usually stoical, unsentimental, and physically courageous. (LAS)

In the same letter to Stevenson, Bishop expresses an inborn affinity with Ernest Hemingway:

> Now I'll be confidential. The Pauline Hemingway mentioned above sent my first book to Ernest in Cuba. He wrote her he liked it, and, referring to "The Fish," I think, "I wish I knew as much about it as she does." Allowing for exaggeration to please his ex-wife—that remark has really meant more to me than any praise in the quarterlies. I knew that underneath Mr. H and I were really a lot alike. I like only his short stories and first two novels—something went tragically wrong with him after that—but he had the right idea about lots of things. (NOT about shooting animals. I used to like deep-sea fishing, too, and still go out once in a while, but without much pleasure, & in my younger tougher days I liked bull-fights, but I don't think I could sit through one now.)

At the bottom of her report of a newsreel about the funeral procession for Brazil's president Getúlio Vargas in 1954—see, in the appendix, "Suicide of a (Moderate) Dictator"—Bishop writes, "My freighter trip might make a sort of short story too. The missionaries, Miss Breen, the awful Uruguayan Consul with all his belongings—the dour engineer, the lovely wireless operator, the three girls working for their dowries—yes—

"—So many people have taken freighter trips by now, I gather, that there may be nothing in this account either to interest or charm—BUT etc—" (VCSC 54.22).

96 "*Young* Man in the Park": Two pages of drafts (VCSC 67.24). The draft is undated, but because of the similarity in phrasing between this and "Arrival at Santos," begun in mid-December 1951, it seems safe to date it from the same period. From "Arrival at Santos":

Oh tourist,
is this how this country is going to answer you

and your immodest demands for a different world,
and a better life, and complete comprehension
of both at last, and immediately,
after eighteen days of suspension?

Near the early drafts of "Arrival at Santos," Bishop writes in her journal, "I thought *I* was travelling in the dark, but no one aboard seems to have the foggiest idea about *anything* ahead of them."

The other page of lines for this poem includes

He thrust his legs through the back
of the park bench. He turned his back
on the spectacular bay, and the [rumpled] back
of his coat to [those passing] in back [strangers]
of him.

The park was postcard-green
after the rain; the flower-beds
all "free-form" & up-to-date:
big commas and kidneys of red—

The statues all bravely looked
the other way—waved their swords or hats or whatever they happened
to have in their hands

(VCSC 68.3)

98 "For M.B.S., buried in Nova Scotia": Three pages of drafts, one handwritten and two typed. The one represented is the last on the second sheet of typed versions (VCSC 68.4). Alternately titled "Aunt M," and "My Dear Aunt," and included on a list of titles with the heading "Poems 1955/1956" in the archive.

M.B.S. is Bishop's aunt Maud Bulmer Shepherdson, in whose home Bishop lived from age seven to sixteen before attending boarding school. Aunt Maud's, and Bishop's mother's, hometown was Great Village, Nova Scotia, described by Bishop to Anne Stevenson (March 1964) as "very small and well-preserved—the last time I saw it, at least—1951, like a small New England village, all white houses, elm trees, one large white church in the middle (designed I believe by great uncle George). It is in the rich farming country around the head of the bay of Fundy: dark red soil, blue fir trees—birches, a pretty river running into the Bay through 'salt marshes'—a few remains of the old Acadian dikes—it is Evangeline country—" (LAS).

In a conversation with Beatriz Schiller for a piece in *Jornal do Brasil* (Rio de Janeiro) on May 8, 1977, Bishop describes her childhood and early youth in unusually stark terms: "My father died when I was eight months old. When I was four years old my mother went mad. I was left alone. My mother's sister, a married aunt with no children, took care of me. Afterwards I was sent to a private school, and later I went off to the university" (CEB, p. 75).

Bishop was in North Carolina in August 1940 when she learned of her aunt's death and made this note in her journal: "Nora Hasecher & I came to Brevard, North Carolina [from Key West]. The next day I got a telegram saying that Aunt Maud had died that afternoon—the 7th" (VCSC 77.3, p. 26).

Victoria Harrison, the author of *Elizabeth Bishop's Poetics of Intimacy*, has made a study of the various typewriters Bishop acquired over the years and dates these drafts and the drafts of the following three poems from the mid-fifties (PI, p. 123).

When Bishop was visiting Nova Scotia in the summer of 1946, she made the following notes in her journal:

> N.S.—where
>
> a million Christmas trees stand
> waiting for Christmas.
>
> I know how they feel—
>
> split short heavy logs with the moonlight
> shining on the split sides— (VCSC 75.3b, p. 109)

During her early years in Brazil, Bishop wrote some of her best work about her Nova Scotia childhood, publishing all of the following in *The New Yorker*: the stories "Gwendolyn" (June 27, 1953) and "In the Village" (December 19, 1953) and the poems "Manners: (Poem for a Child of 1918)" (November 26, 1955) and "Sestina" (September 15, 1956).

She wrote to Katharine White on October 10, 1952, "I am a little embarrassed about having to go to Brazil to experience total recall about Nova Scotia; geography must be more mysterious than we think" (EB/NY).

In "*Mrs. Sullivan Downstairs,*" an unfinished and undated memoir that scholars agree was begun in Brazil in the early 1950s (see appendix for the full text), Bishop describes her aunt Maud in those early years when Maud took care of her: "My aunt was small, worried, nervous, shy . . ." A handwritten draft from Bishop's notebook:

Yes, you are dead now & live,
as I think, only there,
where our clear little river runs into the muddy tide,
by our little countrified graveyard.
But [see how] the Christmas trees have forgathered
with presents they always intended to give,
and your childhood river is curled at your side,
still wetting the child's cold feet that [ ]
and wandered so long in despair;
and so many things you have now— (VCSC 68.4)

Other notes from pages on which Bishop continued to rework this unfinished poem:

helpless memory (weak strong)

remember
each chipped damned dish

you imposed on me

when you talked so much
to my young deaf dreaming deliberately ears

and opposite:

& we lived, with the crowded furniture
whose each last leg
walks or limps through my thoughts always—

National Geographics piled on the sewing machine
Browning / / like a pillow
Shakespeare falling apart

I walked once to see your grave
rainy day

salt marshes
tapped each blueberry
the rain had fingered the blueberries (VCSC 68.4)

From Brett Millier's biography: "Elizabeth said that she began writing poetry and prose at the age of eight, under the influence of Aunt Maud's bookshelves, stocked with Tennyson, Browning, Emerson, Carlyle, and other Victorians. She memorized so many of these poems in her days at home in bed with asthma or bronchitis that in 1978 she conceded that they must be 'an unconscious part' of her" (LM, p. 30).

This same graveyard is described in Bishop's story "Gwendolyn," written in 1953:

The graveyard belonging to the village was surely one of the prettiest in the world. It was on the bank of the river, two miles below us, but where the bank was high. It lay small and green and white, with its firs and cedars and gravestones balancing against the dreaming lavender-red Bay of Fundy. The headstones were mostly rather thin, coarse white marble slabs, frequently leaning slightly, but there was a scattering of small urns and obelisks and broken columns. A few plots were lightly chained in, like the Presbyterian church, or fenced in with wood or iron, like little gardens, and wild rosebushes grew in the grass. Blueberries grew there, too, but I didn't eat them, because I felt I "never knew," as people said, but once when I went there, my grandmother had given me a teacup without a handle and requested me to bring her back some teaberries, which "grew good" on the graves, and I had. (CP, p. 223)

See chapter four ("Gathering in a Childhood") of Victoria Harrison's *Elizabeth Bishop's Poetics of Intimacy* for a thorough discussion of the drafts of this period.

It's worth noting that Joaquim Cardozo's "Cemitério da Infância" ("Cemetery of Childhood") is among the thirteen poems Bishop translated and included in *An Anthology of Twentieth-Century Brazilian Poetry*.

Bishop's first cousin on her mother's side, Phyllis Sutherland, the daughter of her aunt Grace, recalled a visit from Bishop in 1979, which was to be the poet's last to Nova Scotia, and an outing they took to an old cemetery:

Elizabeth used to come in the spring and fall. She loved the fall, the colors. I remember taking her to Scrabble Hill, and we drove the old roads where she used to go. . . . One day, after Mom took sick and when Elizabeth had started at Harvard, she visited. I said, "Let's go for a drive, Elizabeth. Where would you like to go?" "Oh, someplace way back where it is quiet." There's an old cemetery way back up in the woods, so I said, "Let's get a six-pack, Elizabeth, and I'll show you where to go." I took her back to this old, old cemetery. It's just a well-kept and beautiful spot. We sat there and talked all afternoon. She said, "It's so quiet here. All I can hear is the river and the cars in the distance. This is where I'd like to be buried." (OB, p. 346)

In a letter to her friend Dorothee Bowie (June 14, 1970), lamenting the turn in her relationship with a young woman pseudonymously referred to as "Suzanne Bowen" in Millier's biography, Bishop confided her fears for Bowen's child. "Well, thank God for my little Aunt Maud, and I hope she went straight to Heaven—she deserved to, the way she devoted herself to me" (VCSC 27.5).

99 " 'One afternoon my aunt and I . . .' ": Single copy (VCSC 68.3). A draft from the same period—the early fifties—possibly intended for the same elegy for Aunt Maud as above, judging from these lines scribbled below one

of the drafts of that poem (as well as similar lines quoted in the previous note): "The rain had put / a finger on each blueberry." The last two stanzas here were typed at right angles to the left and right (respectively) of the others. Victoria Harrison has identified the type as belonging to Bishop's Royal, acquired at Yaddo in 1950, and used mostly at Samambaia.

101 "Syllables": Four pages of drafts and this single typed copy (VCSC 65.16) (P1, p. 225). Alternately titled "First Syllables" and "Autobiography."

102 " 'Where are the dolls who loved me so . . .' ": Single copy (VCSC 68.2). A forthcoming volume of correspondence between Bishop and her editors at *The New Yorker* includes a letter dated February 1941 from Charles A. Pearce returning "Poem on Dolls" as one that was felt by the editors to be "far too special—or perhaps I should say personal" for the magazine to print (EB/NY).

There are overlaps here (note the bread crumbs, in particular) with a draft of the story "True Confessions," mentioned in a letter from Brazil in 1953 to friends Bishop met at Yaddo three years before, Kit and Ilse Barker. (See the note for "Crossing the Equator" and the appendix for the story itself.)

The "elderly little girl" in the story is based on Pauline (Polly) Hanson, secretary to Elizabeth Ames, the woman who ran Yaddo when Bishop stayed there in 1950. Hanson was a young poet whose first book, *The Forever Young* (1948), Bishop recommended enthusiastically to both Moore ("There are some things in it beautiful enough to break your heart. It's a long sort of *In Memoriam* thing, in the meter of all things of *The Rubaiyat*," OA, p. 206) and Loren MacIver ("I am honestly impressed for the first time in years . . . you get so sick of all this bloody stuff written for effect," OA, p. 208).

In the letter to Kit and Ilse Barker written on July 13, 1953, she describes a passage in her story "True Confessions":

> I found myself saying this about Polly (maybe it's mean, although it isn't meant to be): "As a child, just about at the point where she was able to read Dickens—say, *Little Dorrit*—she and her doll had decided it would be better all around for them to change places. I don't know where the doll had gone—off being an unfaithful wife somewhere, probably—but the doll's looks were very becoming in an unnatural way, so that one looked twice at that tiny chin and those dimples, and the little laugh, opening to have crumbs poked in by birds, perhaps." (OA, pp. 266–67)

In a lecture entitled "Bishop as a Poet of Childhood Recollected," published with other presentations given at the 1997 Elizabeth Bishop Conference at Worcester Polytechnic Institute in *In Worcester, Massachusetts: Essays on Elizabeth Bishop*, Barbara Page contributes the following insights regarding this draft:

> Oddly, and sadly, the opening question is not, Where are the dolls I loved so, but rather, Where are the dolls who loved me so. The

> dolls are remembered as having been the child's imagined caretakers, "early nurses," named Gertrude (her mother's name), Zilpha, and Nokomis (Hiawatha's grandmother and nurse), stand-ins for the absent parents, of a child forced to invent the love and care she cannot expect in life. There is intense, if suppressed, anger in the stated and implied contrast between the dolls and the child: they are asexual and able to play with time; they are good little girls, stoical, smiling, rigidly self-controlled, willingly locked away, untroubled by "unforeseen emotions." They enact a conventional femininity that Bishop felt she "never mastered."

This clutch of drafts—" 'Where are the dolls who loved me so . . .' "; "For M.B.S., buried in Nova Scotia"; "The Grandmothers"; and "Syllables" all seem to date from the early fifties in Brazil.

103 "A Short, Slow Life": (VCSC 58.2). Bishop copied innumerable drafts of this poem in her notebooks over many years in only slightly different versions. (The subject pronoun veered between first person singular and plural and "Till Time" vied with "But Time" again and again.) The poem represented here is in a sheaf that can be dated from the mid- to late fifties because it includes the two initial stanzas (one and four) of "Song for the Rainy Season," which, according to Brett Millier, Bishop said "just happened" to her in 1954.

The poem obviously commemorates Bishop's early childhood in Nova Scotia. According to Millier, "Elizabeth spent a few months at intervals in Great Village before 1916 [when she was five], sometimes with her mother and sometimes without; she was there continuously from spring 1916 until September 1917 and then spent two months of each summer there from 1918 until 1923" (LM, p. 19).

104 "Suicide of a Moderate Dictator": The fifth of five drafts (VCSC 67.14). Bishop wrote both a poem and a prose "report" with this title. (See the appendix for the prose text.)

Thomas Travisano, author of *Elizabeth Bishop: Her Artistic Development*, published this draft in the winter 1992 issue of *The Georgia Review* with commentary that concisely describes its context:

> "Suicide of a Moderate Dictator" represents a category for which examples exist only in Bishop's unpublished *oeuvre*: the political poem. Five drafts survive—the first four in Bishop's minute, steeply slanted, nearly illegible hand, and the last as a typescript with a few handwritten corrections. The poem's "moderate dictator" was Getúlio Vargas, the dominant figure in midcentury Brazilian politics, who ruled as a populist dictator from 1930 to 1945. His support for land reform and social welfare accounts, in part, for Bishop's epithet "moderate," but resistance to his regime grew as he came to depend increasingly on a corrupt political machine and on the military to maintain political control. Although Vargas was deposed in 1945, his machine remained in place. Returned to office as president in 1950 by a democratic election, he faced a rising chorus of criticism over the corruption of his supporters and the frequent brutality of their methods. Eventually, according to Bishop's

> prose account in *Brazil* (Life World Library), "High-ranking members of the armed forces . . . demanded the president's resignation in a dramatic scene in the early morning of August 24, 1954. Vargas, still in pajamas, apparently agreed to resign; he retired to his bedroom—and shot himself through the heart."

In *Brazil*, for which Bishop wrote the text and provided many photographs (although the editing of the volume angered her), the role of her good friend Carlos Lacerda is described:

> The group that returned to power with Vargas was eager for power, fame and money. Getúlio was surrounded by corruption so deep that when he became aware of its extent, he himself referred to it as "the sea of mud." (Vargas was believed to be honest but out of touch, isolated by his own entourage.) Outspoken critics fought bitterly against Vargas and "Getúlismo." Carlos Lacerda, publisher of the newspaper *Tribuna da Imprensa*, was his best-known opponent, exposing graft and chicanery in government circles and even among the members of Vargas' own family. Members of Vargas' bodyguard attempted to assassinate Lacerda. A young air force major, Rubens Florentino Vaz, acting as a bodyguard for Lacerda, was killed; Lacerda managed to escape with only a bullet in the foot. (*Brazil*, Life World Library series, New York: Time Inc., 1962, p. 131)

An early draft of this poem, entitled "August 24th, Rio de Janeiro" (and likewise dedicated to Carlos Lacerda), moves on from the line "At eight two little boys were flying kites" to include "Portuguese Man-of-War climbing the skies" and dogs "no less dogs because the President / lies in his coffin."

Other lines in earlier drafts suggest pathways this poem might have taken: "I used to think of truth / as something like a public monument / that had a great big allegorical meaning / for all to see, & cast no shadows all day long— / Perhaps truth is a shadow, Carlos." Bishop evidently intended to attach notes to the poem. Below the earlier draft, with the line about truth as a shadow, she writes:

- The day after Pres. Getúlio Vargas's suicide.
- Carlos Lacerda is the young editor of *Tribuna da Imprensa*, whose attacks on the Vargas regime were chiefly responsible for its overthrow (& the attempts of the regime upon his life,)— (VCSC 67.14)

In a letter to her friend Pearl Kazin, written on February 22, 1954, several months before the suicide of Vargas, she writes, "I sometimes feel if I could only meet *one* man here who seemed really concerned and honest—I suppose Carlos Lacerda is honest all right, but I think he's got too much ego and will probably end up in about ten years as a cynical politician. (We see a great deal of him, and I must say he's much the most interesting and entertaining person to talk to I've met so far.)" (OA, p. 288).

When Lacerda was forced to flee Brazil in November 1955, Bishop wrote the following to her friend the painter Loren MacIver, in the hope that MacIver would welcome Lacerda in New York:

> Perhaps you did see some notices of the quiet revolution we had last week? It was an anti-revolution revolution. The one *for the better*, that we were expecting, was staved off, and that means that the man who was instigating it, fighting for it in his newspaper, etc., was immediately in great danger and had to get out. . . . His name is Carlos Lacerda. He's 41, a brilliant man, completely honest, wants to be "democratic," certainly; somewhat Catholic; but in the way politicians and journalists often are here, unlike the U.S.A., also interested in culture in general, painting, architecture (his little country house is right near us, built by the same architect as Lota's), gardening, cooking, drinking, etc. He got the Mary Cabot Award for journalism from Columbia University a couple of years ago, and has his own newspaper here, and has been shot at, etc., I don't know how many times, being of course violently anti-dictatorship. (OA, p. 309)

On November 23, 1955, Bishop wrote to Robert Lowell, too, on the same errand: ". . . one of my best friends here was the leader of the revolution that didn't come off—a newspaper editor and Representative who was responsible for getting rid of Vargas last year, almost single-handed. He's a wonderful man, really—41, I think, brave and intelligent, at his best as orator and TV man, and may end up as anything, of course, even dictator" (EB/RL).

105 "To Manuel Bandeira, With Jam and Jelly": The third of three drafts (67.17). In a letter to Robert Lowell (May 20, 1955) Bishop writes, "I am a friend of THE poet [Manuel Bandeira] (at least I keep him provided with marmalade and he has written me a poem and I have written him one) and he gave me a hammock" (EB/RL). About the hammock, she writes to Pearl Kazin (February 22, 1954), "Manuel Bandeira sent me a hammock for Christmas—and since then I've seen pictures of him writing in one, so I guess that's the Brazilian spirit in literature" (OA, p. 289).

In a major summing-up letter to Anne Stevenson, addressing questions the writer posed to her on March 6, 1964 (quoted several times in this section), Bishop writes of her childhood in Great Village and of how "the old Nova Scotian domestic arts" came back to her when she settled in Brazil: "The village was 50 years or so backwards—We made yeast from the hopvine on the barn; had no plumbing, oil lamps etc. My grandmother was a famous butter-maker. Everything is quite changed now, of course. But when I came to live first in Samambaia and we had oil lamps for two or three years, etc. a lot came back to me. I helped design our sitting-room stove, for example (needed up there 'winters'), and without ever having done such things before I found myself baking bread, making marmalade. etc." (LAS).

In the 1977 interview with Beatriz Schiller for *Jornal do Brasil*, Bishop said, "Manuel Bandeira used to come up to sample tidbits. He had a weakness for sweets. He even wrote me a poem, the only one he ever wrote in

English: 'I wish I had two bellies / because of your good jellies.' He told me that those two lines were so good that he could think of nothing that could follow them" (CEB, p. 79).

In 1972, Wesleyan University Press published *An Anthology of Twentieth-Century Brazilian Poetry* (reissued in 2002), edited by Elizabeth Bishop and Emanuel Brasil, with translations by an extraordinary group of American poets—among them Bishop herself, Jane Cooper, Richard Eberhart, Galway Kinnell, James Merrill, W. S. Merwin, Mark Strand, Jean Valentine, Richard Wilbur, and James Wright. The anthology is dedicated "To the memory of Manuel Bandeira," and a note in the table of contents describes Manuel Carneiro de Souza Bandeira Filho (1886–1968):

> He was born in Recife, in the north of Brazil, and his poetry is concerned with memories of his hometown and of the people of the north, even though he lived in Rio de Janeiro nearly all his life. His first book, *Ash of the Hours (Cinza das Horas)*, published in 1917, was a major influence on artists of the Modernist movement, who organized the Modern Art Week of 1922. He taught literature at the Colégio Pedro II in Rio until his retirement. He also made many translations from the French and edited several anthologies of Brazilian poetry. (p. vii)
>
> The first of Bandeira's poems in the book is translated by Bishop:
>
> MY LAST POEM
>
> I would like my last poem thus
>
> That it be gentle saying the simplest and least intended things
> That it be ardent like a tearless sob
> That it have the beauty of almost scentless flowers
> The purity of the flame in which the most limpid diamonds
> are consumed
> The passion of suicides who kill themselves without explanation.
> (Ibid., pp. 2–3)

To Lowell, Bishop wrote on July 28, 1953, about Bandeira's translations of her work:

> I am having some poems in English-Portugese in a literary supplement, here—there are no magazines, so the newspapers cover literature in varying degrees of seriousness. *The* Brazilian poet, a man of about 65, Manuel Bandeira, is doing them and doing them extremely well, I think. I have been trying to return the compliment, I've read quite a lot of Brazilian poetry by now, and it is all graceful, and slight, I think, although Bandeira is sometimes extremely witty, like a gentler Cummings. But how hopeless to write Portugese. But I can read [Luís de] Camões, etc., pretty well now, and he—his sonnets—are superb—as good as any in English, certainly. (EB/RL)

The dedication to Bishop's second collection, *Questions of Travel*, "For Lota de Macedo Soares," is accompanied by this epigraph from Camões: "O dar-vos quanto tenho e quanto posso, / Que quanto mais vos pago, mais vos devo." May Swenson, writing to Bishop on November 6, 1965, about *Questions of Travel*, made this stab at translating the dedication: "though I give you all I have / I cannot give you all I owe" (LMS). Bishop responded on November 10, 1965: "Your translation of the dedication is it, more or less—a bit more like: 'Giving you as much as I have and as much as I can, / the more I pay you the more I owe you—' we wouldn't use *pay* in that way, I suppose" (LMS).

In a notebook labeled "Ouro Prêto, 12/2/61–5/65," Bishop jotted the following: "Translating poetry is like trying to put your feet into gloves—"

107 "The Grandmothers": Drafts of "The Grandmothers" (three pages in all) are fragmentary, but the opening lines and the thematic design for the poem come through clearly. The handwritten sheets are reproduced minus the repetition of the opening lines (VCSC 66.4).

Victoria Harrison dates this "the middle to late 1950s" (P1, p. 125).

A small typed sheet elaborates a bit on each section, as follows:

[Laments]
I had three grandmothers

3.
My day will come.
We wondered what she meant
and did it ever come

Her knee polished blue-veined
smelling of oil of wintergreen
She rose from the rocker saying
Nobody knows

the worst—the great

and all that she could say
was *Ho-hum. Ho-hum, hum-a-day.*

What dismal phrase will come to me?
Hear myself saying

These notebook pages also contain lines for a poem called "Judy":

At school we sat in rows we were all	 we were all
helpless before it even our old martinet principle.	helpless before it, even our dried-up martinet old principle, prayerful

I still am proud
that then I stared so hard
upon the back of Beauty's neck.
I'd know it in a crowd.

In Bishop's story "Memories of Uncle Neddy," based on her mother's younger brother, Arthur ("a tinsmith, a drunkard"), she invokes the figure of her grandmother in the aftermath of one of his visits:

> When Uncle Neddy had finally gone back to his shop, my grandmother would collapse into her kitchen rocking chair. . . . Then she would start rocking, groaning and rocking, wiping her eyes with the edge of her apron, uttering from time to time the mysterious remark that was a sort of chorus in our lives: "Nobody knows . . . *nobody knows* . . ." I often wondered what my grandmother knew that none of the rest of us knew and if she alone knew it, or if it was a total mystery that really nobody knew except perhaps God. I even asked her, "*What* do you know, Gammie, that we don't know? Why don't you tell us? Tell me!" She only laughed, dabbing at her tears. She laughed as easily as she cried, and one very often turned into the other (a trait her children and grandchildren inherited). Then, "Go on with you!" she said. "Scat!" (CP, p. 241)

In 1968, living in San Francisco, Bishop bought a mynah bird she named Jacob. Brett Millier writes that "among the phrases she hoped to teach him were 'Nobody knows' (from grandmother Boomer [*sic*]); 'I, too, dislike it' from Moore; and 'awful, but cheerful' " (LM, p. 406). The second is from Moore's famous poem "Poetry" and the third from Bishop's "The Bight," a phrase she said she'd like to have engraved on her tombstone.

109 "St. John's Day": One typed draft (VCSC 67.6) and three handwritten pages from a sheaf dated 1955–56 by Vassar (VCSC 73.2). The title "St. John's Day" is among those listed with "Poem for a Child" and "The Grandmothers" on a sheet Bishop labeled "Poems: 1955/1956."

From a letter to Dr. Anny Baumann, July 9, 1959: "We've just had two big saint's days—Saint John and Saint Peter. Saint John is the equinox—the longest day in the North, the shortest day here—and there were bonfires and fireworks all along that famous beach, right under our apartment terrace" (OA, p. 372).

In the last line of the fourth quatrain, Bishop had originally used the word "utmost" in place of "power," which is a valuable clue to what she is indicating by "utmost" in the very early poem "A Lovely Finish."

110 "The moon burgled the house—": One draft, two pages, undated (VCSC 65.10). Two pages of draft material contain the fragment represented as well as this shorter one, which obviously belongs with it.

A bump woke me up
it was just a big bug
            kicking his feet
I righted him and he opened wings

much too small and sheer
but they carried him off
bump, into another wall

But there was a burglar
the moon burgled the house
thoroughly and slowly
sidling around the doorways
scanning every paper

all my papers

down on the sidewalk
where the moon reads
        the newspaper

and the moon reads the headlines— (VCSC 65.10)

A fragment entitled "Capricorn," initially called "Tropic of Capricorn," is typed on the same page as the draft "The moon burgled the house . . ." but perpendicular to it:

And the poor never freeze they just starve.	And the poor never freeze— They merely starve.

Well, they have no wars, for one thing—
but they have lots of medals

There is no /   / of snow
but there are deserts—

No real Christmas trees
just imitation ones— (VCSC 65.10)

111 "A Baby Found in the Garbage": The draft represented is the first and fullest of three (VCSC 65.14). The following is labeled "Draft 3" by the Vassar archive and is titled "Death by Exposure":

Two garbage collectors found her:
Wrapped in the very newspaper
whose headlines she would make that day,
newborn, she lay
as good as gold, and the white fumes curled around her.

For in spite of everything they tried,
[Baby, you died,]
she died,
wearing a diaper, breathing pure, expensive oxygen.
Seventy-two hours makes how many deaths?

[Baby,]   the oldest of our deaths,
[and so were driven off again].

Dear, you died the oldest of our deaths
72 hrs. How many breaths?
[Dear,] you died the oldest of our deaths—

The 1962 Life World Library volume on Brazil, written by Bishop, was heavily edited to her dismay and consternation, but she said several times that the first three chapters remained pretty much as she had written them, and in the first, "A Warm and Reasonable People," she immediately addresses "one of Brazil's worst, and certainly most shocking, problems: that of infant mortality." (*Brazil*, p. 10). From Victoria Harrison's *Elizabeth Bishop's Poetics of Intimacy*: "This poem melodramatizes the ride to the dump—'where the buzzards and the poor join forces'—that the baby, found, was spared. Bishop did not resist writing the kind of intentionally political poem she most criticized in interviews. . . . But because she published none of these earnest poems, her publicly stated principles regarding such poetry were effectively served" (PI, p. 166).

113 "Letter to Two Friends": (1957). One draft, one page (VCSC 66.14). Alternately titled "A Letter Home" and "Letter Back." Bishop alludes to this poem in a letter to Robert Lowell, dated December 11, 1957, following her return to Brazil after a six-month stay in New York:

> The one poem I've done anything with since I've been back is a long one I started two years ago, to you and Marianne, called "Letter to Two Friends," or something like that. It began on a rainy day and since it has done nothing but rain since we've been back I took it up again and this time shall try to get it done. It is rather light, though. Oh heavens, when does one begin to write the *real* poems? I certainly feel as if I never had. But of course I don't feel that way about yours—they all seem real as real—and getting more so. (OA, p. 348)

In this letter, she also touches upon the fantastic worth of the American dollar in Brazil and suggests that Lowell might want to invest some money: "I went to bed seeing us all millionaires. . . . What I'm doing will bring about 100% in 2½ years, however—Something quite conservative for here, and quite safe. That is a dreadful paragraph—how did I skid from poetry to percents?"

Writing the next day, she describes the "flying fish" mentioned in her HM *Bowplate* journal of 1951. Lota was apparently very bored on this November 1957 eighteen-day boat trip taking them home from New York: "I like the sea, but the Latin races haven't really liked it since the 15th century, I think . . . We actually did go through the Doldrums—a day of them. The water absolutely slick and flat and the flying fish making sprays of long scratches across it, exactly like fingernail scratches" (OA, pp. 346–49).

115 "New Year's Letter as Auden Says—": One draft (VCSC 66.14). To the right at the top of the page, a few lines are decipherable: "one thing / I seem to be able to bear / is having things up in the air / like a wheezy private plane / but the motor keeps it *up*."

117 "Foreign-Domestic": Two pages of similar drafts (VCSC 65.21). The one represented is the most complete on page two. Alternately titled "Domestic Time." It seems evident that this is an endearing portrait of Lota, one written, I believe, in 1957 or 1958 after their trip to New York. See the commentary quoted below from the Fountain and Brazeau book. Another version of "Foreign-Domestic" can be found in the same sheaf as the draft of "A Short, Slow Life." In the second stanza of that one, the fifth and sixth lines read: "lying there as if you might be dead. / But you are not, thank God. Instead . . ." In the draft labeled number one in the Vassar archive, another stanza is sketched; "you pick up /   / phrases   expressions / like 'rain-check,' 'double-take' / 'tight-schedule' / that sound strange the way you say them." Another phrase: "your pleasure in the ludicrous." And to rhyme with the single word "prevail" jotted below the stanzas about a "detective book" and the record player on draft one: "your vulgar, violent fairy-tales—"

Bishop wrote to Lowell in May 1960 about Anne Sexton's poetry, quoting Lota with delight:

> She [Anne Sexton] *is* good, in spots,—but there is all the difference in the world, I'm afraid, between her kind of simplicity and that of *Life Studies* [Lowell's recent book]. . . . I like some of her really mad ones best; those that sound as though she'd written them all at once. I think she must really have been in what Lota called the other day the "Luna Bin." (You should really cultivate some foreign friends who can startle you like that several times every day.)
>
> (& just now I was asked for a "blanket check") (EB/RL)

In *Elizabeth Bishop: An Oral Biography*, assembled and edited by Gary Fountain and Peter Brazeau, the editors describe how Lota and Elizabeth spent the Christmas holiday of 1957 with friends "in the sea town of Cabo Frio" (northeast of Rio): "They walked the long, deserted beaches, with their salt ponds and windmills, and went deep-sea fishing. Evenings they lay in hammocks while Vivaldi records, which they had finally liberated from customs, played on the victrola" (OB, p. 162).

From a letter to Marianne Moore dated January 13, 1958: "Lota has designed a very handsome cabinet for my hi-fi (eee-fee as they say here) and the whole thing is almost ready to install" (OA, p. 354).

In a letter dated July 16, 1956, from Samambaia, Bishop writes to May Swenson that she is investing her Pulitzer (emended to "Partisan Rev Grant"—she had won both the Pulitzer and a $2,700 fellowship from *Partisan Review* that year) in a "*high-fi*":

> Through an American chemist here I've even been carrying on a correspondence with Mr. Bogen of the Bogen Co., and he has

been extremely kind, telling me exactly what I should order, giving a large discount, etc. That has to be got in somehow or other, too, but I think we're going to try the Brazilian Foreign Affairs—it all costs too much to attempt smuggling. I have a lot of old records here and so has Lota and I've started to acquire new ones—I'll probably never leave the mountainside again, though, once we get it installed. (LMS)

In a letter to Robert Lowell dated "January 29th, I think—1958, I know," Bishop writes of having learned via a letter from his wife, Elizabeth Hardwick, that Lowell has been sick [he was in McLean's]. She also alludes to her joy in the hi-fi she ordered that has just arrived in Brazil:

> Dearest Cal:
> I began to worry a bit when I didn't receive any answer to my two long letters to you before Christmas. . . . I am so dreadfully sorry, as you can imagine—I do hope and pray you are feeling yourself again. (Not that I pray very much, but I mean by that just intensity of hoping. . . .) It is a damned shame; you'd been working so marvelously—but you do have that wonderful group of poems on hand now to console you, and we can all be grateful for them. I've read them over and over again, finally had to stop because I was trying to write some of my own, read them again just now, and every time I find more things I'd like to mention in detail. They are awfully well worked out, *real*, and I like the rather gentle, really, tone . . . more a muted trumpet this time, or even a cello.
>
> I'm thinking in musical terms because last week we finally got the ee-fee, as we call it here, installed. It still has to be adjusted a bit, a little more sponge rubber here, felt there, and some more ground wires—but to me it sounds absolutely superb and now I seem to have everything I want here, except for a few friends I'd like to see more often (EB/RL)

118 "Miami": Three pages of drafts, two of which are represented (VCSC 68.2). The scene here echoes that of " 'In a cheap hotel . . .' " The third page of the drafted material contains the following (the lines in quotation marks are from the last stanza of "The Eve of St. Agnes" by John Keats):

"And they are gone: aye, ages long ago	a
These lovers fled away into the storm."	b
	a
Those buildings you could poke your fingers through,	b
Yellowish, off-white, sullen in the heat	b
	c
tar melting in the street	b
lines	c
pines	c
Burdines—	

And more quotation:

"And they are gone: aye, ages long ago
These lovers fled away into the storm.
That night the Baron dreamt of many a woe,
And all his warrior-guests, with shade and form
Of witch, and demon, and large coffin-worm,
Were long be-nightmar'd. Angela the old
Dide palsy-twitch'd, with meagre face deform;
The Beadsman, after thousand Aves told,
For aye unsought-for slept among his ashes cold."

the two soiled telephone books
that seethed with tiny names beside her head
went unread

seethed with tiny names
and thanked that none of them were theirs.
their stars prayers

In a letter to Robert Lowell from Miami dated February 14, 1948, Bishop mentions the fried potatoes that make an appearance in this draft: "I finally came up here in despair to see if I could find a decent doctor, which I have I am glad to say—a very pleasant young man just out of the army, who has asthma himself & uses a lot of fascinating new drugs. . . . *Miami*, now—I guess it must lack a spiritual nature or something—but the people really look very well, all clean & smelling of toilet waters—but the air smells of fried potatoes & orange-peel—" (EB/RL).

Marjorie Stevens, with whom Bishop was involved from 1941 to 1946, was separated but not divorced from her husband. It's possible that the scene of this draft is a Miami motel en route to or from Key West, where they lived together on and off during those years. But in the same letter to Lowell (dated two years after the breakup with Marjorie), Bishop mentions that she is about to embark on a trip to Haiti, which she took with Pauline Hemingway's sister, Virginia Pfeiffer, on February 19, 1948, and it's possible that they stayed together in Miami on the way to or from Haiti.

In a letter to Carley Dawson dated March 3, 1949, Bishop describes how much she enjoyed that vacation: "WE had a simply wonderful time—in fact I don't believe I've ever had such a good time in my life before" (quoted in LM, p. 211).

I've conjectured that Bishop was at work on this poem in 1958 because of a letter she wrote to Lowell from Brazil on May 8, 1958: "As you see, I don't have much news. We are starting the garage; more like a bridge than a garage, and Lota is happy with 15 'mens' to direct. I seem to be writing poems again at last—they are all such old poems, though, it's like cleaning up the attic. Only one new one, and it's about Miami . . ." (EB/RL).

119 "Keaton": One draft (VCSC 66.11). In a letter to Anne Stevenson, begun on January 8, 1964, and finished on "January 20th—St. Sebastian's Day,"

Bishop formulates some ideas about art that Stevenson quotes directly in her book, ideas so apparently central to Bishop's thinking that the passage is reprinted in *Elizabeth Bishop and Her Art,* edited by Lloyd Schwartz and Sybil P. Estess, under the heading "The 'Darwin' Letter":

> There is no "split" [between the role of consciousness and subconsciousness in art]. Dreams, works of art (some), glimpses of the always-more-successful surrealism of everyday life, unexpected moments of empathy (is it?), catch a peripheral vision of whatever it is one can never really see full-face but that seems enormously important. I can't believe we are wholly irrational—and I do admire Darwin! But reading Darwin, one admires the beautiful solid case being built up out of his endless heroic *observations,* almost unconscious or automatic—and then comes a sudden relaxation, a forgetful phrase, and one *feels* the strangeness of his undertaking, sees the lonely young man, his eyes fixed on facts and minute details, sinking or sliding giddily off into the unknown. What one seems to want in art, in experiencing it, is the same thing that is necessary for its creation, a self-forgetful, perfectly useless concentration. (In this sense it is always "escape," don't you think?)

In the same letter, Bishop alludes to Keaton:

> Postscript. I mentioned that the "surrealism of everyday life" was always more successful,—or more amazing—than any they can think up,—that is for those who have eyes to see. Yesterday I saw such a good example of what I meant by that and some of my other remarks that I must add it. I went to see "O Processo"—"The Trial"—which is absolutely *dreadful.* Have you seen it? I haven't read the book for ages—but in spite of the morbidity of Kafka, etc. I like to remember that when he read his stories out loud to his friends he used to have to stop because he got to laughing so. All the way through the film I kept thinking that any of Buster Keaton's films give one the sense of the tragedy of the human situation, the weirdness of it all, the pathos of man's trying to do the right thing,—all in a twinkling, besides being *fun*—all the very things that poor Orson Welles was trying desperately to illustrate by laying it on with a trowel. I don't like *heaviness*—in general, Germanic art. It seems often to amount to complete self-absorption—like Mann, & Wagner. I think one can be cheerful AND profound!—or, how to be grim without groaning— (LAS)
>
> Hopkins "terrible" sonnets are terrible—but he kept them short, and in form.

Another passage from this important letter: "My outlook is pessimistic. I think we are still barbarians, barbarians who commit a hundred indecencies and cruelties every day of our lives, as just possibly future ages may be able to see. But I think we should be gay in spite of it, sometimes even giddy,—to make life endurable and to keep ourselves 'new, tender, quick' " (LAS).

121 "Mimoso, Near Death": One draft, 3 pp., dated by the archive "1959" (VCSC 64.15).

In a September 12, 1952, letter from Brazil to her *New Yorker* editor, Katharine White, Bishop refers to the donkey of the draft, who "has to be protected from blood-sucking bats with a lantern at night. I am told they don't attack human beings, but I notice my hostess sleeps with her window closed, so I do too, now—anyway—large wet clouds come in if you don't" (EB/NY).

122 "Brasil, 1959": One draft (VCSC 64.16). Brett Millier refers to this draft as among Bishop's "second wave of poems about her adopted country . . . begun in 1959 when, after a year of struggling to write, she again found the voice and tone in which to describe and comment. . . . Bolder and more overtly political than the poems she finished and published, they show her attempts at and her frustrations with trying to speak in poetry about Brazil as a political entity."

In "Brasil, 1959," Millier comments, "she confronts head-on the country's economic crisis and her disgust with the plans for the new capital at Brasília. . . . This is the sort of poem that Elizabeth could never write and that she condemned when other poets did. 'When has politics made good poetry?' she asked in notes for a review of Denise Levertov in 1970" (LM, pp. 300–301).

When Bishop won the Pulitzer Prize in 1956, she was widely featured in the Brazilian press, and in the piece for *O Globo*, the anonymous writer quoted her: " 'Every good writer takes into account the social problems of his times,' she says emphatically at some point in our interview, 'and in one way or another, all good poetry reflects those problems' " (CEB, p. 9).

From the same folder, a single page of untitled, drafted lines, reflecting a kindred sense of discouragement:

the thieves break in

and build a villa twenty miles from town
and paint it pink and make it hideous
with pavements, benches, street lamps, and a niche

for a [twelve] inch Our Lady in ceramic
from Portugal
and carve a name in six-foot letters on the bank
so that the wooshing cars—one car, four gasping trucks

can read, if they can read—

This seems to be admired; not the taste perhaps
but the ability to steal

The biggest crooks are always full of "charm"
or buy Picassos

while their kitchens swarm
with roaches and idle, sweaty cooks—
who're charming, too,
and throw away one third
of every meal— (VCSC 64.16)

124 "On the Amazon": Bishop took a trip down the Amazon River in February 1960 with her friend the Brazilian journalist Rosalina Leão and Rosalina's young nephew. She sent a postcard to May Swenson, which is undated but in the file of correspondence at Washington University placed just after a letter of February 10, 1957: "I'm at Manaus, on the Amazon—or where the Rio Negro (& it really is *black*, too) joins the Solomon, to make the Amazon. Tomorrow we start down to the mouth—Belém—(Bethlehem) on a very *bad* river boat. . . . I've seen some lovely animals—also 4 unlovely Americans—oh, dear, why do we export such awful ones . . ." (LMS).

From the biography of Bishop by Brett Millier: "Elizabeth had been thinking about taking a trip down the Amazon from Manaus to Belém for several years before she finally did it in February 1960. She had been anxious to discover how 'accurate' she had been in 'The Riverman.' "

Written prior to her trip, and in the voice of an Amazonian witch doctor, "The Riverman" appeared in *The New Yorker* in April 1960. It was, Millier notes, Bishop's "Amazon poem written without seeing the Amazon" (LM, pp. 306 and 304).

Bishop's poem "Santarém," also set in Belém (with the opening lines "Of course I may be remembering it all wrong / after, after—how many years?") was begun, Millier documents, after this trip, although it was not completed until 1978. (It was published in a book for the first time, in the section "New Poems," in *The Complete Poems: 1927–1979*, edited by Robert Giroux.)

One wonders whether Bishop's reference is to "On the Amazon" or "Santarém" in her letter to Lowell of April 22, 1960: "You don't have to like the 'Riverman' poem. Lota hates it, and I don't approve of it myself, but once it was written I couldn't seem to get rid of it. Now I am doing an authentic, post-Amazon one that I trust will be better. . . . I want to go back to the Amazon. I dream dreams every night—I don't know quite why I found it so affecting" (OA, pp. 381–82).

Lowell reassures her about "The Riverman" on April 28, 1960: "I wouldn't worry about the Amazon poem—it's the best fairy story in verse I know. It brings back an old dream of yours, you said you felt you were a mermaid scraping barnacles off a wharf-pile. That was Maine, not Brazil. Your new book with this and the Pound and 'The Armadillo' ought to be your very best and all in different styles. . . . I carry 'The Armadillo' in my bill-fold and occasionally amaze people with it" (*LRL*, pp. 363–66).

On May 10, 1960, Bishop wrote to Howard Moss, poetry editor of *The New Yorker*: "Since I last wrote I have made a trip on the Amazon and now I am living to go back there again—it was much more beautiful than I'd imagined and I liked the people very much" (OA, pp. 385–86).

Marvelous details about the boat journey are included in the editors' text in the Fountain and Brazeau oral biography:

> By the time Bishop's boat made its way to Belém, its 250 passengers had increased to 700, most of them hanging in the hammocks below deck. . . . There was livestock on board—turkeys, dogs, and eleven large green turtles in the lifeboats, which the captain had filled with water. He fed them crusts of bread. Egrets and flamingos flew by or waded near the shore, and hundreds of white herons perched on trees beside the river. At one stop along the river, Bishop played with a Peruvian *quati*, with its long nose and striped, erect tail, which rolled, kicked, and bit like a kitten. (OB, p. 166)

Another postcard to May Swenson, dated March 5, 1960, from Belém, gives the basis for the line in this draft "The river, we are told, goes faster than the ship":

> NEVER travel on the Amazon without a pair of binoculars. Also bring along soap, towels, food, toilet-paper, and medicines, and a big warm heart. . . . It was wonderful, and if you weren't off to Europe, probably, I'd suggest that you turn in the Simca for a dugout and paddles and two hammocks and come down the Amazon instead—it's easy paddling—sometimes the river flowed faster than our ship made knots—
>
> I didn't know there were so many birds in the world. We saw a large dead tree, silver, a huge one, completely outlined, every twig, with white herons—against a thunder cloud—It is the 5th day of creation as some Brazilian poet said. (LMS)

Very few letters from Bishop to Lota de Macedo Soares exist, but three written on this trip down the Amazon do. From the third, written from the Hotel Central in Belém, on February 28, 1960:

> We finally got on the *Lauro Sodré* on Tuesday morning, after a few false starts—The trip was one of the most amazing experiences of my life, I think, and I wish to heaven you'd been along—I think we are all proud of ourselves now, very tired. . . . I've never seen Rosinha [Leão] look better and we think that the rough and rigorous life is what she's needed all along—brings out the iron in her character—she was the life of the party and our cabin *de luxo* (thank God we had one—I don't think we could have made it otherwise) became a sort of *salon* where we served Nescafé and biscuits and prunes to the chosen few, and lent books and gave out medicines . . .
>
> The people all stream down to the boat, all the population—in their best clothes, apparently . . . They sell the most unlikely things—dugouts full of *rocking chairs*—live stock of all kinds—fruits and eggs and fried shrimps. . . . The people are wonderful—and so beautiful—they get better and better looking all the time, I swear—particularly the little boys and young girls—But here in Belém they have that city disagreeableness again, alas—in

Manaus they were all like angels. And Santarém—I'd like to go there for a rest cure or something—no pavements, just deep orange sand, beautiful houses and absolute silence—walks along the water front, and two cafés—just the way a town should be laid out . . .

. . . and oh how I hope you are all right—and WHY didn't you write to me?

Love and devotion,
Elizabeth (VCSC 32.8)

126 " 'Let Shakespeare & Milton . . .' ": Dated May 30, 1960. A poem written in the register of the inn in Ouro Prêto owned by a friend of Lota's and Elizabeth's, Lilli Correia de Araújo. (See also the note for " 'Dear, my compass . . .' ") In a piece entitled "Annals of Poetry: Elizabeth Bishop and Brazil" (*The New Yorker*, September 30, 1991), the poet and critic Lloyd Schwartz, a Boston friend of Bishop's in the 1970s, discusses this poem and Bishop's fondness for the eighteenth-century Brazilian colonial town, where she bought a home in 1965:

> Ouro Prêto was just the sort of quiet, unpretentious, out-of-the-way, yet colorful place Bishop loved. She neither trusted nor felt comfortable with any form of grandiosity ("I admire compression, lightness, and agility," her Strayed Crab proclaims [from "Rainy Season; Sub-Tropics"], "all rare in this loose world"); she preferred intimacy to high ambition (Mozart to Beethoven, the Metaphysicals to Milton). Comparing herself to the Great Poets, even in jest, she cannot repress a flash of pride in her own modesty. Her witty quatrain seems a miniature *ars poetica*, a philosophy, an apologia, practically an autobiography, her "view." (p. 88)

126 "(For the window-pane)": Single copy. In his article "Annals of Poetry: Elizabeth Bishop and Brazil" (*The New Yorker*, September 30, 1990), Lloyd Schwartz describes visiting Lilli Correia de Araújo in 1991 and the moment when she presented him with the typed copy of this poem, which Bishop had given to her in celebration of Bishop's purchase of "the house across the way" in Ouro Prêto in 1965.

Fragmentary impressions of Ouro Prêto can be found in the Bishop archive at Vassar—among them: "Sunrise / orange"

> The big yellow tomcat rubbed ingratiatingly around the mountain, made a discovery, quickly lapped up the bowl of thick white mist in the valley and went his way around the world again—his wicked way—bristle—muscular

> Ouro Prêto—the Church of Nossa Senhora do Carmo—the lavabo in the sacristy is of soapstone, very big, sweet sentimental late Baroque—virgin, child, dolphins, angels, sunburst, etc—very pretty. It is the only one in which soapstone is gilded—most of the upper edges. Oblique, hair, rays, etc—The effect is

lovely—gray green, pale gold—like the cauliflowers very early in the morning, in a *heavy* dew, with the sun first on them—same colors

Endless endless treeless mountains or rolling hills—the famous "iron mountain" that looks it—supposed to be enough iron to mine for 2,000 years if Brazil would undertake it. All the minerals along the cuts—glittering, blazing, shaly, dry,—red, black, pinks and whites—a mineral world. Few trees—catatonic—? (VCSC 68.5)

127 "The Blue Chairs (that dream)": From a notebook dated 1961–62 with drafts of "Gypsophilia" and "The Sandpiper" (VCSC 73.4). Below this fragment, Bishop writes, "I longed for day / Darwin said—."

Bishop's notebooks and letters abound with records of dreams, and when the poet Elizabeth Spires interviewed her in June 1978, she spoke of her dedicated interest in dreams predating her college years: "I had a theory at that time that one should write down all one's dreams. That that was the way to write poetry. So I kept a notebook of my dreams and thought if you ate a lot of awful cheese at bedtime you'd have interesting dreams. I went to Vassar with a pot about this big—it did have a cover!—of Roquefort cheese that I kept in the bottom of my bookcase . . . I think everyone's given to eccentricities at that age. I've heard that at Oxford Auden slept with a revolver under his pillow" (CEB, p. 128).

From one of Bishop's Key West notebooks, an entry from the late 1930s: "a chair was making for her through the darkness" (VCSC 75.4b, p. 6). Another entry from this notebook personifying a piece of furniture: "The bureau trapped in the moonlight, like a creature saying 'oh.' "

128 "Gypsophilia": Six pages of drafts and notes from which it is possible to determine the sequence of the most developed stanzas (VCSC 66.5). Other drafted material for this poem can be found in a notebook dated by Vassar 1961–62 (VCSC, 73.4) and containing the fragment "The Blue Chairs (that dream)" and drafts of "The Sandpiper" (published in *The New Yorker* on July 21, 1962):

A star. Oh star, come back!
It's Venus. She appears,
above all earthly sustenance
                    uneasy countenance
blurred   tears   hurrying
and slipping backwards.

A star, Oh, come back star!
It's Venus. She appears
                    uneasy countenance
                    wet tears
above all earthly sustenance
and slipping, slipping backwards   (fear)   (VCSC 66.5)

"Gypsophilia," as one of the drafts tells us, is the plant "Baby's Breath." On several pages, lines about the plant place it at the heart of her questioning meditation, "One thing I've never known: / Is our world luminous like that luminous like them? . . ." and

> One thing I don't know:
> Do we shine, too, or
> a dead black seed   an invisible round seed
> caught somewhere
> caught, somehow, and carried, carried
> in those glimmering sprays about us?
>
> in those minutely-, whitely-blossoming sprays about us?

In these drafts, we again encounter the Manuelzinho of her poem that bears his name.

130 "To the Brook": Four pages of drafts (VCSC 64.17). Vassar dates this draft 1961–62. Rueful and poignant quatrains intended for this poem crop up in several notebooks, one of which contains drafts of the Manuel Bandeira poem written in 1955. Bishop jots down a few titles—"BRAZIL," "Rio, Rainy Day," and "*The Brook* One," among them, along with "Unfinished poems"—on the cover of that notebook, and within it are many variations of parts of this poem, including the following:

> I broke it to the brook
> at half-past nine.
> He cries in his bed,
> [and] I laugh in mine.
>
> Lying down side by side
> [since half-past nine,]
> he cries in his bed,
> & I laugh in mine.
>
> We went to bed happy
> at half-past nine
> but he cries in his bed
> and I laugh in mine.

In another, longer draft similar to the one represented, following the lines "His muscles are longer / but infinitely weaker—" are these: "—My legs are so long! / The bottom of the bed is so warm! / But his are much longer— / The /   / seems endless / Oh poor nature—never quite warm!"

Other alternate titles for this: "To the Brook Below the Window" and "(On having a brook outside the bedroom window)."

On October 28, 1963, Bishop wrote to her aunt Grace about possibly purchasing property in Canada: "How much land goes with that lighthouse? I want some land and some woods and a brook—and a pasture for a cow!" (VCSC 25.11). See also Bishop's "Song for the Rainy Season," published in *The New Yorker*, October 8, 1960, the poem celebrating the house and life she shared with Lota de Macedo Soares in Petrópolis, Brazil. The second stanza of that poem:

> In a dim age
> of water
> the brook sings loud
> from a rib cage
> of giant fern; vapor
> climbs up the thick growth
> effortlessly, turns back,
> holding them both,
> house and rock,
> in a private cloud. (CP, p. 101)

131 "*All afternoon the freighters*—Rio": Eleven pages of drafts and notes and this one fair copy with legible revisions (VCSC 65.5). Other lines to be found in this sheaf of drafted material:

> oh citizens
> why can't you leave
> the blessed whale in peace,
> oh god, in peace, in peace, in peace . . . . . .
>
> in peace, oh God, in peace, in peace, in peace . . . . .

The opening lines can be found in a notebook Bishop dated 1962–64: "I watched the freighters rising from a sea / of pale blue . . . / Their bridges glared like white / like the façades of churches / . . . the loads of oil or ore or grain / theatrical." In the same small notebook, Bishop entered these lines five times, with slight variations: "One of my friends / is shut up in a madhouse, and another / should be there. / Too delicate, determined—what their ends / will be, God knows! (Or, for that matter, mine.)" Bishop mentioned "*All afternoon the freighters*—Rio" in an interview with the poet Elizabeth Spires that took place on June 28, 1978, when discussing the origins of her poem "The Moose." Spires asked, "Do you start a lot of poems and finish very few?" Bishop responded,

> Yes. Alas, yes. I begin lots of things and then I give up on them . . . I wanted to finish it ["The Moose"] because I liked it, but I could never seem to get the middle part, to get from one place to the other. And then when I was still living in Cambridge I was asked to give the Phi Beta Kappa poem at Harvard. I was rather pleased and I remembered that I had another unfinished poem. It's about whales and it was written a long time ago, too. I'm afraid I'll never publish it because it looks as if I were just trying to be up-to-date now that whales are a "cause." . . . I think I could

finish it very easily. I'm going to take it to Maine with me. I think I'll date it or nobody will believe I started it so long ago. (CEB, pp. 117–18)

In many letters to friends, Bishop described the freighters she saw from the apartment in Rio. On August 14, 1959, to May Swenson: ". . . speaking of storms—the biggest one I ever saw, almost, took place while we were in Rio and went on for several days—perhaps it had something to do with that typhoon in the east. The sea came right up across the sidewalks, over the street and to the base of our apartment house—everything covered with sand after each high tide. The freighters going by rolled sickeningly. (Another reason I want binoculars—for the birds here, and the many ships we see from our terrace in Rio.)" (LMS).

From an undated postcard, placed in the Swenson archive between an April 1961 letter from Swenson to Bishop and a June 1961 letter from Bishop to her (evidently after Swenson had sent the longed-for binoculars): "I'm glad you like the rainy season poem—stanzas one and four happened,—more or less—and then they were worked on occasionally, for five years, and I'm still not pleased with two or three spots—it's torture—We have the binoculars here & a little Guide to Ships (like a bird guide)—& keep running to look up what the flags on the freighters going by are saying—rarely very exciting, though—'Dr. aboard' 'All hands on deck' " (LMS).

To Robert Lowell, September 11, 1962, from Rio: ". . . It is getting warmer all the time and I have been swimming almost every morning—except for two marvelous stormy days. Today the sea is like pale blue satin, with a mauve haze—huge freighters and tankers coming in slowly through the haze, like ghosts—lovely" (EB/RL).

From an interview with Ashley Brown, a younger friend of Bishop's who came to know her in Rio, in the Fountain and Brazeau oral biography: "Elizabeth was always seeing things that I didn't immediately see. She was very farsighted, in fact. I remember once we were in the little penthouse she and Lota had in Rio. I said there was a freighter crossing the bay, and Elizabeth immediately described everything that was on the deck" (OB, pp. 197–98).

Peggy Ellsberg, one of Bishop's students at Harvard in the 1970s, visited Bishop at her Lewis Wharf apartment on the Boston waterfront and recalled Bishop's showing her her ship journal: "Elizabeth loved to see the boats. She had a telescope and a small clock on the window, and she had this nautical diary. It was on a stand, like a Bible stand. She would write down the time of day, the name of the boat, the kind of boat and how many masts, and which way it was going. She liked to keep track of details like that" (OB, p. 324).

132 "Mimosas in Bloom": One draft, one page (VCSC 66.19). On June 17, 1963, Bishop wrote to May Swenson: "It was so beautiful in the country early this morning—we hated to leave. We have a whole hillside of mimosa still in bloom—did you see it on your travels? And smelling divinely—like honey. Lots of birds—and 'winter' sunsets now—the sun far to the north, no clouds, the sky getting clearer & clearer and darker, like the lavender-colored window panes on Beacon Hill—" (LMS).

133 "Rainy Day, Rio.": Also titled "Rainy Day, Copacabana" (VCSC, 74.6). Bishop shared the apartment of Lota de Macedo Soares at 5 Rua Antonio Vieira in Leme, Rio de Janeiro, from 1951 to 1967. From a letter to May Swenson dated March 17, 1955:

> Rio is a city of beaches and mts. jumbled together, frequently connected by unexpected tunnels with cars whishing through them, or aqueducts with trolley cars swaying over them (trolley-ducts I suppose, actually) all quite fantastic—but you must have seen pictures of it. It's built along a series of looped beaches, or beaches like scallops. The most famous is Copacabana, really Nossa Senhora de Copacabana. 'Leme' is one end, the quieter and at present more fashionable (but the city changes every week or so) end of Copacabana Beach. (LMS)

134 "Apartment in Leme": 1963. There are some thirty pages of drafts and revisions in the Vassar archive. This one appears to incorporate the latest revisions (VCSC 64.19). The poem was variously titled "Apartment on Copacabana Beach," "From an Apartment in Leme, C.B.," "Apartment in Copacabana," "(Apartment on the Beach)," and "Apartment in Leme, Copacabana (Jan. 1st)."

In her discussion of Bishop's "Pink Dog"—the poem was published in *The New Yorker* in February 1979; Bishop died in October of that year—Brett Millier dates the poem "from the Carnival season of 1963" and writes that "another Rio poem from this year is the unpublished 'Apartment in Leme,' a lovely and more positive consideration of the sea as it dominates life along the Copacabana" (LM, pp. 343–44).

Bishop may be referring to this poem in a letter to Lowell, written on August 2, 1965, in which she thanks him for the passage of praise he'd produced for the jacket of her collection *Questions of Travel* ("You should have seen me, shedding big tears"); tells him she is dedicating "The Armadillo" to him; and mentions "a longer, grimmer one, about Copacabana beach, too, that is to be dedicated to you—but I didn't get it done in time [for inclusion in *Questions of Travel*] . . . Well when it appears, it may be a bit better than 'The Armadillo' " (EB/RL). A transcription of stanza four in Bishop's handwriting in what appears to be a draft prior to the one shown:

> 4. And now the sun. Slowly, as if reluctant,
> you let go of it & it as slowly rises
> huge & red. You sigh
>
> And sigh again. We live at your open mouth,
> with your cold breath blowing warm, your warm breath cold
> as in the fairy tale
>
> —no, in a legend?

Writing to May Swenson on February 19, 1955, Bishop fretted about how Swenson had been addressing letters to her: "I notice on your envelope you have 'Rua Antonio'—and 'Vieira' below—please don't mind my being so fussy, but it's *Rua Antonio Vieira*—like *John Donne Street,* to whom he is roughly equivalent in Portuguese letters! The postal system is so poor that it's best to be accurate. 'Leme' is the beach I live on in Rio—when I live there—and it means 'rudder'—from the shape of the hill behind it. (I think)" (LMS).

In an April 4, 1962, letter to Robert Lowell, from Rio, Bishop tells him that "Antônio Vieria was one of the best early Jesuit writers—a missionary" (EB/RL).

137 "Something I've Meant to Write About for 30 Years": One draft, one page (VCSC 67.12). This draft recalls a train journey to Florida described in Bishop's notebooks of the mid-forties:

These people who
in a lavender gray florescence of
chill dew
lift lanterns like diamonds along
the little platform,
lift black faces to the window
of the long pullman,
just drawing out, still dark & green-curtained
—We hear them talking etc.

while the dew hangs

horses

dew-sodden pickets One is decorated with a broken bit
of mirror nailed to each picket.
—Turpentine // pines //

talking because they love to hear themselves talk

orange tree sloppy, / /, liquid
excited
high laughs—

pass from Georgia into the state
with no cathedrals

soft peninsular air (occasional rhyme?) (VCSC 75.3a, p. 87)

In her biography of Bishop, Brett Millier describes the poet's first trip to Florida, to the Keewaydin fishing camp in Naples, in December 1936, and notes Bishop's delight in the "decoration" she observed there: "Elizabeth's attachment to Florida was instantaneous. Its excesses of scenery, flora, and fauna attracted her painter's eye, and its people's often tasteless attempts at decoration stirred her appreciation for the uniquely awful. . . .

On the trip from Jacksonville to Naples, Elizabeth noted the train's travels through 'swamps and turpentine camps and palm forests' and remarked how 'in a beautiful pink evening it began stopping at several little stations' " (LM, p. 113).

From a chapter of Marit J. MacArthur's unpublished dissertation comparing this draft to Bishop's "Twelfth Morning; or What You Will" (dating from January/February 1964, according to Brett Millier, LM, p. 299): "In 'Twelfth Morning; or What You Will,' the speaker is fascinated by the ramshackle house and fence, as she is by the houses and fence in the Georgia scene in the unfinished poem. In the latter, the fence is wooden and 'once whitewashed,' and everyone is still asleep, while in 'Twelfth Morning,' the whole scene is whitewashed, one black man has come out into the morning, and the fence is barbed wire" (AH, p. 68).

139 "For T.C.B.": One copy, 1964–65 (VCSC 65.20). A poem written to Thomas Barker, the child of her friends Ilse Barker, a writer of fiction, and Kit Barker, a painter, whom Bishop met at Yaddo in 1950. Bishop traveled with Lota to Milan, Florence, and Venice in May 1964, then headed off to England on her own to visit the Barkers in Sussex, after Lota departed Milan for Brazil on June 1. In the Fountain and Brazeau oral biography, Ilse Barker is quoted:

> Elizabeth's stay in 1964 was a very happy one. She was in very good form. She didn't drink. She had been really at the bottom of the world in Yaddo in 1950 to 1951, but in 1964 was a person with a home she had left to travel, with friends. She was relaxed and enjoying herself. She seemed younger than when we had met at Yaddo and was very talkative . . .
>
> My son Thomas was not yet two, and Elizabeth and I went for lots of walks with Thomas in his pushchair. She had this wonderful feeling for babies and small children. Everything to do with them fascinated her, and she was undemonstratively good with them, which was marvelous, because children like that. They don't like to be picked up by a stranger but want everybody's attention, which she loved to give. One day, as we were sitting on the terrace, she asked me, "How far does your land go?" And like a total idiot, I said, "Oh, as far as you can see." She picked me up on that and wrote a poem for Thomas around my remark. (OB, pp. 186–87)

Bishop wrote to Anne Stevenson from the Barkers' home in Sussex on July 10, 1964: "I was awfully busy those two days in London before I came here and it rained abominably—But here it is peaceful and antique and minute, just like pictures in a children's book. I was taken to see Chichester yesterday, and shall probably get to Salisbury to see that church and also George Herbert's little church nearby" (LAS).

Kit Barker drew the watercolor for the limited broadside edition of Bishop's elegy for Robert Lowell, "North Haven," printed in 1979 (VCSC 107.1).

140 " 'Dear, my compass' ": Two identical copies, one handwritten, one typed,

both illustrated by Bishop. Mid-1960s, and probably 1965 (Lloyd Schwartz, "Annals of Poetry: Elizabeth Bishop and Brazil," *The New Yorker*, September 30, 1991). A letter to Robert Lowell dated September 19, 1965, describes Bishop's extended stay in Ouro Prêto, and alludes both to the conversation about haylofts that figures in this poem and to the spring below the house where she is staying that is the setting for "Under the Window: Ouro Prêto," a poem dedicated to Lilli Correia de Araújo and published in *The New Yorker* on December 24, 1966:

> Rio began to get just too much for me again, and so I came off up here—meaning to stay only two weeks. I've been here a month now, and shall probably stay another two weeks. Then possibly Lota can take a few days off, come up, and I'll go back with her. It has been an absolutely killing stretch for her, and I feel guilty at abandoning her—but I wasn't much help, really—moping around the apartment in the heat, and trying to work, very unsuccessfully, while she copes with politicians and crooks and journalists for 18 hours a day. . . . Now I write her almost every day and I'm sure she enjoys my letters more than my company, for the time being, *coitada*! It is very dull here, but I love it.—I stay with our friend Lilli Correia de Araújo—the one who owns the hotel where you stayed; but I live in her house—a huge affair built on a cliff at the edge of the town, with a gold-mine in the back yard—also ruined slave-quarters, gardens away up the hill—level after level—and water running down through a marvellous set of aqueducts, tunnels, fountains, stone tanks, etc.—now all overgrown with ferns and moss. She has a ghastly collection of handcuffs and leg-irons dug up in the grounds. She's Danish, but married a Brazilian painter long ago, as an art student in Paris.—Our languages get very mixed up. I called her *tow-headed*, and she thought I said "Two-headed." She says "Your ass," meaning "Your ace" when we play cards . . .
>
> There's a big spring that runs out just below the house—an iron pipe where there used to be a fountain—and everyone stops, always, to have a drink there—dogs, donkeys, cars—besides all the pedestrians. Just now came a huge truck, painted pink and blue and decorated with rose-buds—On the bumper it says "Here I am, the one you've waited for." Now all hands are taking a drink. . . . I think about you a lot and I have re-read your poems many times already.—I'm always delighted to get a poem! I miss the north very much occasionally—and Lilli and I had one long nostalgic conversation all about bulb plants, birch trees, hay-lofts, etc.—Apparently, "*Up in the hay!*" is an old Danish expression for having a wild good time. She also goes on about *trolls* in a way that reminds me of Auden. (EB/RL)

In 1990, Lloyd Schwartz (see note for " 'Close close all night . . .' ") journeyed to Brazil on the occasion of the tenth anniversary of Bishop's death and the publication of the first bilingual anthology of her poems in that country. He visited with Lilli Correia de Araújo, who showed him two manuscripts of this poem—one handwritten, one typed, and both, as he wrote in "Annals of Poetry: Elizabeth Bishop and Brazil" (*The New Yorker*, September 30, 1991), "illuminated in the roomy margins with small watercolors by Bishop: a square brown house, an apple tree, a goose, a hayloft with a pitchfork, a swan with its head disappearing into the text of the poem, and a fourposter bed."

Describing his trip and his discoveries, Schwartz writes that Bishop

> never published this untitled poem. She abandoned it in Brazil. And, with typical obliqueness, it is even *about* Brazil—or, rather, what Brazil is not. She must have been living there for more than a decade when she wrote it, probably in the mid-nineteen-sixties, and of the poems she wrote there it is the only one—at least, the only one that has come to light—in which she weighs the world of her childhood in Nova Scotia against the life she chose for herself later . . .
>
> Bishop wrote few love poems, and most of them are shadowed by her more customary silences . . . such an overtly erotic poem may still have been too personal to make public. She didn't even keep a copy of it. (p. 86)

Lilli was a distinguished preservationist and designer, the widow of the Brazilian artist Pedro Luiz Correia de Araújo. In her biography of Bishop, Brett Millier describes the relationship between the two women and also Lilli's role in the restoration of Bishop's colonial house in Ouro Prêto:

> Lilli kept her husband's beautiful paintings of women hanging all around her house and inn. [See Bishop's poem about the inn on p. 126.] Since his death in 1955, she had had only lesbian relationships, thereby preserving his memory, she said. Lilli herself was tall, blond, and Nordic looking, and the two women shared an occasional nostalgia for northern things, especially the spring. Among the objects Elizabeth left for Lilli was a poem, framed in her own watercolor illustrations, that speaks to that common nostalgia; the different, yet reminiscent, chill of the mountain air; and the painful compromises their love involved; and the sheer joy of their intimacy. (LM, p. 368)

In 1956 the poet May Swenson, of Swedish Mormon descent, mailed Bishop some photographs of herself, and in reply Bishop described Lilli (October 28, 1956):

> Thank you for the snapshots. In the standing one you look very much like a Danish friend of ours here (only she's at least twice as tall), who wears her hair cut the same way—even blonder than you. It's the same way the Amazonian Indians wear theirs, and some children visiting us at the same time as the Danish Viking asked us, "Is she a *blonde* Indian?" Lota was impressed by the front-face one [of Swenson], and just to show you how we strike

> these Latins, *she* exclaimed, "Why, she's so Nordic she looks like an *eskimo* . . ." (Much funnier-sounding in Portuguese.) (LMS)

In a letter to Swenson nearly a decade later, on May 21, 1965, Bishop describes the delight she takes in Ouro Prêto, in the birdlife at Lilli's, and in the scenes memorialized in her poem "Under the Window: Ouro Prêto," which she shared with Lowell, too, in her letter of September that year. To Swenson, she writes,

> Well, I am back again in Minas for a few days and a change of air, etc. Lilli, our Danish friend here, has a strange assortment of poultry, and a big old-fashioned Brazilian courtyard, laid with black and white brook stones in big daisies. Hens, fan-tailed, white doves, geese (terrifying—they have three eggs now and I keep going to see if there is a 4th and the geese gang up on me, six strong, and hiss and almost bite my legs, but not quite), guinea hens—and I think I once told you about the big wild bird they keep to eat snakes and keep the domestic poultry safe? A tall, stalking, pinkish bird like a heron, with a crest. He eats meat, and Lilli puts a small dish on the kitchen floor for him. He stalks back and forth by the door, looking in, and finally makes up his mind to come in and gobble it up. He's about a yard high—a wonderful creature to have beside one while one eats breakfast . . .
>
> There is also a small water-fall right under my bedroom window—the house sits up high on a ledge overlooking the town—and it is good water, so every passerby, every car and truck almost, stops for a drink of water, and I lean out and eavesdrop on their conversations—mostly talk of sicknesses, funerals, babies, and the cost of living. (LMS)

In a letter to her friends Ilse and Kit Barker, July 20, 1965, Bishop wrote that Lilli "sounds exactly like the early Garbo" (LIKB).

To Anne Stevenson, Bishop wrote on August 15, 1964: "I am staying with a Danish friend here and I have just discovered that 'Kierkegaard' means 'churchyard'—or *grave-yard,* that is. Now probably every other half-educated person in the world already knows that, but I didn't . . . She recites bits of H C Andersen to me in Danish, which is very nice since he has been one of my favorite writers (in English, of course) all my life" (LAS).

In a letter to Swenson, written on November 10, 1965, Bishop speaks of a poem Swenson had written based on Bishop's descriptions of Brazilian birds. The poem is one that Howard Moss, the *New Yorker* poetry editor, felt should have the subtitle "('A Reply to Elizabeth Bishop in Brazil')." The letter makes it clear that Moss and Bishop are at odds about whether *The New Yorker* will print Bishop's dedication of "Under the Window: Ouro Prêto" to Lilli—which the magazine did a year later, on December 24, 1966. To Swenson, Bishop writes, "Howard must have liked it [Swenson's poem], since he just wrote *me* that I couldn't use a dedication line in a recent poem of mine—and yet he let you get away with a very obvious dedication . . ."

In the same letter, Bishop discusses what a refuge Ouro Prêto has been from the stresses of Rio:

> I meant to stay two weeks and ended by staying over two months . . . O P is a wonderful place to work in and the climate is much colder and dryer than here—about 4,000 feet—and I live in great comfort and idleness there—but I did get a lot of work done, for the first time in two or three years, I think. . . . Lota is working so hard these days and going through such a hard time—I am not much use to her in Rio, but also felt I'd abandoned her—even if I don't see her except for the ten minutes it takes to eat dinner. I'm awfully worried about her—although she seems to be bearing up fairly well considering she works about 18 hours a day, has lost her voice, is being violently attacked by some politicians, and this morning started off with a toothache and gumboils, *coitada.* But—even her enemies admit—she's done a marvellous job and sometime I hope you can come here and SEE her park. . . . She finally came and *got* me in Ouro Prêto—a nine hours drive—so I felt she really wanted me back! (LMS)

141 " 'Close close all night' ": Ouro Prêto, late 1960s. This second, then newly discovered, poem was discussed by Lloyd Schwartz in his article "Annals of Poetry: Elizabeth Bishop and Brazil."

Bishop gave this poem to Jose Alberto Nemer, a friend in Brazil, who engraved it as a wedding gift for his bride. Other possible stanzas for this can be found on a single page in the archive under the scratched-out title "Brook One":

Just once in the night
the lovers turned over,
together, asleep.

Once in the night
the lovers turned over
close together
under the cover,

cover.

without waking up

different but like

like a page of a book

Once in the night
the lovers turned over
together, quickly,
under the cover,

Once in the night
the lovers turned over
tightly, together,
under the cover,

—Like a page in a book

142 "The Pretender": Three pages, two drafts. Undated (VCSC 67.4). The poem is set in Petrópolis, where Bishop and Lota shared a country home.

In a letter to Kit and Ilse Barker, February 7, 1952, Bishop described Petrópolis as "the mountain resort about 40–50 miles from Rio where the emperor used to spend the summers."

From another letter to the Barkers, December 16, 1959:

> We had another funny call from "the Pretender"—funnier—It was an awful week-end, hadn't stopped pouring for three days—and we had two guests, one Spanish, who is nice but whom no one can understand in *any* language, and at 5 on Sunday things were getting pretty dismal—We were playing an opera, and Lota, who is always game, had her hair down (she has very long hair) and a straw hat on top and was wearing a pair of bright blue rubber gloves—being a witch (as I said—maybe we *are* turning into witches)—and doing a Witch's Dance. It was very noisy and we were being quite hysterical what with one thing and another when suddenly I realized that right outside the plate glass window, standing in a row staring at us, were Dom Pedro, two little princesses and a prince, and a lady-in-waiting, I guess she is.—English-style, they were all "hiking in the rain." They were polite and puzzled—our reputation for eccentricity soared, probably—it didn't seem *explainable*— (LIKB)

The other draft of this poem:

The Pretender came to breakfast.
(We had been notified two days ahead)
He arrived on the dot, on horseback,
after an eight-mile ride out from the Palace.
The horse was sweating; he was like a daisy

over-awing

tall, big, and blond, blue-eyed, guffawing

He knew the name of each plant in the garden
and where they came from, each tree on the hill

if that isn't patriotism, what is—

he spoke familiarly of his family

and of his law-suits to get back his lands:

"I'm not much in favor of this *regime*" he said   seem
referring to the republic
They say it's all so long ago—but it was my grandmother's
You can't get much closer than that, can you?

He had been to order some new hives of bees
he keeps them on the second floor of the palace
(Like the father of Toulouse-Lautrec)

from the Department of Agriculture
When he gave his name, Prince—
they said "But that's your firm. We want your name,
not the name of your business

His breeches black and white checked breeches, rather loud
a feather in his hat a linen coat
a piqué ascot
and his cufflinks and all his studs were teeth
Hounds teeth? Big and yellow, set in gold.

The Noble Savage with a whip and boots
something left over from another age—

Underneath this draft, Bishop wrote by hand, "democracy has taken its toll."

143 "Inventory": One draft, one page (January 1967) (VCSC 66.9). Bishop's companion of fifteen years, Lota de Macedo Soares, was hospitalized in Rio in late 1966, where she received insulin shock treatments. Overseeing the design and development of Rio's new Flamengo Park from 1961 forward had taken its toll, and trying to negotiate the political shoals surrounding the project as a new regime gained control had exhausted her. The strain on their relationship had caused Bishop to seek affectionate support from others, a transgression confirmed for Soares when she read a letter sent to Bishop in Brazil from "Suzanne Bowen" (a pseudonym), a young woman Bishop had met as she shakily embarked on a teaching stint at the University of Washington in Seattle the previous January. In her biography of Bishop, Brett Millier describes the writing of "Inventory":

> By the first of the year [1967], Elizabeth had packed a suitcase and had moved out of the apartment and into a Rio hotel. She had had to leave on very short notice; her presence was damaging to Lota's attempts to regain her sanity, according to the doctor. She was asked to stay away for a long time—six months to two years. Out "in half an hour," "after fifteen years with a few dirty clothes in a busted suitcase, no home anymore, no claim (legally) to anything here," she sat in her hotel room and tried to get her shock and grief under control. . . .
>
> Unable to stay alone in her hotel and needing supervision to keep from drinking constantly, she checked herself into the Casa de Repouso, where she tried to rest and make plans for the future. . . . Her two impulses—to stay and try to help Lota and to get out of the country as soon as she could—pulled at her all the time. . . . She left the Casa de Repouso in late January and went in the company of her friend Isa Aguirre to Samambaia to pack a trunk. Alone for a few hours in her *estudio* by the waterfall, she typed out a few lines. (LM, pp. 384–85)

The previous fall, Bishop had written about Lota to her own physician, Dr. Anny Baumann, in New York:

> She has had an awful time with the park and the new Governor—and it is even worse now. She did take about two weeks off—then had to come back to work instead of taking a month off as she had planned to do. I can't understand all the details—but I do know she has fought with many people, and is in dreadful shape, physically. I am terribly worried about her but *cannot talk to her.* No one can. She has dizzy spells all the time, even falls down—her medical doctor here (in whom I have no faith whatever) always talks about the liver or the gall bladder and keeps her eating macaroni and gelatin and recommends a certain kind of mineral water . . . (September 1, 1966, OA, pp. 448–49)

> She is really awfully sick, I think, and I don't have the faintest idea what to do for her, really. She has had one blow after another in that park—feels deceived, betrayed, disappointed, etc., all around—and I am on her side in most of it, as far as I can understand it—but she doesn't seem to realize that her increasing violence and rudeness have made things much worse for everyone. . . . I never felt so helpless and ignorant in my life, and unfitted to cope with my life or hers. (September 25, 1966, OA, pp. 450–51)

In the Fountain and Brazeau oral biography, Mary Stearns Morse, to whom Lota left the home in Samambaia in her will, describes Lota's decline. It began, Morse says, when

> a new government came in after Carlos [Lacerda], and they changed a lot of personnel in the park. Lota couldn't get through the things in the park. She was frustrated. She felt that it was her baby, and she wanted to see it done as she wanted. Lota could be very insistent, and she could be aggressive, too. It may have been a combination of Elizabeth's condition, her problems and saying "I'm going away." Lota was afraid of Elizabeth going away. She saw something that she'd wanted to do all her life slipping away from her, and she saw Elizabeth slipping away, too. (OB, p. 200)

V. 1968–1979: San Francisco, Ouro Prêto, Cambridge, Boston

147 " 'Far far away there, where I met . . .' ": One page containing two distinct fragments (1968) (VCSC 68.3).

In the summer of 1967, Bishop was staying at the apartment of her friends Loren MacIver and Lloyd Frankenburg at 61 Perry Street in Greenwich Village. Soares's doctors had urged her not to fly to New York to see Bishop and Bishop herself was deeply concerned, but on September 19, Soares arrived. That night, she took an overdose of pills and slipped into a coma. As Bishop kept a vigil in the days following, she described the tragic sequence of events to her friends Joseph and U. T. Summers: ". . . the minute I saw her I knew she shouldn't have been allowed to come—in fact I think I'll go back to Brazil and shoot her doctor. Anyway—she was exhausted—we passed a quiet afternoon, *no cross words or anything like that*—but I could see she was in a very bad state of depression and [I] didn't know what to do, really, except try to get her to rest. Well—sometime toward dawn she got up and tried to commit suicide—I heard her up in the kitchen about 6:30—she was already almost unconscious. . . . I'm just stunned that's all—this is so totally unlike the Lota of the last 15 years of my life with her" (OA, p. 468).

Soares died in St. Vincent's Hospital on September 25. After Bishop's break with many people she had considered her friends in Rio, who blamed her just as she had told a friend she was "horribly afraid" they would, she moved to San Francisco the following January and took an apartment with Bowen (see the note for "Inventory"), who for the next two years (until their relationship deteriorated) became the mainstay in her life.

The "Rosinha" of the first stanza of this fragment is Rosalina Leão, a Brazilian journalist and landscape architect, with whom Bishop traveled down the Amazon in 1960. (See note for "On the Amazon.") In the Fountain and Brazeau oral biography, Leão is quoted: "Elizabeth, I discovered, is good when she travels. Everything is easy for her. . . . [One day] we saw dolphins, and so [the next day] Elizabeth brought a ball with her and played with them" (OB, pp. 164–65).

Bishop wrote to several friends about the many marvelous birds and animals she and Leão encountered along the way. The lines, "those strange affectionate animals / that seemed to like me too & ate the bread / but who forgot me naturally the moment I left" must have struck her when she wrote them as applicable to the people she'd left behind in Rio a few months earlier. Leão is quoted in the oral biography about Lota's park: "Lota's idea was to have a beautiful park for the people. She imagined a family coming to spend a day there. The little children would be in a playground, and the others would have football, volleyball, swimming, a pool for [sailing] boats, a theater, music, and a place to dance. Elizabeth was fascinated and helped Lota quite a lot. . . . Lota told me that Elizabeth had helped her very, very much" (OB, p. 168).

After a thoroughly discouraging trip to Brazil, Bishop wrote to Lowell from San Francisco on January 9, 1968:

> For about a week I didn't think I could ever make it—thought I'd just leave my bones in Brazil—but somehow I did, after all, even with some loose ends . . .
>
> My young friend Roxanne [elsewhere referred to as "Suzanne Bowen"] came down from Seattle, and we started looking for a place to stay and found a rather funny but comfortable flat on Pacific Avenue—a steam laundry (almost silent) on one side—a body painting (CAR, that is!) place across the street, and also the Cancer Society . . . as she says "a nowhere address," but it has lots of room and will be quite comfortable, I think, when I get some furniture. A pea-green wooden early 20th cent. building—

4 bay windows—2 fireplaces— I really like it . . . Thank God, Cal,
I have such a bright, kind, and funny companion right now—
I don't think I could bear to live alone just yet, or in New York,
and certainly not in Brazil. (EB/RL)

Bishop's old friend Louise Crane wrote to her from New York on January 28, 1969, "I like your account of your 'great lower class American life' with the white Volkswagon and laundrymat [*sic*]" (VCSC, 3.1). Another draft from this moment in San Francisco is quoted in Brett Millier's biography and referred to as possibly anticipating "Five Flights Up," the last poem in *Geography III*, published in 1976:

In the dark night
when the sea shifts over
and leaves a tract
and continents of gravel
never seen
you grit your teeth in sleep

and I am grateful for
your human temperature.

Then one bird, or two?
a crowded hurried song
or two together

The light
It was the moon & not the laundromat
that woke me, love. But soon the laundromat
opens its doors and all the lonely people
will come to wash their clothes. (LM, p. 412)

Bishop wrote an account of attending a rock-and-roll practice session by a group called The Threshold in an apartment "belonging, I think, to the girl friends of two of them," and her disaffection with the milieu in which she had suddenly found herself is evident in this passage:

All the sexuality is in the bumping & grinding bodies and of course in the music driving to a climax—the sexuality of the instrument, guitars, violins etc (think of the cubists, etc), the serenade, flamenco—all gone—the sexual quality of the human voice and all its infinite variety of appeals, caresses, even gratitudes, and so on—none of that—nothing of it left in the instruments and only the mechanical physical working part of it in the performers—all has been transferred to a machine . . .

But—they obviously don't want to think, or feel anything but the animal driving power—and wearing themselves out with the violence of the noise and the grinding hips and dirty distorted grinding twisting bodies—when they stop they probably say nothing to each other—each one, like the midget dreamy dirty silent smiling girls—exhausted before they start. It is hard to imagine any delicate sex-play—flirtation—a kiss that is led up to by looks and round-about remarks, any delicately growing heightening excitement—no—just grind and bang nag nag and then blank exhaustion—wordless, skill-less—no use of charm, retreats, the lovely game of love—pretty games. (VCSC 53.9)

149 "Aubade and Elegy": (VCSC 64.20). This is the single extant draft of Bishop's intended elegy for Lota de Macedo Soares, with whom she lived in Brazil for nearly fifteen years. (Three pages of notes for the elegy can be found in the appendix along with all sixteen drafts of the poem "One Art.")

Brett Millier states that "Aubade and Elegy" was written in spring 1970, during a stretch when Bishop was alone in her home in Ouro Prêto after "Suzanne Bowen" had returned to Seattle (LM, p. 427). Note the overlap of phrasing with that of the draft of "St. John's Day": "But no, no prayer / can wake him."

A short account of Lota Soares's suicide in September 1967 is given in the note above for "Far far away there, where I met . . . " When her will was opened, this quotation from Voltaire was discovered: "*Si le Bon Dieu existe, il me pardonnera. C'est son métier.*" ("If God exists, he'll forgive me. That's his job.")

On December 5, 1967, Bishop wrote to Dr. Anny Baumann from Rio de Janeiro: ". . . The tale—natural, I suppose, but hard to listen to and deny calmly—that I did something so awful that day, September 17, that Lota committed suicide. If that were true, how could I possibly be here, I wonder—or still alive myself, even?" (OA, p. 483). (Note: Bishop mistakenly believed Soares arrived in New York on September 17 rather than the nineteenth.)

The heartbreak and guilt Bishop experienced are documented in many letters to friends and in the many books written about her. The epigraph on the dedication page to *Questions of Travel* (see note for "On the *Prince of Fundy*") expressed her love and infinite gratitude to Lota, and friends testified to Bishop's feeling that Lota had rescued her.

Joseph Summers is quoted in the Fountain and Brazeau oral biography speaking about a visit Bishop paid in 1957, some six years after she'd settled in Brazil, to Storrs, Connecticut, where Summers and his wife, U.T., were living: "She said, 'It's just heaven. I don't know what I've done to deserve heaven.' . . . Elizabeth brought all these pictures of Samambaia and told stories about Lota, the household, and the adopted son. She made a great point about this boy. Elizabeth said that Lota thought she had done two good things in her life. Lota felt as if she had saved two people, this boy and Elizabeth" (OB, pp. 151–52).

In a March 5, 1963, letter to Robert Lowell, from Rio, Bishop expresses both her admiration for Lota and her growing desire to distance herself from the political cauldron in which Lota found herself: "Lota is flabbergasting me more every day. Her latest triumph is too long to go into—but she has really saved a big hunk of the city, done a crook out of a few extra millions, all in about 48 hours. And while she saves the doomed city of Rio, I shut myself up with my air conditioner and try to forget it" (EB/RL).

To Ashley Brown, Bishop wrote on October 3, 1967, after Lota's death:

> As you probably realized, I only came to N.Y. because the doctor there wanted me to get away—thought he could treat her better without me, also that I might have another breakdown myself, hadn't done any work in 18 months, etc. She wanted to come so badly, however, that instead of waiting six months, until December, as we had planned, she finally came [on Sunday] September 17. I couldn't say no to her cables—and I wrote and cabled the doctor over and over, and never got any reply. Friends wrote me they didn't think she was well at all. It was hard to tell from her letters—two or three good ones, then one very obsessive one, etc.
>
> Well, she came—the plane three hours late—I saw at once she was very sick and depressed. We had only a few hours together that Sunday afternoon and they were thank heavens very peaceful and affectionate, and I tried to cheer her up with plans for N.Y., for Venice next spring, and so on. We were both extremely tired and went to bed early. Sometime in the night she got up and took an overdose of sedatives. I woke up and heard her upstairs here, around 6:30—already almost unconscious. . . . She lived for a week, but never regained consciousness. (OA, p. 473)

In December of 1967, two months after Lota's death, the duo pianists Robert Fizdale and Arthur Gold wrote to Bishop:

> All the things we wanted to say to you and couldn't, somehow, remain unsaid. I think you know what a special place Lota had in our hearts. It was love at first sight when we met (was it 22 or 23 years ago?) and we adored her from that moment on . . .
>
> I hope you know how much you brought into her life. She was so proud of you (and of herself for being your friend). I remember when she first told us about you she was a bit timid thinking we might not know who you were and when we both said, "But Lota, she's one of the great poets of the world and our absolute favorite and we know every word she's written" the sweetness of the pleasure she took in all that was adorable to see. (VCSC 4.1)

When Fizdale and Gold were interviewed in July of 1984, the exchange between them revealed an aspect of their response to the tragedy that must have been painfully evident to Bishop on some level. The two men had been aware of the pressures that Lota was under as overseer of Flamingo Park in Rio, when a new government made it harder and harder for her to fulfill her vision for the project, and she must also have confided to them her knowledge of a love affair Bishop had begun in 1966 while teaching at the University of Washington.

> *Robert Fizdale* [Elizabeth told us that] Lota had been in a sort of sanitarium and she sort of broke out. Lota had been exhausted when she left, and the plane was delayed twelve hours. Elizabeth said Lota just took an overdose of sleeping pills. Lota was in a coma, and Elizabeth kept calling. It was a terrible, terrible thing for all.
>
> *Arthur Gold* Elizabeth called it "suicide." One of the reasons Lota killed herself was because the men just simply brushed her aside. Lota's generation was a generation of women absolutely five yards behind carrying the luggage. Elizabeth was going to lead her own life because the love affair was over, which did nothing not to hasten Lota's demise. She wasn't exemplary in the situation. Elizabeth simply didn't handle it as well as Lota might have, had the roles been reversed.
>
> *Fizdale* That's impossible to say. If one person leaves another, and the other one commits suicide, you can never say there's any way to handle that. I think Elizabeth always felt a little guilty that we would judge her treatment of Lota.
>
> *Gold* Which we did. (OB, pp. 233–34)

Bishop wrote to her doctor in New York, Anny Baumann, on Washington's Birthday 1970, from Ouro Prêto:

> I try to keep remembering that I had about 15 really happy years until Lota got so sick—and I should be grateful—most people don't have that much, I know. But since she died, Anny—I just don't seem to care whether I live or die. I seem to miss her more every day of my life. I try hard to live in the present, as everyone always says—but the present is so hideous to me. . . . I am sorry to have unburdened myself to you this way—you are the only person I can tell these things to, however. Send me some strength of character. (OA, pp. 514–15)

150 "A Drunkard": One developed draft (represented) plus a fragment closely echoing the first nine lines of the draft, handwritten on Harvard's Kirkland House stationery (VCSC 64.22). (Bishop moved into Kirkland House on October 3, 1970, to begin her career as a teacher at Harvard.) This poem is mentioned in a letter from Bishop to Lowell, dated February 15, 1960: "Please send me the poem called 'The Drinker'—I have a sort of sonnet called 'The Drunkard' but I've never been able to decide whether it's any good or not" (EB/RL).

On April 22, 1960, she again brought up the poem to Lowell: "Oh, I think your drunkenness poem is going to be superb! It started me off on mine again—mine is more personal and yet a bit more abstract, I think" (OA, p. 384).

Thomas Travisano, author of *Elizabeth Bishop: Her Artistic Development,* and the editor of a forthcoming volume of correspondence between Elizabeth Bishop and Robert Lowell, published a piece in the winter 1991 issue of *The Georgia Review* about three Bishop drafts: "A Drunkard," "Salem Willows," and "Suicide of a Moderate Dictator." From his careful analysis of both the context for the poem and the draft that exists:

> "A Drunkard," which dates from the 1970s, describes a terrifying historical incident, the Great Salem Fire, from the perspective of a three-year-old child. The fire took place on 25 June 1914 and is termed in Frances Diane Robotti's *Chonicles of Old Salem* (1948) "the greatest disaster in Salem's history." The fire devastated 252 acres, destroyed 1,800 buildings, and rendered 15,000 people homeless. . . . "A Drunkard" links Bishop's problem with alcohol to a traumatic early moment when her mother is still present but is ignoring her to meet the more pressing needs of others. Overtones of abandonment, betrayal, incomprehensible danger, and inadvertent transgression run through a piece that is among the most personally revealing that Bishop ever produced. (pp. 614–15)

152 "Vague Poem (*Vaguely love poem*)": Draft two of two (VCSC 67.23). Bishop uses the phrase "far inland" (see line eleven of this draft) in her draft of "Brasil, 1959," her poem registering her skepticism about the plans for Brazil's new capital of Brasília and contrasting the country's terrible problems with the vision of this extravagant "bauble."

But it is Bishop's use of the phrase "far inland" in her (April 9, 1976) speech accepting the 1976 Books Abroad/Neustadt International Prize for Literature along with a passage from Victoria Harrison's *Elizabeth Bishop's Poetics of Intimacy* that has persuaded me to Harrison's point of view about the origin and probable date of the composition of this draft as circa 1973. From Bishop's speech: "I have always felt I couldn't *possibly* live very far inland, away from the ocean; and I *have* always lived near it, frequently in sight of it . . . The first time I came to Norman, Oklahoma, in 1973—it was the farthest I had ever been inland in my life" (VCSC 39.5).

Harrison traces the imagery of "rock roses" in Bishop's prose and poetry from 1939 forward (particularly in Bishop's memoir of Gregorio Valdes and her poem "Faustina, or Rock Roses") and states that in this draft, "The word slips and reverses, becoming rose rocks, a crystal common in Oklahoma, where Bishop gave a reading [in February 1973]; as such they are the excuse for a visit to the home of an eager student and an entry into conversation" (PI, pp. 204–205).

The student and the visit do not, I think, provide the basis for the poem. The occasion "Just now, when I saw you . . ." provokes the remembrance. In the first draft, Bishop scrawls at the bottom "exacting roses from your body & you give them to me," a phrase replaced by "to give them to me."

A March 9, 1964, letter to May Swenson, from Rio, thanking Swenson for sending her a puzzle, touches on Bishop's interest in crystallography: "I try mathematics and crystallography and crystal-growing and other such hobbies here once in a while—have a fine growth of alum in the cupboard now—can write you the formula.—Lota, poor dear, doesn't even know the multiplication-table, you know!—the result of high-class convents—" (LMS).

Bishop (as noted) wrote or left behind very little explicitly erotic writing. "Breakfast Song" (see note on page 347) is distinctly candid for her, and the following fragment, dated 1965 by the Vassar archive, is also similarly arresting:

> *After Bonnard*
>
> The small shell-pink roses have opened so far, after two days in their bottle of water, that they are tired. The pink is fleeing—it is more mauve this afternoon.—The centers stick up further and are faded, too, almost brown. Still delicate, but reaching out, out, thinner, vaguer, wearier—like those wide beautiful pale nipples I saw somewhere, on white, white and strong, but tired nevertheless, breasts—Time smeared them, with a loving but heavy thumb—
>
> Time has smeared them, spoiled them; his thumb is loving but heavy—(VCSC 73.7)

154 "For Grandfather": The fourth of four drafts (mid-1970s) (VCSC 65.19). The first draft that is preserved carries the initials of Bishop's maternal grandfather, William Bulmer:

> "For My Grandfather *W.B.*
> died 1927?"

Note the overlap in imagery with the crusted snow in the draft for " 'A mother made of dress-goods . . .' "

155 "Swan-Boat Ride": (VCSC 68.2). The cleanest of several drafts scattered among Bishop's papers. Bishop wrote a review of Wallace Fowlie's "Pantomime: A Journal of Rehearsals," which was published in *Poetry* in January 1952 and entitled "What the Young Man Said to the Psalmist." In the review she invokes her vivid memory of the swan boat ride of this draft: "Tremont Temple and its Baptist sermons, Symphony Hall, the Harvard Glee Club, the Museum of Fine Arts—all these were part of my own childhood background. . . . My own first ride on a swan boat occurred at the age of three and is chiefly memorable for the fact that one of the live swans paddling around us bit my mother's finger when she offered it a peanut. I remember the hole in the black kid glove and a drop of blood" (*Elizabeth Bishop and Her Art*, p. 282).

From an interview with Elizabeth Spires, published first in *The Vassar Quarterly* in 1979 and subsequently in an expanded version in *The Paris Review*, Summer 1981:

> I remember my mother taking me for a ride on the swan boats here in Boston. I think I was three then. It was before we went back to Canada. Mother was dressed all in black—widows were in those days. She had a box of mixed peanuts and raisins. There were real swans floating around. I don't think they have them anymore. A swan came up and she fed it and it bit her finger. Maybe she just told me this, but I believed it because she showed me her black kid glove and said, "See." The finger was split. Well, I was thrilled to death! Robert Lowell put those swan boats in two or three of the *Lord Weary's Castle* poems. (CEB, p. 126)

One of the early drafts is just four lines long: "Boston. The Public Gardens. There was time / to take a swan-boat ride: The half an hour, / or fifteen minutes, perhaps, easily time enough / to hold a summer afternoon to hold a summer."

Victoria Harrison discusses drafts of "Swan-Boat Ride" and " 'A mother made of dress-goods . . .' " with reference to "Homesickness" in *Elizabeth Bishop's Poetics of Intimacy.* From her analysis of the typed draft of "Swan-Boat Ride": "The child faces a terrifying thought: perhaps her mother's 'madness & death' began here in this bloody hole; having witnessed this biting, she herself is irrevocably linked to this horror" (PI, p. 135).

Bishop's notebook labeled "(some 1934–36)" contains the following notes: "The white swan bit the finger of her glove"; "White swan—destruction in the quiet park—She raised her veil over her nose to kiss me." And from the Key West notebooks, from the 1940s, a dream entry reflecting "the fear [and] repulsion" Harrison identifies in "the child's response in 'Swan-Boat Ride,' " but not the "ambivalence." The central figure here is Bishop's father's sister, Florence, but the dream is similarly anchored in a violent detail about gloves: "In a black sedan with high windows. A tall woman, Aunt Florence, only I knew it wasn't really Aunt Florence, stood outside, wanting to get in, talking, talking. I screwed up the window, hurriedly, and caught the tips of her gloved fingers in the crack at the top—she kept on talking, talking, begging me to let her in the car, and I felt nauseated. She was dressed all in black, with a large black hat, the gloves were soiled gray" (VCSC 75.4a, p. 38).

On April 21, 1972, Bishop wrote to her friend the painter Loren MacIver, from Boston: "It occured to me the other day that you simply must paint a picture of a Boston Garden Swan boat. You'd do a lovely one. Did I send you one of those postcards? If you could get over for a short visit, when it is warmer, we'd go and take a ride on them" (OA, p. 566).

156 " 'A mother made of dress-goods . . .' ": (VCSC 68.3). Victoria Harrison considers this to be another, later, version of "Swan-Boat Ride," but the development is sufficiently different to present this draft on its own. The drafts are undated, but there is general agreement (among scholars and the Vassar archive) that both were written in the mid-1970s.

158 "Breakfast Song": 1974; single copy. In a note to me, Bishop's friend Lloyd Schwartz (author of the article "Annals of Poetry: Elizabeth Bishop and Brazil," *The New Yorker,* September 30, 1991) and co-editor of *Elizabeth*

Bishop and Her Art described the way he discovered and preserved this poem:

> Early in January, 1974, I was visiting Elizabeth Bishop in the Harvard infirmary. She had broken her shoulder falling down a flight of steps and asked me to bring her some things—her mail, her handbag—from her nearby apartment. One of the items she particularly requested was the steno pad she had left on her coffee table. I was happy I could help. When she was taken out of her hospital room (for X-rays?), I couldn't resist peeking into the notebook. The first couple of pages had what looked like final drafts for a new poem, "Breakfast Song." I was moved by it—and shaken. I had never seen a poem by her in which she dealt so directly with sexual love and her fear of death (she was a month away from her 63rd birthday). I had to have a copy—I wanted to read it over and over. I also had the queasy suspicion that if I waited to see the poem in print, I might never see it again. I knew she was capable of not publishing anything so profoundly personal, capable even of destroying it. So I copied it and hoped it would soon come to light. I kept it to myself for more than 20 years, and neither the poem nor the notebook ever surfaced. Though several drafts of the opening lines have been found in other notebooks, as far as I know, my copy is the only extant version of the complete poem.
>
> "Breakfast Song" is one of a small number of erotic lyrics that have turned up since Bishop's death—poems she completed but never published. It would be a great loss if it didn't exist, though I still feel a little guilty about how I came to have it.
>
> "Breakfast Song" has been set to music—a haunting waltz—by the American composer John Harbison, as part of his Bishop song cycle *North & South,* which concludes with another love poem " 'Dear, my compass' " and includes four other Bishop poems with images of either love or music or both, the first two of the four "Songs for a Colored Singer," "Late Air," and "Song."

Tucked in among the sheaf of drafts of "Salem Willows" is a page with the following typed lines entitled "*SIMPLE-MINDED MORNING SONG*": "My love, my saving grace, / your eyes are very blue."

"Breakfast Song" appeared in the December 23/30, 2002, issue of *The New Yorker.*

159 "Belated Dedication": One draft (VCSC 65.8). A poem to Bishop's doctor in New York, Anny Baumann, the title of which is included on the list she drew up and labeled "Poems 1955/1956."

In her book *Elizabeth Bishop: The Biography of a Poetry,* Lorrie Goldensohn reasonably speculates that this draft was "begun perhaps in the mid or late seventies when she was seeing more of Anny Baumann, and recording images of slatestone angels to friends as she walked past the Harvard Yard cemetery, or the Copp's Hill graveyard in Boston." Goldensohn writes of "Bishop's sense of what it is that Dr. Baumann's 'clean' blue eyes have helped her to see and survive" (BP, p. 240).

From Bishop's January 5, 1977, letter to her friend the painter Loren MacIver: "Yesterday and the day before were beautiful here—lots of snow (12 inches while I was away), but sunny and not too cold and the harbor a pale, pale, milky blue. Seven ducks seem to be wintering here. I walk to my allergy doctor for a weekly shot—about a mile, I suppose—along the waterfront. Yesterday I walked back the long way, around by 'Copp's Hill' graveyard—very ancient, and very beautiful—all the faint, slatestone angels eyeing one out of their depths in the snow" (OA, pp. 610–11).

To the right of the opening lines, the handwritten notes, "everything / had to be *close* / (Zoology study) / In the laboratory / I looked down / & /   / the / under the lenses / & copied them with a hard gray pencil."

To the right of the line "under the promised hand," the handwritten notes: "or held / on the palm of the hand / its [personal message] [   ] labyrinth"; and her instruction to herself about the poem:

> I looked down: (all beginning stanzas)   Then—*Now*   (2 or 3 times only)
> The reasonable prophecy   Now, under the rainbow's

160 "Memory of Baltimore": One draft, one page (VCSC 66.17). Undated; grouped with the poems above because of the typeface. Alternately titled "A Vision of Baltimore." The last line on the page reads "now you see them now you don't."

Bishop visited her friend Jane Dewey on the Dewey farm outside Baltimore in Havre de Grace, Maryland, from the 1940s on. Millier reports in her biography that for Bishop the farm "was always a favorite place to work." The phrasing at the close, "and it was still," summons up the end of her poem "In the Waiting Room."

162 "Travelling, A Love Poem": Draft three of three in the archive, all undated (VCSC 67.19). One of the phrases in what is labeled the second draft—"None of these will tax our imaginations"—brings to mind "None of these will bring disaster," from Bishop's villanelle of 1975, "One Art."

Letters to friends in the early 1970s speak of sightseeing trips around Boston. In one to her friend Dorothee Bowie, dated November 15, 1973, in anticipation of her visit, Bishop mentions touring around Boston with her friends Ilse and Kit Barker: "I had a lovely time with the Barkers & I think they enjoyed it, too—I gave a Halloween party—a sort of *romp*, I'm afraid; rather noisy, with ping-pong, false noses & moustaches, etc. . . . They thought the sight-seeing trip was so good that I shall take it with you—we might even take *two* of them. . . . The trouble is there is really too much to see here & around here—*How long can you stay?*" (VCSC 28.2).

I've concluded that these drafts date from the 1970s but can't be more specific as to the year. The version marked "Draft 1" by the archive is handwritten and differently titled, as follows:

> (N.E. October?)—
>
> I went to see
> 1. the "exquisite Congregational Church",

2. "the Octagonal House",
3. "the swaying Suspension Bridge"—
the *footbridge*—
above the dark fast
secretive water
where? (someone) died
Yes the "exquisite Congregational Church"
& the motel & this motel & that motel—
false ceiling—false ceilings
false bath-tubs—new horse
not old or out to pasture—

& miles & miles & miles of [?] woods—
that *red*!—& that exquisite church—

small tombstones off there—through the fog
oh no—three sheep?

The second is also handwritten and is more extensive than the third, and "Traveling" has been crossed out and replaced by "Love Poem" as a title. It's similar to the draft represented in this book up through the lines about "*Mechanic* Street," after which it develops in a different way:

The street, *Mechanic* street, I wonder why?
goes straight up from the harbor
the asphalt sidewalk black "asphalt"
my grandmother once told me, seems to have melted
and hardened again; it rises
and gently falls; there are also cracks.
That elm-tree stump wd. serve nicely
for a dolls' tea-party. Oh that one
would serve for adults or giant dolls
(Oh giant children have been at work)
on the church. That's not "the Exquisite
Congregational"—that's the Methodist.
Well, it's rather pretty but the top of its steeple
lies beside it, clad in copper
and the middle of it sits beside that,
like a round white
Well now here it is. I don't think *that's*
so exquisite. Well, I guess it's *allright.*
The windows seem out of proportion, I think
Last Sunday's sermon was "Rise and be not Weary."
Oh dear, Well—what do you expect?
Hinks Street. I thought it said *Thinks* Street!
That's the tin bent over.

In the 1964 letter to Anne Stevenson much quoted here ("Answers to your questions of March 6th"), which includes information about her ancestry, Bishop mentions the Tories on her maternal grandfather's side of the family: "Of the Bulmer side I don't know very much. As I said—there were Tories from N.Y. state, given farms in N S at the time of the Revolution, and more recent Scotch, Scotch-Irish, and English additions" (LAS). Brett Millier quotes Bishop as having said that it was "her English Tory blood" that "had helped her recover from Lota's death and survive the pain and humiliation in Brazil" (LM, p. 399).

164 "Salem Willows": Fourteen pages of drafts (VCSC 67.7). In her biography of Bishop, Brett Millier quotes another draft with a slightly different ending: "Yes, through the windows glittered, / really, a glassy sea, / and Aunt Maud sat and knitted / and knitted, waiting for me" (LM, p. 29).

From a version of a talk Bishop gave on December 13, 1977, in a series of "Conversations" sponsored by the Academy of American Poets, edited by the poet Henri Cole: "There's one hymn I'm very fond of, just the one line, which has influenced me a great deal. The author's name is Heber [Reginald Heber] and he wrote a good many hymns: 'Holy, Holy, Holy,' 'Early in the Morning,' 'Lord God Almighty,' and others. I don't care for most of them. But it's the second stanza of 'Holy, Holy, Holy' that I like: 'Holy, Holy, Holy! all the saints adore thee! casting down their golden crowns around the glassy sea.' When I was a child that absolutely *got* me! And I can still imagine it" (*American Poetry Review*, Vol. 14, no. 7, 1985).

Thomas Travisano published the draft represented as part of a triptych that included drafts of "Suicide of a Moderate Dictator" and "A Drunkard" in the winter 1992 issue of *The Georgia Review*. The poem began, he writes, "as a handwritten draft of two stanzas" on the stationery of Kirkland House, Harvard University, where Bishop lived when she first taught at Harvard in the fall of 1970, and where she continued to enjoy working after she'd found another apartment. Travisano describes the "twelve subsequent drafts, all typescripts, showing a poem that was going through a steady process of refinement left uncompleted at Bishop's death."

He also describes the amusement park itself, located at Salem Neck, Massachusetts, as a place that dated back to Native American times: "Surrounded by a 'glassy sea' on three sides, the park featured the famous 'Brown's Carousel,' with its handsomely hand-carved animals that went to a New York toy store when the ride's seventy-year life ended in 1945."

Bishop notes the date "1919" on one of the drafts. In 1918, when she was seven, she embarked on her seven-year residence with her aunt Maud and uncle George Shepherdson in Revere, Massachusetts, before her student years at Walnut Hill boarding school.

In the March 1964 letter to Anne Stevenson Bishop writes of her early years when sickness kept her from a regular school regime: "I went to school off and on, but remember chiefly lying in bed wheezing and reading—and my dear aunt Maud going out to buy me more books. When I was 13 I was well enough, summers, to go to camp, and it wasn't until then, briefly, and then at Walnut Hill, that I met girls who were as clever, or cleverer, than I was, and made friends, and began to cheer up a bit" (LAS).

167 "Just North of Boston": The second of two drafts (66.10). This is dated by

the archive 1974–77. The facsimile gives us a greater sense of the scale of the poem she envisioned, but the subsequent and abbreviated draft transcribed shows us how she was revising the opening lines.

Both "Dicky and Sister" and "Mrs. Sullivan Downstairs" describe Bishop's years living with her aunt and uncle "on the outskirts of an old but hideously ugly city north of Boston," and her memory of these years certainly informs the poem. But I accept the view of Marit MacArthur that this draft may have been occasioned by a drive back to Boston from a cross-country skiing trip with Alice Methfessel in the mid-1970s.

It's apparent that Bishop had Robert Frost in mind when she substituted "Just North of Boston" for her original title, "Back to Boston." MacArthur wrote to me describing her sense that "the poem is a direct response to Frost." The "small brown hill—historic hill, no doubt—" may be on Frost's farm, MacArthur feels, as "that highway passes very near Derry, and Frost's former farm there, which was, I believe, quite neglected in the 70s. (A car junkyard was all over the lawn for a while.)" "But Bishop," she adds, "could have been referring to any abandoned farmhouse she saw along the way. It does seem quite clear from the title that she was referring to Frost, and she was teaching him a lot in the 70s at Harvard" (Marit MacArthur to Alice Quinn, September 22, 2004).

At Harvard, Bishop asked her students to memorize several of Frost's longer poems—among them "A Servant to Servants" and "Directive." She wrote to Robert Lowell in August 1950 about the records Frost made while she was Poetry Consultant in Washington: "those and Dylan T[homas]'s have been the high points of my sojourn" (EB/RL). From Rio, on February 16, 1964, she wrote to Anne Stevenson:

> Frost is a complicated case—a lot of what he wrote about was just homely to me, after my Nova Scotia days, but the kind of thing I have tried to avoid sentimentalizing. I hate his philosophy, what I understand of it—I find it *mean*—while admiring his technique enormously. "Two Tramps at Mudtime" for example—what is it but a refusal to be charitable? (And he was hideously uncharitable, conversationally, at least.) Well—as Cal says frequently—"We're all flawed,"—and as far as poetry goes I think we have to be grateful for what we do get. They all rise above their flaws, on occasion. (LAS)

On August 4, 1963, Bishop wrote to May Swenson from Brazil:

> I was born and raised mostly in and around Boston, you know and know it pretty well—but every time I get back it seems to me they're putting up uglier and uglier buildings. My grandpa B was a big contractor there—built the Public Library and the Museum of Fine Arts—my uncle Jack built the newer wing to the Museum—also lots of old movie houses, public buildings and the *jail* . . . oh dear, how could he. (In fact, I think my father got malaria building that ghastly Charlestown jail which you see if you go in by train . . .) (OA, p. 594)

168 "Dicky and Sister": Seven small notebook pages of drafted stanzas (VCSC 74.9). All the drafted lines (save a few absolute repeats following one another in tight succession) are presented in the page order of the notebook in which they can be found, one Bishop used in the mid to late 1970s, when she was still hoping to finish poems whose titles appeared in it: "Gypsophilia," "Florida Revisited," "Sammy," "Elegy," and others referred to as "old whale one" and "4 sonnets." She also returned to the poem, "Homesickness" in this little notebook (see the note on that poem for lines found here), and set down a few lines of "North Haven," a poem to Robert Lowell that developed into an elegy after his death.

Many of the details in these pages of drafts about life with her aunt Maud and uncle George Shepherdson, from 1918 to 1927, when she left for boarding school at age sixteen, can also be found in the draft of her memoir "Mrs. Sullivan Downstairs," reproduced in the appendix.

According to Victoria Harrison, author of *Elizabeth Bishop's Poetics of Intimacy,* these drafts are 1970s revisions of a poem begun in the 1950s, when Bishop worked on two other poems about her aunt Maud ("For M.B.S., buried in Nova Scotia" and " 'One afternoon my aunt and I . . .' "). Harrison quotes the 1950s draft:

we had time
on winter afternoons

when the Singer sang; the canary sang eagerly
and Magee Ideal flashed red & her [coal], joints
[. . .]
and the water thumped and banged in the long brass pipes
& the [neighbor] Irish downstairs were / / up housekeeping freely
din

we lifted our voices in many a hymn.
You took the alto. straight through the hymnbook—

The pipes and the knobs of the faucets framed us
in gold & the Jello studded in ruby
& the stew took on form & joined in the

(PI, p. 124)

Notes on various poems and a possible story are appended to the description of a newsreel Bishop watched on September 1 or 2, 1954—see the appendix, "Suicide of a (Moderate) Dictator"—among them the following:

To My Dear Aunt: "Food, Clothes, Animals" "all his hallows."

The canaries, Sister and Dicky dining room suite
consolidating minute gains

The endless rearrangements of life, the constant dream of a new
spring suit or when we get the chair upholstered will it go better

with the rug? or repairing the Wedgwood the one Wedgwood piece

God knows you got little enough—the lemon peel over the sink for whitening the hands, the "suprafatted soap" the small tin of crystallized ginger the so-called luxuries—the games with the aunts of "When my Ship Comes In"

177 "(Florida Revisited)?": Three pages of drafts (VCSC 64.24). "(Florida Revisited)?" is one of the poems listed on the first page of the little notebook with the extensive drafts of "Dicky and Sister." Brett Millier dates this draft from August 1976 (LM, p. 523). The poem as transcribed represents an earnest attempt to follow Bishop's instructions for ordering stanzas and lines on the draft. This is by far the most challenging of the poems represented in the book.

179 "Sammy": Five pages of drafts and notes grouped together (VCSC 67.8). Bishop's letters abound with exuberant descriptions of her toucan, Sammy, whom she accidentally poisoned in 1958. The first of the drafts that survive clearly dates from the early or mid-fifties, when he was alive.

From a letter to Robert Lowell, dated April Fool's Day, 1958, describing what happened when she attempted to treat the bird for fleas: "My darling toucan died; I still can't bear to think about it. It was all my fault. I used an insecticide the man in the store said was 'inoffensive' to animals, and it killed him. There he lay, just like life only with his feet up in the air. I want to get another one, but Lota says we're having a little vacation from toucans now. I am trying to write Sammy an ode—incorporating a lot of poems I wrote about him from time to time—'Most comical of all in death' " (EB/RL).

Ten years later, in a letter to May Swenson dated November 16, 1968, Bishop mentions the poem again: "I am trying to finish up a poem about Sammy, the toucan who died several years ago now, to go in my 'Collected' to be published in March—I hope I can get him in. . . . But I really haven't written a poem since I can't remember when. However—one always does start again, it seems—Stevens says in his letters (just read them all) that translating is a waste of time—but I don't agree with him completely—it gets one to going through dictionaries and that is a helpful activity" (LMS).

On March 10, 1969, she wrote to her old friend Louise Crane, mentioning a new bird she'd acquired, and referring to Sammy: "Jacob, the mynah, is talking quite a lot. He says, 'My name is Jacob,' 'I love you,' and my favorite line from my own works, 'Awful but cheerful.' . . . I wish you had known the toucan, Sammy, I had for years in Brazil, though. They don't talk, but are really the funniest birds in the world" (OA, p. 504).

On January 1, 1974, Bishop wrote to her friend the painter Loren MacIver: "I'm at last going on with a long one about Sam, the toucan I used to have. It's sad, too, but fairly funny, I think—since *he* was so funny" (OA, p. 583).

Four years later, in a letter to Frank Bidart on July 9, 1978, from North Haven, Maine, Bishop enclosed her poem "North Haven—In memoriam: Robert Lowell" and mentioned both her ode to Sammy and the poem about the Carlyles: "I am now doing two [poems] at once. 'Sammy' (the toucan), and a very slight affair about the Carlyles I started long ago—it's almost done" (OA, p. 625).

Another page of drafts, largely handwritten, includes these lines:

I did behold
my toucan dead & cold.

reached toward the skies

It's true I cried & cried
the day that Sammy died
& still when I remember
the tears come to my eyes

how he lay on his back
his feet towards the skies
the tears come to my eyes

I thought that he had fleas
The pharmacist assured me—
it was "inoffensive"
I didn't
read the finest print
I cried, I took to my bed—

The cook, to comfort me,
went & made gingerbread
I ate it [ ]
but Sammy lay there dead—

and fly, & fly away
& perch on a high tree
and shriek with purest joy

and laugh at us
and laugh at us always—?
& shriek & shriek & shriek

Sammy was a birthday present from neighbors in Petrópolis in the first year of Bishop's life there. On February 9, 1952, she wrote to her friends Ilse and Kit Barker about that day:

> Heavens—yesterday was my birthday & I am fonder of Brazilians than ever. Friends of Lota's came bringing a large cake (we're straight up the side of a mountain and can only be reached by jeep, or as they say here, jeepy—an English "Land Rover" Kit will be pleased to hear). And then later on a neighbor whom I scarcely know—because we have no known language in common,

for one thing—came bringing me my lifelong dream—a TOUCAN. . . . He has brilliant, electric-blue eyes, gray-blue legs and feet. Most of him is black, except the base of the enormous bill is green and yellow and he has a bright gold bib and bunches of red feathers on his stomach and under his tail. He eats six bananas a day. I must say they seem to go right through him & come out practically as good as new—meat, grapes—to see him swallowing grapes is rather like playing a pinball machine. And something I'd never known—they sleep with their tails straight up over their heads, and their heads under a wing, so the silhouette is just like an inverted comma. I am calling him Uncle Sam, or Sammy. He steals everything, particularly something bright, but so far the favorite toy is a champagne bottle cork, also from the birthday. (OA, pp. 233–34)

On March 20, 1953, she wrote to May Swenson: "The toucan's eyes are brilliant blue—like neon almost—He 'eats fruit' all right—6–10 bananas a day, that go *right through* him—plus a cup or two of rice, several tomatoes, ground meat, hard boiled eggs—& jewelry, diamonds, & money, if left around—& once he even killed a small mouse,—I don't know how because that tremendous beak is really very brittle & useless. (He swallows grapes just like balls rolling down a pin-ball-game)" (LMS).

A page of notes about Sammy, apparently written while he was alive (and typed on the reverse of a draft of "Giant Toad"), contains the following:

Almost the only idea I have of god—a vague light coming around the
corners in the
darks of the heavens—

In my toucan's bright blue eye
I see sky
His black body, his sun-like breast
bursting yellow then into red flames

His blue-armored feet
and underneath his blue blue skin like denims like blue jeans
his work clothes underneath his symbolic feather dress
like a Peruvian King—his feather cape
His huge false nose to make a joke—
His [queer fine] reed-like tongue that gets stuck—
The way he sleeps the blaze of feathers behind we don't know whether
he's really male or female
—He is brave and tough; he lives cheerfully in his cage
He attacks the cat or any dog that comes too close
he can't bite an orange properly, but he once killed a mouse
and left it lying in his rice bowl

Avuncular dear Sammy, Uncle Sam—
I am.

he adores jewelry, coins, or diamonds if he could get them—
let him pick your ring
scratch his head or smooth his enamel-like beak—it seems to itch—
and his rattle of pleasure soft and self-satisfied
Bright colors—when he sees a tomato he shrieks or a section of
orange
he adjusts himself firmly for the night, grasping his perch
and shifting this way and that like someone getting a good
grip on the handle bars—
up goes his tail, his head settling slumps finally it [disappears heaven]
knows where—beak and all, under an inadequate short wing—
A little turban of feathers for the night—

Every day he takes a bath in his bright tin basin
and showers himself well and uses his oil bag thoroughly
until he is gleaming and bluish his black feathers—

Handwritten notes below this include the lines "Brave and cheerful" and "Dear Sammy, Uncle Sam, / though I cage you, yet I love you."

180 "Mr. and Mrs. Carlyle": Eight pages of drafts (VCSC 67.22). On the cover of a 1962–64 notebook, which exists as a group of loose pages, Bishop jots down the title "Carlyle," but no notes on the poem survive here. See the note for "Sammy" indicating (in the letter to Frank Bidart of July 9, 1978) that the later drafts here can be fairly confidently dated to the summer of 1978. The story that occasioned the poem seems to be reflected in these notes of Bishop's based on letters or a memoir by Mrs. Carlyle: " 'This seems to me one of the most indubitable proofs of genius which he has ever manifested' she says, and I agree with her—"; "In hurrying along the Strand pretty sure of being too late, amidst all the imaginable and unimaginable phenomena which the immense thoroughfare of a street presents—his eye had lighted on my trunk . . ."; and "C's face, beautifully set off by a new broad-brimmed white hat."

Other notes of Bishop's for the poem:

(But now when one comes to think of it,
it may not have been that way at all
Perhaps the trunk had CARLYLE on it
in red letters eighteen inches tall.)

I have known several geniuses, five or six
absent-minded, present-minded
all distracted
some too sane for comfort, [others] too dotty
their powers of observation are [remarkably] spotty

and

he was not just looking at his boots
and brooding about Robespierre
Even if it was only to his own name
he was a *little* aware

Among the boys in buttons, footmen,
dirty tail-coats, stained cravats,
crossing (swipers), beggars smell of horses
tinkling harness, creaking harness
beaten horses, farting horses stinking horses
the golden clouds of stinging manure-dust
the cracks of whips and carters curses—
the dirt, dirt it is early September

dust ginger-colored dust
(he was mad for ginger bread) nuts
with his heart-burn and his horse-urine bile
and his brand new white beaver hat?
And she exhausted, in the mail all night
smelling of
her face washed to the edges with toilet vinegar
bringing him her headache
praying for rest, for no complaints

Bishop characteristically set down a string of words as possible rhymes for "Necks"—among them "flex, sex, complex, perplex, pecks, wrecks."

An alternate title: "The Nicest Thing I Know About Carlyle."

A few more stray notes on another page:

she saw him
against the light
wearing a new white beaver with a broad brim

The sun rays her head was splitting
  as he got on
                        looked beautiful
the head of a swan—

on the dry hot haze at the end of the street
  he superimposed on the scene
            blood and the guillotine

The last stanza represented in the draft appears to be the one Bishop envisioned as the climax of the poem.

In a letter to her old friend Frani Blough Muser, on St. Valentine's Day 1970, Bishop writes, "I was also a bit cheered to read in some of Carlyle (loathe him but like those letters) that he got stuck in 'The French Revolution' and 'read trash for 4 weeks'—meaning novels" (OA, p. 514).

In a letter to James Merrill, on May 5, 1970, anticipating his visit to

Ouro Prêto and requesting items she couldn't obtain in Brazil, Bishop mentions powdered ginger, adding, "I can get the roots here occasionally, but not the powdered and, like Carlyle, my favorite food is gingerbread" (OA, pp. 520–22).

Bishop wrote to Robert Lowell from Ouro Prêto on May 13, 1970, during a particularly difficult stretch:

> Courage!—as Carlyle keeps saying to himself . . . I've been reading Carlyle's life—I have a poem about him I've had around for years and thought maybe I'd finish it—very slight. What a man—And inadvertently so funny, *coitado* . . . I do like this
>
> "Today I am full of dyspepsia, but also of hope."
>
> "The world gets even madder with its choppings and changings and never-ending innovations, not for the better. My collars, too, are all on a new principle."
>
> Courage! More courage! . . . (EB/RL)

In a letter to Arthur Gold and Robert Fizdale, written on July 8, 1971, from Ouro Prêto, Bishop mentions her forthcoming fall class at Harvard: "I have to get to Cambridge early in September to arrange my new flat—and do some work on my new seminar, on 'Letters'! . . . Just *letters*—as an art form or something. I'm hoping to select a nicely incongruous assortment of people—Mrs. Carlyle, Chekhov, my Aunt Grace, Keats, a letter found in the street, etc. etc. But I need some ideas from you both—just on the subject of letters, the dying 'form of communication' " (OA, pp. 544–45).

Bibliography

Collections in Libraries

Bishop, Elizabeth. Letters to Ilse and Kit Barker. Manuscripts Division, Department of Rare Books and Special Collections, Princeton University Library. Quotations from materials in this collection are published with permission of the Princeton University Library.

———. Letters to Dorothee Bowie. Special Collections, Vassar College Libraries, Poughkeepsie, N.Y. Quotations from materials in this collection are used with permission from the library and from Alice Methfessel.

———. Letters to Anne Stevenson. The Elizabeth Bishop Papers, Washington University Library Special Collections, St. Louis, Mo. Quotations from materials in this collection are used with permission from the library and from Alice Methfessel, executor of the literary estate of Elizabeth Bishop.

———. Letters to May Swenson; and May Swenson letters to Elizabeth Bishop. The May Swenson Papers, Washington University Library Special Collections, St. Louis, Mo. Quotations from materials in this collection are used with permission from the library and from Rozanne Knudson, executor of the literary estate of May Swenson, and Alice Methfessel, executor of the literary estate of Elizabeth Bishop.

———. Notebooks and papers. Special Collections, Vassar College Libraries, Poughkeepsie, N.Y. Quotations from materials in this collection are used with permission from the library and from Alice Methfessel.

Merrill, James. Letters to Elizabeth Bishop. Special Collections, Vassar College Libraries, Poughkeepsie, N.Y. Quotations from materials in this collection are used with permission from J. D. McClatchy and Stephen Yenser, co-executors of the literary estate of James Merrill.

Miller, Margaret. Letters to Elizabeth Bishop. Special Collections, Vassar College Libraries, Poughkeepsie, N.Y. Quotations from materials in this collection are used with permission from the library and from Alice Methfessel.

Moore, Marianne. Letters to Elizabeth Bishop. Special Collections, Vassar College Libraries, Poughkeepsie, N.Y. Quotations from materials in this collection are used with permission from the library and from the estate of Marianne Moore.

Books and Articles

Anderson, Linda, and Jo Shapcott, eds. *Elizabeth Bishop: Poet of the Periphery.* Newcastle upon Tyne, England: University of Newcastle and Bloodaxe Books, Ltd., 2002.

Baudelaire, Charles. *Baudelaire as a Literary Critic: Selected Essays.* Introduced and translated by Lois Boe Hyslop and Francis E. Hyslop, Jr. University Park: Pennsylvania State University Press, 1964.

Bishop, Elizabeth. *A Cold Spring.* Boston: Houghton Mifflin, 1956.

———. *Brazil.* With the editors of *Life.* Life World Library series. New York: Time Inc., 1962.

———*The Collected Prose.* Edited, with an introduction, by Robert Giroux. New York: Farrar, Straus and Giroux, 1984.

———. *The Complete Poems: 1927–1979.* New York: Farrar, Straus and Giroux, 1979.

———. *Exchanging Hats: Paintings.* Edited and with an introduction by William Benton. New York: Farrar, Straus and Giroux, 1996.

———. *Geography III.* New York: Farrar, Straus and Giroux, 1976.

———. *North & South.* Boston: Houghton Mifflin, 1946.

———. *One Art: Letters.* Selected and edited, with an introduction, by Robert Giroux. New York: Farrar, Straus and Giroux, 1994.

———. *Poems: North & South—A Cold Spring.* Boston: Houghton Mifflin, 1955.

———. *Questions of Travel.* New York: Farrar, Straus and Giroux, 1965.

Bishop, Elizabeth, and Emanuel Brasil, eds. *An Anthology of Twentieth-Century Brazilian Poetry.* Introduction by Elizabeth Bishop. Middletown, Conn.: Wesleyan University Press, 1972.

———. *The Diary of "Helena Morley."* Translated and with an introduction by Elizabeth Bishop. New York: Farrar, Straus and Cudahy, 1957.

Bloom, Harold, ed. *Elizabeth Bishop.* Modern Critical Views. New York: Chelsea House, 1985.

Brown, Ashley. "Elizabeth Bishop and Carlos Drummond De Andrade." *Verse* 4, no. 3 (November 1987).

Carroll, Lewis. *Alice's Adventures in Wonderland and Through the Looking Glass.* Illustrated by John Tenniel, with an introduction and notes by Martin Gardner. New York: Clarkson N. Potter, 1960.

Cole, Henri, ed. "Elizabeth Bishop: Influences." A version of a December 13, 1977, talk given by Elizabeth Bishop. Academy of American Poets "Conversations." In *American Poetry Review* (January/February 1985).

Costello, Bonnie. *Elizabeth Bishop: Questions of Mastery.* Cambridge, Massachusetts, and London: Harvard University Press, 1991.

Donoghue, Denis. *Connoisseurs of Chaos: Ideas of Order in Modern American Poetry.* New York: Columbia University Press, 1984.

Fountain, Gary, and Peter Brazeau. *Remembering Elizabeth Bishop: An Oral Biography.* Amherst: University of Massachusetts Press, 1994.

Gioia, Dana. "Studying with Miss Bishop." *The New Yorker,* September 15, 1986.

Goldensohn, Lorrie. *Elizabeth Bishop: The Biography of a Poetry.* New York: Columbia University Press, 1992.

Harrison, Victoria. *Elizabeth Bishop's Poetics of Intimacy.* New York: Cambridge University Press, 1993.

Hecht, Anthony. "The Ambiguities of Light." *Verse* 4, no. 3 (November 1987).

Hyslop, Lois Boc, and Francis E. Hyslop, Jr., eds. and trans. *Baudelaire as a Literary Critic: Selected Essays.* University Park: Pennsylvania State University Press, 1964.

Javadizadeh, Kamran. "An Audience May Be Found: Letters to T. C. Wilson." *The Yale Review* 93, no. 4 (October 2005).

Kalstone, David. *Becoming a Poet: Elizabeth Bishop with Marianne Moore and Robert Lowell.* Edited, with a preface, by Robert Hemenway. Afterword by James Merrill. New York: Farrar, Straus and Giroux, 1989.

———. *Five Temperaments: Elizabeth Bishop, Robert Lowell, James Merrill, Adrienne Rich, John Ashbery.* New York: Oxford University Press, 1977.

Keats, John. *Keats: Selected Poetry.* With an introduction by Howard Moss. The Laurel Poetry Series. New York: Dell Publishing, 1959.

Lowell, Robert. *The Letters of Elizabeth Bishop and Robert Lowell.* Edited by Thomas Travisano. New York: Farrar, Straus and Giroux, forthcoming.

———. *The Letters of Robert Lowell.* Edited by Saskia Hamilton. New York: Farrar, Straus and Giroux, 2005.

MacArthur, Marit J. "Abandoning the House: Landscape Meditation in Twentieth Century American Poetry." Dissertation. University of California at Davis, 2005.

MacMahon, Candace W. *Elizabeth Bishop: A Bibliography, 1927–1979.* Charlottesville: University Press of Virginia, 1980.

Millier, Brett C. *Elizabeth Bishop: Life and the Memory of It.* Berkeley and Los Angeles: University of California Press, 1993.

———. "Elusive Mastery: The Drafts of Elizabeth Bishop's 'One Art.' " *New England Review* 13, no. 2 (Spring 1991).

———. "A Modest Challenge: Elizabeth Bishop Meets Ezra Pound." *Verse* 4, no. 3 (November 1987).

Monteiro, George, ed. *Conversations with Elizabeth Bishop.* Jackson: University Press of Mississippi, 1996.

Moore, Marianne. *The Complete Prose.* Edited and with an introduction by Patricia C. Willis. New York: Viking Penguin Inc., 1986.

Moss, Howard. "Elizabeth Bishop: All Praise." In *Writing Against Time: Critical Essays and Reviews.* New York: William Morrow & Company, Inc., 1969.

———. "Elizabeth Bishop: A Tribute." *Verse* 4, no. 3 (November 1987).

———. "Elizabeth Bishop: The Canada-Brazil Connection." In *Whatever Is Moving.* Boston and Toronto: Little, Brown and Company, 1981.

Oliveira, Carmen L. *Rare and Commonplace Flowers: The Story of Elizabeth Bishop and Lota de Macedo Soares.* Translated by Neil K. Besner. New Brunswick, N.J., and London: Rutgers University Press, 2002.

Page, Barbara. "Off-Beat Claves, Oblique Realities: The Key West Notebooks of Elizabeth Bishop." From *Elizabeth Bishop: The Geography of Gender*, edited by Marilyn May Lombardi. Charlottesville and London: University Press of Virginia, 1993.

———. "Bishop as a Poet of Childhood Recollected." From *In Worcester, Massachusetts: Essays on Elizabeth Bishop from the 1997 Elizabeth Bishop Conference at Worcester Polytechnic Institute*, edited by Laura J. Menides and Angela G. Dorenkamp. New York: Peter Lang, 1999.

Poe, Edgar Allan. *The Complete Poems and Stories of Edgar Allan Poe.* With selections from his critical writings. Edited by Arthur Hobson Quinn and Edward H. O'Neill. New York: Alfred A. Knopf, 1946.

Pritchard, William H. "Bishop and Jarrell." *Verse* 4, no. 3 (November 1987).

Rich, Adrienne. "The Eye of the Outsider: The Poetry of Elizabeth Bishop." Review of *The Complete Poems: 1927–1979* by Elizabeth Bishop. *Boston Review*, April 1983.

Roman, Camille. *Elizabeth Bishop's World War II—Cold War View.* New York: Palgrave / St. Martin's, 2001.

Schwartz, Lloyd. "Annals of Poetry: Elizabeth Bishop and Brazil." *The New Yorker*, September 30, 1991.

———. *Elizabeth Bishop and Her Art.* Edited with Sybil P. Estess. Ann Arbor: University of Michigan Press, 1983.

Spires, Elizabeth. "An Afternoon with Elizabeth Bishop." *Vassar Quarterly* (Winter 1979). Revised and reprinted as "The Art of Poetry XXVII: Elizabeth Bishop." *Paris Review* 80 (Summer 1981).

———. "The Things I'd Like to Write." *Gettysburg Review* (Winter 1992).

Stanford, Donald E. "From the Letters of Elizabeth Bishop, 1933–1934." *Verse* 4, no. 3 (November 1987).

Stevenson, Anne. *Elizabeth Bishop.* New York: Twayne's United States Authors Series, 1966.

Travisano, Thomas J. *Elizabeth Bishop: Her Artistic Development.* Charlottesville: University Press of Virginia, 1988.

———. "The Elizabeth Bishop Phenomenon." *New Literary History* (Autumn 1995).

———. "Emerging Genius: Elizabeth Bishop and the Blue Pencil, 1927–1930." *Gettysburg Review* (Winter 1992).

———. "Heavenly Dragons: A Newly Discovered Poem by Elizabeth Bishop." *Western Humanities Review* (Spring 1991).

———. " 'With an Eye of Flemish Accuracy': An Afterword." *Georgia Review* (Winter 1992).

Acknowledgments

I'm profoundly grateful to Robert Giroux for asking me to assemble this book, and for setting such a high standard with the Bishop books he has edited with the utmost devotion, sensitivity, and skill. I want to thank the superb staff at Farrar, Straus and Giroux, starting with the president and publisher, Jonathan Galassi, whose deep personal feeling for Elizabeth Bishop and her work proved a source of strength to me time and again. I'm indebted to Annie Wedekind for her scrupulous attention to this book and to Jenna Dolan and Don McConnell for their good work.

My thanks to Susan Mitchell and to Jonathan D. Lippincott for a wonderful jacket and the excellent design of the book, to Jeff Seroy for his friendship and support, to Cary Goldstein for his enthusiasm and care, and to Spenser Lee for his marvelous energy and welcome advice.

It is impossible to overstate—as will be abundantly clear from the notes—my debt to the Bishop scholars whose work has contributed so much to this book. I'd like to thank, in particular, the late Peter Brazeau, Bonnie Costello, Sybil P. Estess, Gary Fountain, Lorrie Goldensohn, Victoria Harrison, the late David Kalstone, Marit J. MacArthur, Candace W. MacMahon, Brett C. Millier, the late Howard Moss (my predecessor at *The New Yorker* and an important champion in Bishop's life), Barbara Page, and Thomas Travisano.

I am indebted to William Logan for pioneering the effort to gather Elizabeth Bishop's uncollected and unfinished work and for preparing a manuscript that helped me in the early stages of this book. I'm grateful for both his labor and his graciousness.

The Department of Special Collections, Vassar College Libraries, has the quality of a cherished sanctuary for me, and I am infinitely grateful to Nancy MacKechnie, Ron Patkus, and Dean Rogers, the librarians who have made working there such a rich and pleasurable experience. I am also indebted to Chatham Ewing, formerly of the Department of Special Collections at the Washington University Library, and Meg Rich of the Princeton University Library.

Many thanks to the editors who have welcomed so much of the material in this book—among them David Bonanno and Arthur Vogelsang of the *American Poetry Review*; David Barber and Tess Taylor of *The Atlantic Monthly*; Brad Morrow of *Conjunctions*; Stanley W. Lindberg of *The Georgia Review*; Philip Gourevitch, Meghan O'Rourke, and Charles Simic of *The Paris Review*; David Remnick of *The New Yorker*, and Barbara Epstein and Robert Silvers of *The New York Review of Books*.

I also want to thank Tracey O'Shaughnessy for writing with such penetration and sympathy about the many challenges of this undertaking for me.

Frank Bidart, Lloyd Schwartz, and Beth Spires have been abiding and encouraging presences. Henri Cole read the manuscript at a crucial juncture and helped me tremendously, and as is the case with so many others, I have benefited from Alice Methfessel's gracious generosity and her commitment to the work of Elizabeth Bishop.

My friends have been (as they always will be) infinitely important to me, and they include my former colleagues at Alfred A. Knopf, my home base, and my colleagues at *The New Yorker*, the Poetry Society of America, and Columbia University's School of the Arts. I'd like to thank Betsey Schmidt for her constant encouragement and her discerning eye on the contents of this book, and I'm grateful for the thoughtful response of David Semanki, an early reader of the manuscript.

Among the multitudes who cheered me on, I wish to thank Jo Ann Beard, Eavan Boland, Rosemary, Barry, and Farley Chase, Carmela Ciuraru, Rachel Cohen, Mary Davin, Mac and Mary Dewart, Marigny Dupuy, Joost Elffers, David Emil, Sarah Fitzharding, Emily Fragos, Marianne Galvin and Larry Maness, Deborah Garrison, Marijo Gillen, Ann Goldstein, Dana Goodyear, all my friends at the Gotham Book Mart, Bob Gottlieb, Nicky Gottlieb and Maria Tucci, Roselyne Gregor, Eamon Grennan, Saskia Hamilton, Jeanne

Heifetz, Edward Hirsch, Katherine Hourigan, Roz Jacobs, Audrey Jacobson, Juris Jurjevics, Martha Kaplan, Jonathan Kandell, Jenna Krajeski, Jeelu and Elliott Kaufman, Barry Lennan, William Louis-Dreyfus, Tom Lynch, Ben Lytal, Elizabeth Macklin, Faith, Dan, and Natira McDermott, Ellen McNeilly, Gwyn Metz, Emily Moore, William Moran, Bob Palermo, Joann Pheasant, Marie Ponsot, Laurie and Mark Quinn, Juanin Reid, Charles Ruas, Gigi and Revan Schendler, Michael Schmidt, Scott Spencer, Pat Steir, Regina Tierney, Deborah Treisman, Alice Truax, Laurie Weisman, Wendy Williams, Joan Witek, and Rob Wynne.

I'm grateful to Kathy Novak for her affectionate wise counsel, and my thanks always to Nina Bourne and Vicky Wilson, both so dear to me.

I feel the deepest gratitude to my father, Raymond Quinn, and to Laurie Kerr, my mainstay, a wonderful writer and an inspired architect, who created two beautiful spaces in which much of the work on this book was done.

Index of Titles and First Lines